PERSPECTIVES

ON CORRECTION

Selected Studies in Social Problems

Bernard Rosenberg, GENERAL EDITOR

Societal Guidance: A New Approach to Social Problems
EDITED BY *Sarajane Heidt and Amitai Etzioni*

Juvenile Delinquency
EDITED BY *Richard R. Korn*

Perspectives on Correction
EDITED BY *Donal E. J. MacNamara and Edward Sagarin*

Problems of Sex Behavior
EDITED BY *Edward Sagarin and Donal E. J. MacNamara*

Aspects of Poverty
EDITED BY *Ben B. Seligman*

The Social Control of Mental Illness
EDITED BY *Harry Silverstein*

PERSPECTIVES
ON CORRECTION

EDITED BY

Donal E. J. MacNamara

*The John Jay College of
Criminal Justice of the
City University of New York*

Edward Sagarin

*The City College of the
City University of New York*

THOMAS Y. CROWELL COMPANY
NEW YORK
Established 1834

L.C. No. 72-107305
ISBN 0-690-61536-1

SERIES DESIGN BY *Margaret F. Plympton*

MANUFACTURED IN THE UNITED STATES OF AMERICA

Editor's Foreword

A Chilean leader with much experience of the world once remarked that all political problems could be reduced to those that solved themselves and those for which there is no solution. Such limited wisdom applies, *pari passu*, to many so-called social problems. How often, if we only let them be, will they disappear. A thoughtful president of the United States may reflect that when he decides to stay out of Indonesia, things go his way; but when he plunges into Indochina, the results are disastrous. Spirited intervention might sometimes be required; but just as often, it boomerangs. Little problems or illusory problems suddenly become big and real for no other reason than that we have acted when it would have been advisable not to act. Prohibiting the consumption of alcohol or the ingestion of narcotics drives these substances inexorably into the organized underworld which battens on an illicit traffic that need never have existed in the first place. Outlaw prostitution, abortion, fornication and cohabitation, or legislate anywhere else in the sphere of private morals, or criminalize previous legal and possibly uncontrollable behavior, and you get a society of inveterate offenders. Ours is such a society. We, who like to believe that the American government is not one of men but of law, have piled law upon punitive law until countless inconsistent criminal codes produce juridical elephantiasis, and men become lawbreakers by definition. Our partially lawless police, trying, and then not trying, to contain "vice" are thrust into collusion with professional thieves, venal politicians, corrupt judges, and a wide assortment of reputable citizens similarly involved in the maladministration of criminal justice.

And all this accounts for only a fraction of the energy expended in unmaking problems initially made by misguided attempts to solve them. The impulse to do something, almost anything, in an apparently intolerable situation (which worsens

v

as we proliferate our blunders) alternates with blindness, fatigue, indifference, and apathy.

Herbert Spencer, the founder of Anglo-American sociology, understood the desirability of inaction. His followers, inspired by that great proponent of laissez faire ideology, favored hands off a problem when the laying on of hands could only be fatal. These liberals, who did not wish to meddle with the economy, the polity, or the society at large, and who, when pushed, found themselves exposed as anarchists, were not in possession of the whole truth. Yet, that part of the truth which they did grasp seems largely to have been forgotten. We go on fatuously defining, and thereby creating, problems beyond our capacity to solve except by generating even graver problems. Finally, the myth of absolute omnipotence yields to the myth of absolute impotence. Then, with neither action nor inaction as a purposive and effective principle, the world is allowed to drift. At that stage, things, as the Poles say, are worse than they were but better than they're going to be.

When to do something and when not to are the major questions of our time. They weigh heavily on the mind of this writer as he launches still another and, he hopes, better series of books, each devoted to a social problem.

And what, pray, is a social problem? Or better, in a totally problematic situation, what is *not* a social problem? As the categorical imperative within disappears and man literally reaches for the starry heavens above, while awaiting oblivion by self-destruction, anything and everything may be regarded as a problem. That, like all human enterprises, it is also social to some no doubt large extent, goes without saying.

If the editors and authors of this series are at all able to distinguish between remediable and irremediable problems, if they can admit the immense and universal ignorance that prevails as we all grope our way in darkness toward a little bit of light, if sociological arrogance is eschewed in favor of a more becoming modesty, and above all, if a hierarchy of values is sustained—such that well-subsidized trifles do not eclipse impoverished areas of investigation—then these books will have been worth our while. If not, let the reader beware.

BERNARD ROSENBERG

Contents

INTRODUCTION

Ever since the law of crimes displaced the law of torts and society-imposed penalties replaced individual or family-arranged compensation, mankind's ingenuity in devising ever more brutal and vicious as well as, in the case of the gas chamber, guillotine, and electric chair, more fiendishly efficient punishments has known few bounds. It has been exceeded only by the creativity of theologians, jurists, and penologists among many others, in developing even more specious, but convincing, justifications, or improved rationalizations, for our inhumane and demonstrably ineffective methods of dealing with those who are unable or unwilling to adjust to society's mores and to comply with its laws.

Even Thomas Aquinas, philosopher, scholar, and saint, was able to justify not only slavery and the taking of human life as punishments for crimes but also the gouging out of the culprit's eyes, the amputation of his limbs, and the application of torture. He reasoned that as the good of the individual is subordinate to the good and well-being of the community, and the good of the human body is subordinate to the saving of the human soul, so too the good of any part of the body is subordinate to the good of the whole. Hence, eyes, hands, tongue, or testicles might be severed, if necessary, to prevent the whole body from sinning (committing crimes) through use of that part.

Many and varied groups in our society and others have, over the years, either consciously accepted this Thomistic paralogic or unknowingly adopted it as their inarticulate basic premise: the lynch mobs who savagely mutilated their Negro victim; our colonial forebears who branded the adulteress; the Middle Eastern caid who ordered the amputation of the thief's hand; and, in our own time, the highly vocal legislators who call for the castration of the sex offender, and sadistic elements in the public who demand increased use of the death penalty and the restoration of corporal punishment to its once dominant role in the home and schools, in juvenile detention facilities, and in prisons.

Early tribal societies, reasoning *post hoc ergo propter hoc*, interpreted natural catastrophes (earthquakes, floods, plagues, droughts) as punishments decreed by an avenging deity for the misconduct of one or more tribesmen or group members (witness Sodom and Gomorrah). They sought to allay the wrath of the gods and avoid future disasters by seeking out and punishing their erring brethren. In the same way, they attempted to forestall retaliatory raids, destruction of cattle and crops, and despoilment of tribal womenfolk by more powerful neighboring tribes against whom a wrong had been committed. Closely related was the feeling that failure of the group to impose penalties would encourage private vengeance; or that society's lust for punishment, presumably omnipresent, might if unrequited manifest itself in lynching or even rebellion.

Early Christian writers felt punishment necessary to restore the natural equilibrium destroyed by the criminal act; and later theologians declared that punishment not only provided expiation of guilt but was also a necessary first step in the moral regeneration of the offender.

More pragmatic justifications were not lacking. Defense of the death penalty, amputations, and castration was seen as reducing or eliminating the criminal's capacity for harm (two of these penalties also appealed to the "race purifiers," who would eliminate unfit strains). Branding was a warning to potential victims. Exile, ostracism, or transportation to distant penal colonies was a cleansing of the community of undesirable elements as well as a positive economic good in providing cheap labor in dangerous or unhealthful lands.

More recently, great stress has been placed on the deterrent values of punishment: deterring the offender from repeating his offenses and deterring others by example. Furthermore, imprisonment has been seen as a means of making the culprit amenable and available for what is loosely termed rehabilitation, so that one speaks less frequently of penology, more frequently of corrections.

Few would contest the proposition that the prospect of punishment deters some normal citizens from engaging in criminal acts of little emotional content; but the case for a demonstrably effective deterrent value in punishments, no matter how severe, founders badly when one consults history. "I call upon you to remember that cruel punishments have an inevitable tendency to produce cruelty in the people," said Samuel Romilly, arguing for the reform of England's "Bloody Code" in 1813. The efforts of Bentham and Beccaria (or indeed of Gilbert and Sullivan) to calculate punishments that "fit the crime" presuppose a rational man acting as a free moral agent, computing the "hedonistic calculus" and determining a course of lawful or criminal conduct thereby. If punishment followed criminality with certainty, celerity, and consistency, and if the "rationality" of the offender at the time of weighing the felicity calculus were not affected by emotional stress, alcohol, or drugs, or conditioned by environmental factors, neither of his choosing nor of his making, even relatively light penalties would prove deterrent. That these necessary prerequisites do not maintain is too obvious to merit restatement, yet our legislative bodies all too frequently attest their faith in the deterrent approach by increasing penalties. These overly rigorous if ineffective penalties are used as a substitute for more complex and, at least temporarily, more costly programs which might well reduce or eliminate the social pathologies and the individual deprivations and disadvantages of which crime is symptomatic.

Fyodor Dostoevsky and Victor Hugo have clearly depicted the reciprocal pathologies inherent in the crime-punishment sequence: the guilt-ridden, punishment-seeking, masochistic, self-destructive offender balancing, albeit quite unevenly, the authoritarian, judgmental, punitive, and sadistically vengeful police agent, prosecutor, and prison warden. Indeed, the number of suicides and attempted suicides, some immediately following the misdeed committed, others after apprehension or conviction or while serving a term of confinement, and others consisting of a small number of heavily guarded "quare fellows" (Irish prison slang for those awaiting execution), as well as the large number of voluntary confessors (some, as Marcel Frym has pointed out, pathological false confessors) and those who, in Freudian terms, confess and seek punishment by inadvertently leaving direct evidence of their identity at the crime scene, support at least to some degree the theological proposition that conscience imposes its own penance and that the intervention of human justice is in many cases a superfluity.

Supporting Samuel Romilly's penal reform bills in the House of Commons in 1821 (although Romilly had himself committed suicide two years earlier), Sir Thomas Powell Buxton warned his colleagues: "We rest our hopes on the hangman; and in this vain and deceitful confidence in the ultimate punishment of crime, forget the very first of our duties—its prevention."

Almost a century and a half later, on March 8, 1965, Lyndon B. Johnson, in a special message to another punishment-oriented legislature, declared, "We cannot tolerate an endless, self-defeating cycle of imprisonment, release, and reimprisonment which fails to alter undesirable attitudes and behavior."

The editors of this volume categorically reject retributive punishment and question the efficacy of threatened penalties, no matter how dire, in seriously reducing crime and delinquency. They condemn capital and corporal punishment as immoral and ineffective, tending to harden and degrade not only the victims but those who impose the penalties, including all the citizens of a society that authorizes and tolerates their use.

Detention in a truly therapeutic community for the shortest term consistent with the offender's rehabilitation, maximum utilization of extra-institutional methods of supervision and support (probation and parole), research into methods of earlier diagnosis of criminal potentiality, greater tolerance of deviant behavior not clearly dangerous to others or to the society, more attention to the psychologically sound concept of encouraging desirable attitudes and behavior through reward-oriented pro-grams, and the focusing of energy, ingenuity, and money on a major and continuing effort to modify the sociogenic factors in crime causation—these are suggested as feasible alternatives to our present overdependence on punishment.

To accomplish these admittedly difficult ends, one must first accumulate knowledge: facts, theories, the teachings of those who have studied and experienced. If, in order to know, one must approach a subject or look at an object from a variety of perspectives, then how true this is of punishment. Once the domain of the theologian and later the philosopher, still later to be studied by legal authorities, sociologists, psychiatrists and psychologists, muckrakers, social thinkers, humanitarians, judges, penal reformers, and even victims of the criminal, to this group there is now added that important missing dimension: the perspective of the insider, the man answering for his transgressions, be they supposed or real.

It is this variety of perspectives that we have sought to capture, or at least to sample, in this collection. Here is Eldridge Cleaver and his cry of anguish, with a view of iron bars and prison walls from within the cage; here is Erving Goffman, with the perceptive analysis of the rituals, ceremonies, and degradations of the inmate world. With these views, there converge those of a professor of law, a philosopher, a social critic, an historian, a psychiatrist, and a would-be reformer and experimentalist who became America's best-known spokesman for the psychedelic revolution. Meld together their different orientations, their divergent preparations for the world they are examining, and out of these perspectives on correction it is hoped that there will emerge a single perspective, enriched by these many, and that can be as effective as it is humane.

LETTER FROM FOLSOM PRISON

Eldridge Cleaver

Eldridge Cleaver—unsuccessful candidate for the presidency of the United States, convicted rapist, refugee or fugitive from his native land, exile or expatriate first in Cuba and later Algeria, leader of the militant Black Panther party or movement—was wanted by prison authorities and failed to show. Eldridge Cleaver —his *Soul on Ice* has won wide acclaim as a work of profundity and of eloquence.

When the story of man's inhumanity to man is recounted, we shall all have to learn from the victim; and when the story is told of the anguish and torture, the cruelty and the bitterness of a world in which millions are kept behind barbed wire and enclosed in locked cells, we shall all have to listen to the sufferers. Among them, hear the voice of Eldridge Cleaver.

It is ironic that a land that has abandoned the word "penology," and in its stead embraced the word "correction," should have caused this man to flee from its shores. For seldom can society point to such a remarkable example of rehabilitation. Once demoralized and hopeless, this self-confessed rapist had become a thinker, a writer, and a political leader. It would seem

Source: Eldridge Cleaver, *Soul on Ice* (New York: McGraw-Hill Book Company, 1968) pp. 18–25. Copyright © 1968 by Eldridge Cleaver. Reprinted by permission of McGraw-Hill Book Company.

apparent that he had forsaken the road of antisocial activities, unless his struggle for black liberation and for the unity of black and white radicals were to be defined as antisocial. And how else could it be defined, when those responsible for the definition were the courts, police, prison authorities, and others who were part of the system that had driven Cleaver to prison (or at least to the act which had brought him there) and were determined to see him behind bars again?

Addressing a San Francisco meeting five days before he became a fugitive from justice, Cleaver described as piggish and criminal a system that he termed the enemy of people: "This very system that we live in and function in every day. This system that we are in and under at this very moment. *Our* system! Each and every one of your systems. If you happen to be from another country, it's still your system, because the system in your country is part of this. This system is *evil*. It is criminal; it is murderous. And it is in control. It is in power. It is arrogant. It is crazy."

But not crazy enough to fail to realize that Eldridge Cleaver's was a voice that had to be silenced!

Folsom Prison
October 9, 1965

I'm perfectly aware that I'm in prison, that I'm a Negro, that I've been a rapist, and that I have a Higher Uneducation. I never know what significance I'm supposed to attach to these factors. But I have a suspicion that, because of these aspects of my character, "free-normal-educated" people rather expect me to be more reserved, penitent, remorseful, and not too quick to shoot off my mouth on certain subjects. But I let them down, disappoint them, make them gape at me in a sort of stupor, as if they're thinking: "You've got your nerve! Don't you realize that you owe a debt to society?" My answer to all such thoughts lurking in their split-level heads, crouching behind their squinting bombardier eyes, is that the blood of Vietnamese peasants has paid off all my debts; that the Vietnamese people, afflicted with a rampant disease called Yankees, through their sufferings —as opposed to the "frustration" of fat-assed American geeks safe at home worrying over whether to have bacon, ham, or sausage with their grade-A eggs in the morning, while Vietnamese worry each morning whether the Yankees will gas them, burn them up, or blow away their humble pads in a hail of bombs—have canceled all my IOUs.

In beginning this letter I could just as easily have mentioned other aspects of my situation; I could have said: I'm perfectly aware that I'm tall, that I'm skinny, that I need a shave, that I'm hard-up enough to suck my grandmother's old withered tits, and that I would dig (deeper than deeply) getting *clean* once more—not only in the steam-bath sense, but in getting sharp as an *Esquire* square with a Harlem touch—or that I would like to put on a pair of bib overalls and become a Snicker, or that I'd like to leap the whole last mile and grow a beard and don whatever threads the local nationalism might require and comrade with Che Guevara, and share his fate, blazing a new pathfinder's trail through the stymied upbeat brain of the New Left, or how I'd just love to be in Berkeley right now, to roll in that mud, frolic in that sty of funky revolution, to breathe in its heady fumes, and look with roving eyes for a new John Brown, Eugene Debs, a blacker-meaner-keener Malcolm X, a Robert Franklin Williams with less rabbit in his hot blood, an American Lenin, Fidel, a Mao-Mao, A MAO MAO, A MAO MAO, A MAO MAO, A MAO MAO, A MAO MAO, A MAO MAO. . . . All of which is true.

But what matters is that I have fallen in love with my lawyer! Is that surprising? A convict is expected to have a high regard for *anyone* who comes to his aid, who tries to help him and who expends time, energy, and money in an effort to set him free. But can a convict really love a lawyer? It goes against the grain. Convicts hate lawyers. To walk around a prison yard and speak well of a lawyer is to raise the downcast eyebrows of felons who've been bitten by members of the Bar and Grill. Convicts are convinced that lawyers must have a secret little black book which no one else is ever allowed to see, a book that schools lawyers in an esoteric morality in which the Highest Good is treachery and crossing one's dumb and trusting client the noblest of deeds. It was learned by the convicts that I'd gotten busted with some magazines given to me by my lawyer and that I was thrown in the Hole for it. Convicts smiled knowingly and told me that I had gone for the greasy pig, that my lawyer had set me up, and that if I couldn't see through the plot I was so stupid that I would buy not only the Golden Gate Bridge but some fried ice cream.

It was my turn to smile knowingly. A convict's paranoia is as thick as the prison wall—and just as necessary. Why should we have faith in anyone? Even our wives and lovers whose beds we have shared, with whom we have shared the tenderest moments and most delicate relations, leave us after a while, put us down, cut us clean aloose and treat us like they hate us, won't even write us a letter, send us a Christmas card every other year, or a quarter for a pack of cigarettes or a tube of toothpaste now and then. All society shows the convict its ass and expects him to kiss it: the convict feels like kicking it or putting a bullet in it. A convict sees man's fangs and claws and learns quickly to bare and unsheath his own, for real and final. To maintain a hold on the ideals and sentiments of civilization in such circumstances is probably impossible. How much more incredible is it, then, while rooted in this pit, to fall in love, and with a lawyer! Use a lawyer, yes: use anybody. Even tell the lawyer that you're in love. But you will always know when you are lying and even if you could manage to fool the lawyer you could never manage to fool yourself.

And why does it make you sad to see how everything hangs by such thin and whimsical threads? Because you're a dreamer, an incredible dreamer, with a tiny spark hidden somewhere inside you which cannot die, which even you cannot kill or quench and which tortures you horribly because all the odds are against its continual burning. In the midst of the foulest decay and putrid savagery, this spark speaks to you of beauty, of human warmth and kindness, of goodness, of greatness, of heroism, of martyrdom, and it speaks to you of love.

So I love my lawyer. My lawyer is not an ordinary person. My lawyer is a rebel, a revolutionary who is alienated fundamentally

from the *status quo*, probably with as great an intensity, conviction, and irretrievability as I am alienated from it—and probably
with more intelligence, compassion, and humanity. If you read
the papers, you are no doubt aware of my lawyer's incessant in-
volvement in agitation against all manifestations of the mon-
strous evil of our system, such as our intervention in the internal
affairs of the Vietnamese people or the invasion of the Domini-
can Republic by U.S. Marines. And my lawyer defends civil
rights demonstrators, sit-iners, and the Free Speech students
who rebelled against the Kerr–Strong machine at the University
of California. My love for my lawyer is due, in part, to these
activities and involvements, because we are always on the same
side of the issues. And I love all my allies. But this, which may
be the beginning of an explanation, does not nearly explain what
goes on between my lawyer and me.

I suppose that I should be honest and, before going any
further, admit that my lawyer is a woman—or maybe I should
have held back with that piece of the puzzle—a very excellent,
unusual, and beautiful woman. I know that *she* believes that I
do not really love her and that I am confusing a combination
of lust and gratitude for love. Lust and gratitude I feel abun-
dantly, but I also love this woman. And I fear that, believing
that I do not love her, she will act according to that belief.

At night, I talk with her in my sleep, long dialogues in which
she answers back. We alternate in speaking, like in the script of
a play. And let me say that I don't believe a word she says.
While we are talking, I participate and believe everything,
taking her word as her bond. But when I awake, I repudiate
the conversation and disbelieve her. I awake refreshed, and
though my sleep has been restless, I am not tired. Except for a
few lost hours in which she slips away and I fall into a deep
sleep, I hover on a level between consciousness and peace, and
the dialogue ensues. It does not bother me now. I have often
gone through this when something seizes my mind.

I place a great deal of emphasis on people really listening
to each other, to what the other person has to say, because you
very seldom encounter a person who is capable of taking either
you or himself seriously. Of course, when I was out of prison I

was not really like this; the seeds were there, but there was too much confusion and madness mixed in. I had a profound desire for communicating with and getting to know other people, but I was incapable of doing so. I didn't know how.

Getting to know someone, entering that new world, is an ultimate, irretrievable leap into the unknown. The prospect is terrifying. The stakes are high. The emotions are overwhelming. The two people are reluctant really to strip themselves naked in front of each other, because in doing so they make themselves vulnerable and give enormous power over themselves one to the other. How often they inflict pain and torment upon each other! Better to maintain shallow, superficial affairs; that way the scars are not too deep. No blood is hacked from the soul.

But I do not believe a beautiful relationship has to end always in carnage, or that we have to be fraudulent and pretentious with one another. If we project fraudulent, pretentious images, or if we fantasize each other into distorted caricatures of what we really are, then, when we awake from the trance and see beyond the sham and front, all will dissolve, all will die or be transformed into bitterness and hate. I know that sometimes people fake on each other out of genuine motives to hold onto the object of their tenderest feelings. They see themselves as so inadequate that they feel forced to wear a mask in order continuously to impress the second party.

If a man is free—not in prison, the Army, a monastery, hospital, spaceship, submarine—and living a normal life with the usual multiplicity of social relations with individuals of both sexes, it may be that he is incapable of experiencing the total impact of another individual upon himself. The competing influences and conflicting forces of other personalities may dilute one's psychic and emotional perception, to the extent that one does not and cannot receive all that the other person is capable of sending.

Yet I may believe that a man whose soul or emotional apparatus had lain dormant in a deadening limbo of desuetude is capable of responding from some great sunken well of his being, as though a potent catalyst had been tossed into a critical mass, when an exciting, lovely, and lovable woman enters the range of his feelings. What a deep, slow, torturous, reluctant, frightened stirring! He feels a certain part of himself in a state of flux, as if a bodiless stranger has stolen inside his body, startling him by doing calisthenics, and he feels himself coming slowly back to life. His body chemistry changes and he is flushed with new strength.

When she first comes to him his heart is empty, a desolate place, a dehydrated oasis, unsolaced, and he's craving woman-food, without which sustenance the tension of his manhood has unwound and relaxed. He has imperative need of the kindness, sympathy, understanding, and conversation of a woman, to hear a woman's laughter at his words, to answer her questions and be answered by her, to look into her eyes, to sniff her primeval fragrance, to hear—with slaughtered ears—the sensuous rustling of frivolous garments as legs are crossed and uncrossed beneath a table, to feel the delicate, shy weight of her hand in his—how painfully and totally aware is he of her presence, her every movement! It is as if one had been left to die beneath a bush on a lonely trail. The sun is hot and the shade of the bush, if not offering an extension of life, offers at least a slowing-down of death. And just when one feels the next breath will surely be the last, a rare and rainbow-colored bird settles on a delicate twig of the bush and, with the magic of melodious trillings and beauty of plumage, charms the dying one back to life. The dying man feels the strength flowing into and through the conduits of his body from the charged atmosphere created by the presence of the bird, and he knows intuitively in his clinging to life that if the bird remains he will regain his strength and health—and live.

Seeing her image slipping away from the weak fingers of his mind as soon as she has gone, his mind fights for a token of her on which to peg memory. Jealously, he hoards the fading memory of their encounter, like a miser gloating over a folio of blue-chip stock. The unfathomable machinery of the subconscious projects an image onto the conscious mind: her bare right arm, from a curve of shoulder to fingertip. (Had his lips quivered with desire to brand that soft, cool-looking flesh with a kiss of fire, had his fingers itched to caress?) Such is the magic of a woman, the female principle of nature which she embodies, and her power to resurrect and revitalize a long-isolated and lonely man.

I was twenty-two when I came to prison and of course I have changed tremendously over the years. But I had always had a strong sense of myself and in the last few years I felt I was losing my identity. There was a deadness in my body that eluded me, as though I could not exactly locate its site. I would be aware of this numbness, this feeling of atrophy, and it haunted the back of my mind. Because of this numb spot, I felt peculiarly off balance, the awareness of something missing, of a blank spot, a certain intimation of emptiness. Now I know what it was. After eight years in prison, I was visited by a woman, a woman who was interested in my work and cared about what happened to me. And since encountering her, I feel life, strength flowing back into that spot. My step, the tread of my stride, which was becoming tentative and uncertain, has begun to recover a definiteness, a confidence, a boldness which makes me want to kick over a few tables. I may even swagger a little, and, as I read in a book somewhere, "push myself forward like a train."

OUR PRISONS
ARE CRIMINAL

Bruce Jackson

It has often been said that in America we coddle our criminals.
This is the kind of remark that was heard frequently, but with
little justification, during the years that the Warren Court was
extending to the accused certain constitutional rights formerly
denied them. But although the public may use the words "criminals" and "prisoners" loosely, often confusing the two, no one
would accuse Americans of coddling their prisoners. Just the
reverse: prison administrations and the prison system itself are
constantly being charged with brutality and savagery.

Perhaps the reason for these charges is that our prison system is
mainly retributive, only slightly deterrent, and rehabilitative in so
few instances and even then despite itself. Few countries have
attempted to have a prison program that would not dehumanize,
one that would contain the dangerous and deter the tempted, but
not wreak vengeance on the transgressor. Sweden, perhaps, has
come closest to this ideal, but it is a smaller nation than America,
with a relatively homogeneous population.

But surely the American prison system can introduce reforms.
If brutality dehumanizes the victimizer as well as the victim, then

Source: *The New York Times Magazine,* September 22, 1968. Copyright
© 1968 by The New York Times Company. Reprinted by permission of
the publisher and author.

it also dehumanizes the society that sponsors, tolerates, conceals, and protects that brutality. This is the essence of Bruce Jackson's remarks in the article reprinted here, which is based on his personal observations as an outsider, a college professor, who had been permitted to visit a prison and investigate. Put his comments together with Eldridge Cleaver's, the outsider looking in and the insider looking out, and the result is not a pretty picture; but it is a picture that all of us must be forced to view if correction as a concept is to be taken seriously.

❦

During the summer of 1963 I visited a Midwestern prison that had had a particularly devastating week in the wake of riots that swept American prisons a decade or so earlier. Many buildings had been destroyed and many inmates had been killed or injured, and even in 1963 portions of the yard were scarred by the ruined foundations of buildings that had not yet been rebuilt. Some of the inmates with whom I spoke doubted that a riot could again happen there. "They've gone just the other way," one man said, "they don't bother us at all."

"They" was the administration, and he was pretty much right. The warden never went inside the prison itself and the primary rule for inmates seemed to be: *Don't go over the wall.* Other than that, they pretty much ran their own show. But I wondered: If all those inmates were so adept at self-government, what were they doing in prison in the first place? My concern was increased when I learned that at least 30 inmates had been stabbed in separate incidents during the previous month, hardly a sign of social stability.

When I returned for my second visit in 1964, the warden said, "You planning to go inside and just wander around, like last time?"

"Yes. Any reason I shouldn't?"

"Oh, no."

"Any trouble lately?"

"No, no. Everything's fine. Fine."

I left his office and walked downstairs through the trap, the double gates bracketing the control booth. The gates are rigged so only one set may open at a time, preventing a rush to the outside. When I reached the inner prison I was greeted by two inmates I had met on my previous visit.

"Hi, Bruce," one said. "We heard you was out in front and figured you'd be on your way in, so we waited here."

"What's new?"

"You hear about them niggers all got stabbed a couple days ago?"

"Yeah," the second man said. "*Every*body's been carrying a shank here all week."

"Just starting to cool off now."

"But it still might blow. You can't tell with these goddam people."

The entire prison, I found, narrowly missed exploding in a massive race riot. Inmates, white and black, who had got on well for years, were ready to slice each other to ribbons. The production total at the license-plate plant one day was down about 20 per cent—the machine operators were too busy turning out diagonal pieces of sheet steel for knives.

The administration had decided to integrate the prison, they told me. Black inmates were six or eight to a cell; white inmates were one or two to a cell. Almost all cells were the same size. (Once, when I had asked a prison official why the blacks were so overcrowded, he said, "Aw, they're all queer in here anyway." When I suggested that the overcrowding might contribute to the development of situational homosexuality, he told me I didn't understand people.) When the word went out, there was some grumbling among a few inmates, but they were quickly silenced by others who told them, in the words of one of the men who met me by the gates, "If it's gotta come, it's gotta come. We work with those guys every day. We play ball with them. What's the big deal living in the next cell anyway?" The inmates were ready for the move.

But the administration wasn't. It made the worst mistake possible in a prison: it tested the inmates. Instead of making a large-scale reassignment of cells, it moved a very small group of blacks into a white cell block. The inmates immediately saw this as an indication that the administration was afraid. "You *never* challenge anybody in this place," one old-timer said. "That's the surest way to get it. Even if the guy's a creep. A challenge is a challenge."

Inmates who had previously accepted the integration decision found themselves in heated discussions about it. A few beat everyone to the conclusion—they ganged up on a small group of blacks who were walking back to the cell block from the messhall. They killed one and injured the others seriously.

The entire prison began arming itself. Some men walked around with more armor than they ever carried on the streets. As fast as guards discovered knives in cell shakedowns, more were manufactured. At one point knives were leaving the tag plants by the bucketful.

A major disaster was finally averted when an inmate group pointed out to the administration that if integration was to occur, and it had to, it must be done on a large scale. When word went out that the administration was talking with a group of white and black inmates, tensions cooled some. The knives were hidden away and the tag plant once again began stamping out license plates. Not long after, the integration was put into effect on a fairly wide scale, as it should have been at first, and there wasn't a murmur from the inmate population or even a minor slowdown in license-plate production.

Prisons are most peculiar societies, and although they regularly emit signals for the general public (to tell how well or badly things are going), one has to understand the situation before the meaning of those signals is at all useful. The most important signal is how many men commit new crimes after release, but that signal is not easily picked up. To know only that a man is returned to prison does not help us, because we have to know if he committed a new crime or violated parole, and if the latter we have to know if that violation was serious or trivial (did he assault someone viciously or did he stay out too late at night once or twice), etc. It takes a long time for the information to accumulate, and longer still to evaluate that information. As a result, that signal, which is the one that affects the public most, is rarely read meaningfully. Far more dramatic are riots and near-riots, which are often monologues trying to be dialogues.

Inmates and administrators alike are quite aware that, given the proper situation, prisons can suddenly become major news copy. Sometimes inmates will riot, hoping that their complaints (real or imagined) will be taken up by a newsman somewhere, as was partly the case in the recent escape attempt/riot at Atlanta Federal Penitentiary; sometimes an administrator will reveal atrocities committed by a previous administration, hoping that the press will give the state legislature the stimulus it needs to act civilized. Newspapers have been full of such stories from North Carolina and Arkansas.

Although prison disturbances are sometimes a reaction to bad conditions, they are often a reaction to improvements, reflecting inmate resistance to change. The North Carolina experience is a case in point. Commissioner V. Lee Bounds is one of the more intelligent and perceptive prison administrators in this country. He runs a fairly good prison system, has established a work-release program that permits some inmates to work in the outside society during the day and return to the prison at night (not only does this have obvious economic advantages, but it helps avoid the psychological re-entry trauma many inmates have on release). There is a weekend leave program that permits some inmates to go home for visits (which is not only an incentive for good behavior within the prison, but helps maintain family stability); and there is a program that permits some inmates to attend day classes at nearby colleges.

All these amenities were made feasible by removing the more troublesome and aggressive inmates from the general prison population and relocating them in one building or complex of buildings. Bounds was then able to have conditions in the other buildings relaxed considerably. But there is a price for such consolidation. It concentrates the troublemakers and may create a dangerous kind of "élitism." (That was once the case with the Federal system's Alcatraz, now closed.) In North Carolina's Central Prison, where 1,038 dangerous inmates were held, a riot broke out in April over visiting hours, hot lunches, pay for inmate labor, and the number of allotted TV sets in each wing (there were two, the rioters wanted four). In the melee 78 inmates were injured and five killed.

In some states this problem is avoided by taking all the inmates defined as dangerous (which sometimes includes inmates someone dislikes or wants out of the way) and locking them in a deep segregation unit. Unlike the solitary confinement punishment cells, these living units are not too brutal: they do have mattresses and the inmates are fed regular meals. The only thing is, they are sometimes left there for years at a time.

There are interesting regional differences in the actions and attitudes of inmates and administrators. In the North, angry or frustrated inmates usually wreck buildings when they riot; in the South, they wreck themselves, by cutting heel tendons or lopping off fingers or toes or hands or feet. Administrators in the North punish by limiting options (i.e., resorting to deep lockups), in the South by hurting bodies (an Arkansas committee recommended recently that the prison system reintroduce the whip). Each group acts in terms of what the local economy considers most valuable—material things, freedoms, the physical being. Since in the North there is nothing for most inmates to *do*, the Northern prison places no value on the body of the inmate and doesn't perceive it as an object for formal revenge; destroying or damaging something valueless never satisfies the vengeful.

Prisons in the North and South also re-enact in a way their areas' moral histories. Concerned with sin, the North in the 19th century locked men in solitary confinement to meditate upon their faults; inmates were forbidden conversation with anyone and denied any reading matter except the Bible. The word *penitentiary* used to carry a heavy religious connotation, at least for the administrators. Gradually that restrictiveness has been changed, but not without considerable resentment in the outside world. Attempts to increase the work opportunities for inmates (if properly designed, prison labor can be educational) are still savagely opposed by manufacturers and unions. Lobbyists have got on the books a Federal law that prohibits the interstate shipment of goods manufactured by state prison inmates.

In the South, prison was modeled on the plantation at its

worst; the prison manager did not even have the responsibility of getting his employer's investment out of his slaves—they came free, sent in an unending stream by a host of judges and juries. Similarities between the brutal Southern prisons of the past (and a few of the present) and plantation slavery are obvious: human beings are perceived as chattel goods; they exist mainly to work the land. The manager of the plantation was answerable to the owner, who wanted to know about profits; the prison administrator was answerable to the state legislature, which wanted to know about costs. But there was that one important difference—in slavery, the physical fitness of the worker was important to the manager; he didn't care if the worker was happy, but he did care if the worker was healthy, since his boss had a cash investment in that body. The plantation manager kept the slaves as well as his economy permitted, but didn't worry about much else. However, in the brutal plantation prisons (I stress that these are on the way out and that in places like North Carolina there was no cash investment in the labor) on the contrary, the live bodies represented something of a liability.

Like other Southern states, Arkansas after the Civil War had a system in which convicts were leased out to private firms. This seemed to make everyone but the convicts happy—the state could punish without cost, sometimes it made a profit, and politicians and their friends could make a great deal of money. Convicts were leased to almost anyone having the price and the connections, the Arkansas Penitentiary Study Commission reported earlier this year, including "farmers, railway companies, building contractors, coal-mine operators, brick manufacturers, and others. The men were thus widely scattered and supervision was difficult. Investigations showed that prisoners were often neglected and mistreated. In the coal mines, convicts were worked through the winter barefooted in icy water, and flogged if they failed to dig as much coal as the contractor wanted. A fourth of the prisoners died every year."

Few people worried about the deaths. It was cheaper to let those men die than supply decent clothing, adequate living conditions and competent medical care. In revulsion, Gov. George

W. Donaghey in 1912 turned loose 361 convicts at once; that aroused such concern that the lease system was abolished until the nineteen-twenties, when it was reinstated.

It was stopped again, but another, equally exploitative, practice emerged. Inmates were paroled to specific firms or individuals, and unless they worked to the satisfaction of their employer they were returned to the prison. Often conditions on the job were as bad as or worse than conditions on the prison farm. Medical treatment was so poor that almost any injury or malady could result in death (and for this reason a vague statement of illness was often used to cover up a murder).

The scandals over unexplained bodies in Arkansas's two prison farms, Tucker and Cummins, is not quite so fresh as recent newspaper coverage would suggest. In August, 1966, Gov. Orval Faubus sent Arkansas state police to investigate irregularities at Tucker; the report of that investigation was suppressed, but the police temporarily took over management of the farm. After his election, Gov. Winthrop Rockefeller released the state police report and appointed a study commission to suggest changes in management of both Tucker and Cummins farms. Early in 1967, Thomas Murton, an ex-professor, was appointed to run Tucker; in January, 1968, he was put in charge of both farms. The former superintendent of Tucker and two other former wardens were, in the meantime, indicted on criminal charges.

After Murton's appointment, the prisons were in the headlines regularly as reports of past beatings, murders and general corruption were released. A number of unexplained bodies were uncovered and predictions were made that scores more would be found. Former convicts around the country began seeking out reporters to give statements about brutality and killings. (A favorite torture device of the Arkansas prison, the "Tucker Telephone," was developed by a prison doctor. It consisted of a crank telephone and a generator wired to an inmate's big toe and scrotum.)

Winthrop Rockefeller ordered another state police investigation and put a lid on further press releases. On March 7, Murton was fired. It is hard to say just why. The most obvious inference is that he was uncovering too many cadavers for political comfort. Some have said that it wasn't the bodies so much as his tendency to tell the press about them before he was sure how they got there. His supporters reply to this by pointing out that it is hard to tell much of anything about the Arkansas prison system, for records are quite scanty, and what records do exist sometimes conflict with obvious facts. The official statement accused Murton of turning the whole affair into a "circus."

Certainly some of the deaths were murders, but probably fewer than it appears. Some of the men the records say were killed trying to escape may really have been trying to escape —given the atrocious living conditions on the two farms, it is not surprising that some inmates should make such attempts. But here is a press problem: If you start out with rumors of several hundred murdered men and it turns out that you in fact can document 20 to 30, it is hard to convince the people outside that when you go after the men responsible for the 20 or 30, you aren't covering up for many others. Of course that doesn't always matter: on May 19 the Arkansas prosecutor handling the case said that no action would be taken as a result of the reported prison murders.

Things will change a little in Arkansas now, but I am not optimistic that they will change much. The main result of the scandal is that once again the old image of the Southern labor camps has been revived in the minds of Northern observers. It is an image that does not belong to Arkansas only. A few years ago a man who had spent some time in a Louisiana prison told me about his experiences there:

"I know of instances where arms and legs were broken during an afternoon's work, anything to be able to get into the hospital. I remember one time we were working on the levee with the object of bringing whole trees and logs floating in the Mississippi to land, let them dry out, cut them up and use them that winter as firewood for the wood-burning boilers. If you can imagine in rainy weather, trying to carry whole trees and haul huge logs on your shoulder. . . . One of the boys happened to wander over and say, 'I wish I had a broken leg. I'd get into the hospital.'

"Well, at the time we were joking about it and one of us said, 'Well, you want your leg broken?'

" 'Yeah.'

" 'Well, we can take care of it for you.'

"And that man thought about it for a minute and he said, 'I'm serious. Can you break it?'

"We laid the lower part of his leg from the knee down over two logs and dropped another in the middle. Word got around. Before the day was over we'd done away with something like half a dozen arms, even more legs.

"Finally, the Man decided to take the whole damned bunch of us in before we crippled the whole force. The Man knew what was going on, but there wasn't anything he could do about it."

It isn't work itself that inmates hate (often the worst prisons are those in which there is no work at all), but work that is humiliating, or exploitative, or senseless. Texas inmates toil the fields and build their own buildings, but working conditions are reasonable and the labor results in excellent institutional food and first-rate housing, so few of the men resent the work. Also, many of the inmates in the construction project appreciate the chance to learn high-paying trades, such as bricklaying or plumbing.

But it is not prisons like those in Texas that get attention; it is rather those in the more barbaric states. And the South does in fact have more than one of these. But so does the North, and no one talks about that at all.

Even now Massachusetts has one of the most wretched institutions in the country, the Correctional Institution at Bridgewater, designed to handle the "criminally insane." Fred Wiseman's portrayal of this place in "Titicut Follies" did not exaggerate; it is the worst place I have visited, North or South. I remember one building in particular with row on row of door-lined corridors, and board floors and brick walls. Every few feet there was a wooden door braced shut by a beam and a Judas-hole to peek through. Some of the rooms had a bed and a pan, none had running water, some had nothing at all but a naked man wrapped in an army blanket.

Through one of the Judas-holes one could see a man walking in a small circle, round and round and round and round. "He doesn't talk to anyone anymore," my guide said. "He just walks in circles now."

"And before?"

"I don't know just what he's supposed to have done. He used to be all right though. I remember when he came in, he was rational, could carry on a conversation, all that stuff. Then the doctor started telling him he'd be out of here soon. Every month or so they'd say he'd get out that month. Went on like that for two years. Then one day he stopped talking. No contact with anyone after that. He's been like this for years now."

We walked on down the hall. The guide told me about one 60-year-old inmate who had been in since the age of 7. His offense: running away from home.

A thin man, old and dry, stopped the guide and said, "When the hell you gonna get me a suit and let me outa here. How about it?" And to me: "I got a job on the Brockton Police Department if I can just get out of here. You ask the chief, he'll tell you. Old buddy of mine. Soon as I get outa here." The guide said something indefinite and the man walked away, nodding. This was the section for the killers, I had been told, so I asked what the thin man had done.

"He painted a horse."

"He what?"

"He painted a horse."

"What's wrong with that?"

"It was in a field. A live horse. He was drunk and somebody bet him he couldn't make a horse look like a zebra, I think, so he painted it and they put him in here. For being drunk, probably."

"How long has he been in?"

"Thirty-seven years. By the time they got around to letting him out he really *was* crazy. He couldn't take care of himself outside now. For his own good we just can't let him go out of here."

As for the plain old-fashioned brutality, the North has some of that, too. One Midwestern prison I visited had concrete blocks in a dungeon to which troublesome inmates were chained naked; the dungeon was next to the prison generators and hummed and vibrated intermittently, a total body massage equivalent of the Chinese water torture. Several inmates told me that those not made docile by the chains in the dungeon were subsequently given multiple electroshock therapy "treatments" on the upper floor of the infirmary building. I couldn't check out the story: guards stopped me when I tried to wander out of the shiny public part of the infirmary. I met a man who had been up there for treatments many times, but he didn't remember very much about it; he didn't seem to remember much about *any-thing*. "He was a truck driver in————for 18 years before he came up here, but he don't remember any street names," an inmate said. I asked why. "Those treatments, man. Like they dissolve the front end of your head." They all laughed, including the man who couldn't remember street names.

I find myself amazed not that such idiocies and brutalities go on in our prisons, but that they do not occur more often than they do. I am amazed that so many competent men go into the correctional field despite all the obstacles put in their way by politics, thoughtlessness and by stupid economies. In this morass where almost every lesson of the social sciences is ignored, a prison system like California's, which attempts to apply all the knowledge it can, stands out as anomalous.

Among the men who stand out is George Beto, director of Texas's massive prison system (12,000 inmates, 14 prisons, 100,000 acres of land). Beto is a former teacher and college president; he is a Lutheran minister with an M.A. in medieval history and a doctorate in educational administration. His methods of work best describe him. He is in his office around dawn, clearing up the paperwork on his desk; he then spends a good portion of his day visiting the individual prisons, talking with Austin officials about matters concerning the prison system and its relations with the rest of the state government (everything from guard salaries to parole requirements), arranging to get more inmates into the college programs, improving the extensive pre-release programs, seeing inmates. He is usually home for dinner around 5:30, but quite often shoots out again to meet with inmates or wander around the units. He is willing to talk with anyone, an important factor in inmate relations. All the inmates trust him, even the most cynical. Sometimes, when his sensors pick up feelings of discontent or possibilities of trouble at one of the prisons he turns up with apparent casualness.

("Just happened to be in the neighborhood." Fifteen miles from nowhere at 3 A.M.)

Beto points out that since 95 per cent of all the people in prison are going to come out again *sometime*, and most of these will be out after serving less than two years, society's self-interest should dictate that a good portion of a prison's effort would be toward restructuring the thinking of those inmates who need such restructuring, and training for a useful life those who can be trained.

But society doesn't respond the way it should; it isn't quite that rational. Fewer than 7 per cent of all correctional employees (psychologists, social workers, vocational and academic teachers, and chaplains) are qualified to treat inmates. Half the states have no educational requirements at all for custodial officers; in 28 per cent of the prisons, according to the report done for the President's crime commission, "One can be a 'professional worker' without having graduated from high school. In at least one [prison system] the mail clerk is called a social worker."

Part of the problem in America, I suspect, is a naive faith in the "principle" of deterrence: "If someone is deterred by a certain threat of punishment, twice as many people will be doubly deterred by twice the punishment." The symmetry may be nice, but the sociology is defective. States with death penalties have no smaller homicide rates than states without them; in Texas, where you can do more time for possessing marijuana than for second-degree murder, there are still more people smoking pot than killing each other; in Colorado, where you get 20 years for setting fire to a house but only 10 years for blowing it up, there are still more fires than explosions.

America has the longest prison sentences in the West, yet the only condition long sentences demonstrably cure is heterosexuality. (This assault on heterosexuality begins early in most prison careers. In fact, the worst places for challenges to sexual normality are the county jails, where the innocent and the guilty are often jammed together under brutal conditions for long periods of time. This month's scandalous revelations of homosexual assaults in Philadelphia prisons surprise no professionals in the field; such revelations could have occurred in a thousand county jails had local investigators cared to be as honest.) Long sentences inflict a double punishment; the man who gets one not only serves it, but finds that when he gets out he has no place in the world, for his wife and children usually belong to someone else and technology has passed him by.

Other countries—such as Denmark and Sweden—have immensely improved prison education. Yet in the United States— with all its fancy schools and its splendid mass media, with all its technology and experts—prison education barely makes up for the basic reading and writing skills the inmate never got on the outside. England is about to legalize conjugal visiting rights for married inmate men, because it realizes that there is much social value in keeping an inmate's family together. But in this country people trying to make the prison experience more socially beneficial in almost any way are accused of "coddling" criminals.

The nature of the myopia, though disheartening, is not hard to determine. With rare exceptions, our approach to the problem of crime and correction is an approach to the symptom rather than the cure.

Maybe we should be honest with ourselves; if what we want is vengeance, we've got pretty good models going in several places right now. If what we want is to make the streets safer, our property more secure, our nights more tranquil, if we want to help those people (and at the same time ourselves), we had best redefine what those places with their walls, their wires, their guns and their bars are required to do.

It is useless to talk about prisons as if they were miniworlds of their own. A prison is a part of our whole social complex, and it can only function well if there is harmony with the rest of the complex. A state may have an excellent prison system, with modern rehabilitative processes and splendid treatment programs, but if the sentencing procedures in the courts are primitive (flat, rather than indeterminate, sentences, and few presentence hearings to determine whether a convicted felon needs prison in the first place) and the parole procedures are restrictive (overloaded parole officers do none of their charges any good; a parole board which lets few men out refuses to give most inmates help at the time they need it most—i.e., when they first return to the outside world), then that prison system can do little.

There is still great resistance to in-community pre-release programs and work-release programs. Both of these permit the inmates and treatment staff to deal with the inmates' problems as they manifest themselves in the outside world, rather than the prison world. An individual may make a satisfactory adjustment to prison, enhancing his chances of parole, but this tells us nothing about how he will behave on the streets.

The direct cost of keeping a man in prison is about 10 times the cost of having him on parole, under supervision in the community. Further, a man on parole may contribute to the economy, while a man in prison is a complete debit. In addition, the inmate's family is often (inadequately) supported by one humiliating welfare program or another, and his children grow up without a permanent male in the household. Between a third and a half of all prison inmates could be paroled tomorrow with no risk to society, but they won't be.

Most wardens I know favor shorter sentences and more parole, not to make their own jobs easier (those reforms make their jobs harder, for the more unmanageable residual group of inmates loses the healthy influence of those who are qualified for parole), but because they think society is better served. But wardens are not so vocal or public a lobby as police and prosecutors, and it is the last who tend to get heard at legislative sessions. Police, for all their recent complaints about maltreatment by the courts, really are the object of a great deal of sentimental respect in this country. However, respect earned by hazardous duty well performed need not put above criticism the testimony of policemen on subjects in which they have little or no expertness. Further, the understandable goals of the police (re addicts, for example: "Keep those people off the streets") do not always coincide with society's interests. It is fitting that legislators should consult with police when they have crime problems, but they should know that there are only certain kinds of information police can offer (they can talk about crime control and criminal apprehension, but not expertly about the effectiveness of rehabilitation programs or the appropriateness of sentences). The policeman never sees the man the prison system happens to help—he sees the failures only.

Prison should be a home for two groups of people; those who take a calculated risk that they can get away with something our society tells them they should not do, and those who need a regimented society of the prison type to survive at all in this world. Ideally, the corrections process halts the development of a criminal career and, in the process, substitutes skills and goals that permit or encourage the criminal to support himself and maintain a life style acceptable to the general population. Far more often, the corrections process merely causes a time gap in the criminal development; in too many cases it accelerates rather than slows or ends that development.

I can think of no prison in the United States that really does its job. The best—like California and Texas—do what they can, but they are trapped in a conceptual nightmare created by outsiders who neither understand the prison's potential nor care very much about its limitations. As long as prisons are filled with inmates who should not be there and as long as prison administrations are handed the job of patching or hiding the major failures of other social agencies, they are going to continue failing.

What, in sum, do we need? This: (1) rational sentencing inspired by the realization that unnecessary or overlong prison terms can make a career criminal or career convict out of a one-time offender; (2) adequate funds for services that will let "correction" be a function rather than a title; (3) humane dwelling places for those citizens who, for whatever reason, cannot survive in any world but prison; and (4) public awareness that prison, any prison, however modern and well-run, is a punishing place to be and that we need add no savagery to it.

ON THE CHARACTERISTICS OF TOTAL INSTITUTIONS: THE INMATE WORLD

Erving Goffman

It would be difficult to name another sociologist who, with the insights and profundity of Erving Goffman, penetrates as deeply into the inner self of man and the manner in which society shapes him. Taking a cue, perhaps, from the psychoanalysts, Goffman's image of man is that of the human animal who wears a mask; he,

Source: Donald Cressey, *The Prison: Studies in Institutional Organization and Change* (New York: Holt, Rinehart & Winston, 1961), pp. 22–48. Copyright © 1961 by Holt, Rinehart and Winston, Inc. Reprinted by permission of the publisher. The excerpt reproduced here forms about one-half of the essay, "Inmate World," which is the opening section of Goffman's *Asylums: Essays on the Social Situation of Mental Patients and Other Inmates.*

Goffman, seeks to look behind the mask and discover man's hidden identity. It is not so much the conscious and the unconscious that he seeks to unravel, as the public and the private man, the interplay between the two, and the constant effect of others (those known and those who might be described as "them") on one's self and oneself. Reading Goffman, a line of poet and essayist Kenneth Patchen's comes to mind: "I have forgotten my mask, and my face was in it."

It is of more than passing interest that Goffman's essay included here does not pertain specifically to prisons, nor even to inmates who are undergoing punishment. Goffman's conceptual formation is broader: he sees total institutions as being of several different types. Their major differences are denoted by the nature of the resident or "inmate"—for example, soldier, student, or patient—but they have more in common than most of us realize. What the orphan asylum, the mental hospital, the prison, and the boarding school share is that in each, an inmate's life pattern (at least for a limited period of time), and in particular the activities of play, work, and sleep, are conducted in one place, with one set of companions, under one authority, and within the framework of a single rational plan. Given this frame of reference, Goffman penetrates into the minds of those who inhabit these total institutions—what, to the outsider, are worlds of regimentation and confinement.

Prisons share many of the attributes of other total institutions, but not all total institutions share the attributes of prisons. Almost no one is in a prison voluntarily; just being there is a sign of transgression and carries with it overwhelming stigma. The "mortification of the self," of which Goffman speaks, is seldom more clearly encountered than in prison. Only self-righteous political prisoners, carrying a mantle of martyrdom, seem to be able to escape it.

Works on penology, or specific aspects thereof, usually begin by viewing society as threatened, abused, in search of a means of self-defense. Goffman focuses instead on those who have been confined by that society. He captures the spirit of their world and looks at the outside from within. Students seeking to probe further into the inmate world, particularly of prisoners, are referred to Gresham M. Sykes, *The Society of Captives* (1958), Donald Clemmer, *The Prison Community* (1940), as well as to the rich literature that has come from the writings of ex-prisoners.

Some of the more renowned include Jean Genet, Brendan Behan, and Albie Sachs, but there are many others, less talented as writers, who have vividly described their prison experiences.

It is characteristic of inmates that they come to the institution with a "presenting culture" (to modify a psychiatric phrase) derived from a *home world*—a way of life and a round of activities taken for granted until the point of admission to the institution. (There is reason, then, to exclude orphanages and foundling homes from the list of total institutions, except insofar as the orphan comes to be socialized into the outside world by some process of cultural osmosis, even while this world is being systematically denied him.) Whatever the stability of the recruit's personal organization, it was part of a wider framework lodged in his civil environment—a round of experience that confirmed a tolerable conception of self, and allowed for a set of defensive maneuvers, exercised at his own discretion, for coping with conflicts, discreditings, and failures.

Now, it appears that total institutions do not substitute their own unique culture for something already formed; we deal with something more restricted than acculturation or assimilation. (If cultural change does occur, it has to do, perhaps, with the removal of certain behavior opportunities and the failure to keep pace with recent social changes on the outside. Thus if the inmate's stay is long, what has been called *disculturation*[1] may occur—that is, an "untraining" which renders him temporarily incapable of managing certain features of daily life on the outside, if and when he gets back to it.) The full meaning for the inmate of being "in" or "on the inside" does not exist apart from the special meaning to him of "getting out" or "getting on

[1] A term employed by Robert Sommer, "Patients Who Grow Old in a Mental Hospital," *Geriatrics*, XIV (1959), pp. 586–87. The term "desocialization," sometimes used in this context, would seem to be too strong, implying loss of fundamental capacities to communicate and cooperate.

the outside." In this sense, total institutions do not really look for cultural victory. They create and sustain a particular kind of tension between the home world and the institutional world and use this persistent tension as strategic leverage in the management of men.

The recruit, then, comes into the establishment with a conception of himself made possible by certain stable social arrangements in his home world. Upon entrance, he is immediately stripped of the support provided by these arrangements. In the accurate language of some of our oldest total institutions, he begins a series of abasements, degradations, humiliations, and profanations of self. His self is systematically, if often unintentionally, mortified. He begins some radical shifts in his *moral career*, a career composed of the progressive changes that occur in the beliefs that he has concerning himself and significant others.

The Process of Mortification

The processes by which a person's self is mortified are fairly standard in total institutions.[2] Analysis of these processes can help us to see the arrangements that ordinary establishments must guarantee if members are to preserve their civilian selves.

The barrier that total institutions place between the inmate and the wider world marks the first curtailment of self. In civil life, the sequential scheduling of the individual's roles, both in the life cycle and in the repeated daily round, ensures that no one role he plays will block his performance and ties in another. In total institutions, in contrast, membership automatically disrupts role scheduling, since the inmate's separation from the wider world lasts around the clock and may continue for years. *Role dispossession* therefore occurs. In many total institutions, the privilege of visiting away from the establishment or having visitors come to the establishment is completely withheld at first, ensuring a deep initial break with past roles and an appre-

---

[2] An example of the description of these processes may be found in Gresham M. Sykes, *The Society of Captives* (Princeton: Princeton University Press, 1958), Ch. IV, "The Pains of Imprisonment," pp. 63–83.

ciation of role dispossession. A report on cadet life in a military academy provides an illustration:

This clean break with the past must be achieved in a relatively short period. For two months, therefore, the swab is not allowed to leave the base or to engage in social intercourse with non-cadets. This complete isolation helps to produce a unified group of swabs, rather than a heterogeneous collection of persons of high and low status. Uniforms are issued on the first day, and discussions of wealth and family background are taboo. Although the pay of the cadet is very low, he is not permitted to receive money from home. The role of cadet must supersede other roles the individual has been accustomed to play. There are few clues left which will reveal social status in the outside world.[3]

I might add that when entrance is voluntary, the recruit has already partially withdrawn from his home world: what is cleanly severed by the institution is something that had already started to decay.

While some roles can be re-established by the inmate if and when he returns to the world, it is plain that other losses are irrevocable and may be painfully experienced as such. It may not be possible to make up, at a later phase of the life cycle, the time not now spent in educational or job advancement, in courting, or in socializing one's children. A legal aspect of this permanent dispossession is found in the concept of "civil death": prison inmates may face not only a temporary loss of the rights to will money and write checks, to contest divorce or adoption proceedings, and to vote, but may have some of these rights permanently abrogated.[4]

The inmate, then, finds that certain roles are lost to him by

[3] Sanford M. Dornbusch, "The Military Academy as an Assimilating Institution," Social Forces, XXXIII (1955), p. 317. For an example of initial visiting restrictions in a mental hospital, see D. McI. Johnson and N. Dodds, eds., The Plea for the Silent (London: Christopher Johnson, 1957), p. 16. Compare the rule against having visitors which has often bound domestic servants to their total institution. See J. Jean Hecht, The Domestic Servant Class in Eighteenth-Century England (London: Routledge and Kegan Paul, 1956), pp. 127–28.

[4] A useful review in the case of American prisons may be found in Paul W. Tappan, "The Legal Rights of Prisoners," The Annals, CCXCIII (May 1954), pp. 99–111.

virtue of the barrier that separates him from the outside world. The process of entrance typically brings other kinds of loss and mortification as well. We very generally find what are called *admission procedures*, such as taking a life history, photographing, weighing, fingerprinting, number-assigning, searching, signing away of personal possessions, undressing, bathing, disinfecting, haircutting, issuing institutional clothing and instruction as to rules, and assigning to quarters.[5] Admission procedures might better be called "trimming" or "programming" because in thus being squared-away the new arrival allows himself to become shaped and coded into the kind of object that can be fed into the administrative machinery of the establishment, to be worked on smoothly by routine operations. Many of these procedures depend upon attributes such as weight or fingerprints which the individual possesses merely because he is a member of the largest and most abstract of social categories, that of the human being. Action taken on the basis of such attributes necessarily ignores most of his previous basis of self-identification.

Because a total institution deals with its inmates in so many connections, with a complex squaring away at admission, there is a special need to obtain initial cooperativeness from the recruit. Staff often feel that a recruit's readiness to be appropriately deferential in his initial face-to-face encounters with them is a sign that he will pliantly take the role of the routinely usable inmate. The occasion on which staff members first tell the inmate of his deference obligations may be structured to challenge the inmate to balk or to hold his peace forever. Thus these initial moments of socialization may involve an *obedience test* and even a *will-breaking contest*: an inmate who shows defiance receives immediate visible punishment, which increases until he openly "cries uncle" and humbles himself.

An engaging illustration is provided by Brendan Behan in his review of his contest with two warders upon his admission to Walton prison:

[5] See, for example, J. Kerkhoff, *How Thin the Veil: A Newspaperman's Story of His Own Mental Crack-up and Recovery* (New York: Greenberg, 1952), p. 110; Elie A. Cohen, *Human Behaviour in the Concentration Camp* (London: Jonathan Cape, 1954), pp. 118–122; Eugen Kogon, *The Theory and Practice of Hell* (New York: Berkley Publishing Corp., n.d.), pp. 63–68.

"And 'old up your 'ead, when I speak to you."

" 'Old up your 'ead, when Mr. Whitbread speaks to you," said Mr. Holmes.

I looked round at Charlie. His eyes met mine and he quickly lowered them to the ground.

"What are you looking round at, Behan? Look at me."

I looked at Mr. Whitbread. "I am looking at you," I said. . . .

"You are looking at Mr. Whitbread—what?" said Mr. Holmes.

"I am looking at Mr. Whitbread."

Mr. Holmes looked gravely at Mr. Whitbread, drew back his open hand, and struck me on the face, held me with his other hand and struck me again.

My head spun and burned and pained and I wondered would it happen again. I forgot and felt another smack, and forgot, and another, and moved, and was held by a steadying, almost kindly hand, and another, and my sight was a vision of red and white and pity-coloured flashes.

"You are looking at Mr. Whitbread—what, Behan?"

I gulped and got together my voice and tried again till I got it out. "I, sir, please, sir, I am looking at you, I mean, I am looking at Mr. Whitbread, sir."[6]

Admission procedures and obedience tests may be elaborated into a form of initiation that has been called *the welcome*, where staff or inmates, or both, go out of their way to give the recruit a clear notion of his plight.[7] As part of this *rite de passage* he may be called by a term, such as "fish" or "swab," which tells him that he is merely an inmate, and, what is more, that he has a special low status even in this low group.

The admission procedure may be characterized as a leaving off and a taking on, with the midpoint marked by physical nakedness. Leaving off, of course, entails a *dispossession* of property, important here because persons invest self-feelings in their possessions. Perhaps the most significant of these possessions is

---

[6] Brendan Behan, *Borstal Boy* (London: Hutchinson, 1958), p. 40. See also Anthony Heckstall-Smith, *Eighteen Months* (London: Allan Wingate, 1954), p. 26.

[7] For a version of this process in concentration camps, see Cohen, *op. cit.*, p. 120, and Kogon, *op. cit.*, pp. 64–65. For a fictionalized treatment of the welcome in a girls' reformatory, see Sara Harris, *The Wayward Ones* (New York: New American Library, 1952), pp. 31–34. A prison version, less explicit, is found in George Dendrickson and Frederick Thomas, *The Truth About Dartmoor* (London: Gollancz, 1954), pp. 42–57.

not physical at all, that is, one's full name; whatever one is thereafter called, loss of one's name can be a great curtailment of the self.[8]

Once the inmate is stripped of his possessions, at least some replacements must be made by the establishment, but these take the form of standard issue, uniform in character and uniformly distributed. These substitute possessions are clearly marked as really belonging to the institution and in some cases are recalled at regular intervals to be, as it were, disinfected of identifications. With objects that can be used up, for example pencils, the inmate may be required to return the remnants before obtaining a re-issue.[9] Failure to provide inmates with individual lockers, and periodic searches and confiscations of accumulated personal property[10] reinforce property dispossession. Religious orders have appreciated the implications for self of such separation from belongings. Inmates may be required to change their cells once a year so as not to become attached to them. The Benedictine Rule is explicit:

For their bedding let a mattress, a blanket, a coverlet, and a pillow suffice. These beds must be frequently inspected by the Abbot, because of private property which may be found therein. If anyone be discovered to have what he has not received from the Abbot, let him be most severely punished. And in order that this vice of private ownership may be completely rooted out, let all things that are necessary be supplied by the Abbot: that is, cowl, tunic, stockings, shoes, girdle, knife, pen, needle, handkerchief, and tablets; so that all plea of necessity may be taken away. And let the Abbot always consider that passage in the Acts of the Apostles: "Distribution was made to each according as anyone had need."[11]

One set of the individual's possessions has a special relation to self. The individual ordinarily expects to exert some control over the guise in which he appears before others. For this he needs cosmetic and clothing supplies, tools for applying, arranging,

[8] For example, Thomas Merton, *The Seven Storey Mountain* (New York: Harcourt, Brace and Company, 1948), pp. 290–91; Cohen, *op. cit.*, pp. 145–47.

[9] Dendrickson and Thomas, *op. cit.*, pp. 83–84; also *The Holy Rule of Saint Benedict*, Ch. 55.

[10] Kogon, *op. cit.*, p. 69.

[11] *The Holy Rule of Saint Benedict*, Ch. 55.

and repairing them, and an accessible, secure place to store these supplies and tools—in short, for the management of his personal front, the individual possesses an identity kit. He also has access to services offered by barbers and clothiers.

On admission to a total institution, however, the individual is likely to be stripped of his usual appearance and of the equipment and services by which he maintains it, suffering, thus, a *personal defacement*. Clothing, combs, needle and thread, cosmetics, towels, soap, shaving sets, bathing facilities—all these may be taken away or denied him, although some may be kept in inaccessible storage, to be returned if and when he leaves. In the words of Saint Benedict's Holy Rule:

> Then forthwith he shall, there in the oratory, be divested of his own garments with which he is clothed and be clad in those of the monastery. Those garments of which he is divested shall be placed in the wardrobe, there to be kept, so that if, perchance, he should ever be persuaded by the devil to leave the monastery (which God forbid), he may be stripped of the monastic habit and cast forth.[12]

As suggested, the institutional issue provided as a substitute for what has been taken away is typically of a "coarse" variety, ill-suited, often old, and the same for large categories of inmates. The impact of this substitution is described in a report on imprisoned prostitutes:

> First, there is the shower officer who forces them to undress, takes their own clothes away, sees to it that they take showers and get their prison clothes—one pair of black oxfords with cuban heels, two pairs of much-mended ankle socks, three cotton dresses, two cotton slips, two pairs of panties, and a couple of bras. Practically all the bras are flat and useless. No corsets or girdles are issued.
>
> There is not a sadder sight than some of the obese prisoners who, if nothing else, have been managing to keep themselves looking decent on the outside, confronted by the first sight of themselves in prison issue.[13]

[12] *Ibid.*, Ch. 58.

[13] John M. Murtagh and Sara Harris, *Cast the First Stone* (New York: Pocket Books, 1958), pp. 239–40. On mental hospitals see, for example, Kerkhoff, *op. cit.*, p. 10. Mary Jane Ward, *The Snake Pit* (New York: New American Library, 1955), p. 60, makes the reasonable suggestion that men in our society suffer less defacement in total institutions than do women.

In addition to personal defacement that comes from being stripped of one's identity kit, there is *personal disfigurement* that comes from such direct and permanent mutilations of the body as brands or loss of limbs. Although this mortification of the self by way of the body is found in few total institutions, still, loss of a sense of personal safety is common and provides a basis for anxieties about disfigurement. Beatings, surgery or shock therapy—whatever the intent of staff in providing these services for some inmates—may lead many inmates to feel that they are in an environment that does not guarantee their physical integrity.

At admission, then, loss of identity equipment can prevent the individual from presenting his usual image of himself to others. After admission, the image of himself he presents is attacked in another way.

Given the expressive idiom of a particular civil society, certain movements, postures, and stances will convey lowly images of the individual and be avoided as demeaning. Any regulation, command, or task that forces the individual to adopt these movements or postures may thus mortify the self. In total institutions, such physical indignities abound. In mental hospitals, for example, patients may be forced to eat all food with a spoon.[14] In military prisons, inmates may be required to stand at attention whenever an officer enters the compound.[15] In religious institutions, there are such classic gestures of penitence as the kissing of feet,[16] and the posture required of an erring monk —that he must "lie prostrate at the door of the oratory in silence; and thus, with his face to the ground and his body prone, let him cast himself at the feet of all as they go forth from the oratory."[17] In some penal institutions, we find the humiliation of bending over to receive a birching.[18]

Just as the individual can be required to hold his body in a

[14] Johnson and Dodds, *op. cit.*, p. 15; for a prison version see Alfred Hassler, *Diary of a Self-Made Convict* (Chicago: Regnery, 1954), p. 33.

[15] L. D. Hankoff, "Interaction Patterns Among Military Prison Personnel," *U.S. Armed Forces Medical Journal*, X (1959), p. 1419.

[16] Kathryn Hulme, *The Nun's Story* (London: Muller, 1957), p. 52.

[17] *The Holy Rule of Saint Benedict*, Ch. 44.

[18] Dendrickson and Thomas, *op. cit.*, p. 76.

humiliating pose, so he may have to provide humiliating verbal responses. An important instance of this is the forced deference pattern of total institutions; inmates are often required to punctuate their social intercourse with staff by verbal acts of deference, such as saying "Sir." Another instance is the necessity to beg, importune, or humbly ask for little things such as a light for a cigarette, a drink of water, or permission to use the telephone.

Corresponding to the indignities of speech and action required of the inmate are the indignities of treatment others accord him. The standard examples here are *verbal or gestural profanations*: staff or fellow inmates call the individual obscene names, curse him, point out his negative attributes, tease him, or talk about him or his fellow-inmates as if he were not present.

Whatever the form or the source of these various indignities, the individual has to engage in activity whose symbolic implications are incompatible with his conception of self. A more diffuse example of this kind of mortification occurs when the individual is required to undertake a daily round of life that he considers alien to him—to undertake a *disidentifying role*. Thus in prisons denial of heterosexual activity can induce the fear of losing one's masculinity.[19] In military establishments, the patently useless make-work forced on fatigue details can cause men to feel their time and effort are worthless.[20] In religious institutions, there are special arrangements to ensure that all inmates take a turn performing the more menial aspects of the servant role.[21] An extreme is the concentration camp practice requiring prisoners to administer whippings to other prisoners.[22]

There is another form of mortification in total institutions; beginning with admission, a kind of *contaminative exposure* occurs. On the outside, the individual can hold objects of self-feeling—such as his body, his immediate actions, his thoughts, and some of his possessions—clear of contact with alien and

[19] Sykes, *op. cit.*, pp. 70–72.

[20] For example, T. E. Lawrence, *The Mint* (London: Jonathan Cape, 1955), pp. 34–35.

[21] *The Holy Rule of Saint Benedict*, Ch. 35.

[22] Kogon, *op. cit.*, p. 102.

contaminating things. But in total institutions these territories of the self are violated: the boundary that the individual places between his being and the environment is invaded and the embodiments of self profaned.

There is, first, a violation of one's informational preserve regarding self. During admission, facts about the inmate's social statuses and past behavior—especially discreditable facts—are collected and recorded in a dossier available to staff. Later, insofar as the establishment officially expects to alter the self-regulating inner-tendencies of the inmate, there may be dyadic or group confession—psychiatric, political, military or religious —according to the type of institution. On these occasions the inmate has to expose facts and feelings about self to new kinds of audiences. The most spectacular examples of such exposure come to us from Communist confession camps and from the *culpa* sessions that form part of the routine of Catholic religious institutions.[23] The dynamics of the process have been explicitly considered by those engaged in so-called milieu therapy.

Not only do new audiences learn discreditable facts about oneself that are ordinarily concealed, but they are also in a position to perceive some of these facts directly. Thus prisoners and mental patients cannot prevent their visitors from seeing them in humiliating circumstances.[24] Another example is the shoulder-patch of ethnic identification worn by concentration camp inmates.[25] Medical and security examinations often expose the inmate physically, sometimes to persons of both sexes. Collective sleeping arrangements cause a similar exposure, as do doorless toilets.[26] An extreme here, perhaps, is the situation of the mental patient who is stripped naked for what is felt to be his own protection and placed in a constantly-lit seclusion room, into whose judas-window any person passing on the ward can peer.

[23] Hulme, *op. cit.*, pp. 48–51.

[24] Wider communities in Western society, of course, have employed this technique too, in the form of public floggings and public hangings, the pillory and stocks. Functionally correlated with the public emphasis on mortifications in total institutions is the commonly found strict ruling that staff is not to be humiliated by staff in the presence of inmates.

[25] Kogon, *op. cit.*, pp. 41–42.

[26] Behan, *op. cit.*, p. 23.

In general, of course, the inmate is never fully alone; he is always within sight and often within earshot of someone, if only his fellow-inmates.[27] Prison cages with bars for walls fully realize such exposure.

Perhaps the most obvious type of contaminative exposure is the directly physical kind—the besmearing and defiling of the body or of other objects closely identified with the self. Sometimes this involves a breakdown of the usual environmental arrangements for insulating oneself from one's own source of contamination, as in having to empty one's own slops[28] or having to subject one's evacuation to regimentation, as reported in Chinese political prisons:

An aspect of their isolation regimen which is especially onerous to Western prisoners is the arrangement for the elimination of urine and feces. The "slop jar" that is usually present in Russian cells is often absent in China. It is a Chinese custom to allow defecation and urination only at one or two specified times each day—usually in the morning after breakfast. The prisoner is hustled from his cell by a guard, double-timed down a long corridor, and given approximately two minutes to squat over an open Chinese latrine and attend to all of his wants. The haste and the public scrutiny are especially difficult for women to tolerate. If the prisoners cannot complete their action in about two minutes, they are abruptly dragged away and back to their cells.[29]

A very common form of physical contamination is reflected in complaints about unclean food, messy quarters, soiled towels, shoes and clothing impregnated with previous users' sweat,

[27] For example, Kogon, *op. cit.*, p. 128; Hassler, *op. cit.*, p. 16. For the situation in a religious institution, see Hulme, *op. cit.*, p. 48. She also describes a lack of aural privacy since thin cotton hangings are used as the only door closing off the individual sleeping cells (p. 20).

[28] Heckstall-Smith, *op. cit.*, p. 21; Dendrickson and Thomas, *op. cit.*, p. 53.

[29] L. E. Hinkle, Jr. and H. G. Wolff, "Communist Interrogation and Indoctrination of 'Enemies of the State,'" A.M.A. *Archives of Neurology and Psychiatry*, LXXVI (1956), p. 153. An extremely useful report on the profanizing role of fecal matter, and the social necessity of personal as well as environmental control, is provided in C. E. Orbach, *et. al.*, "Fears and Defensive Adaptations to the Loss of Anal Sphincter Control," *The Psychoanalytic Review*, XLIV (1957), pp. 121–75.

toilets without seats, and dirty bath facilities.[30] Orwell's comments on his boarding school may be taken as illustrative:

> For example, there were the pewter bowls out of which we had our porridge. They had overhanging rims, and under the rims there were accumulations of sour porridge, which could be flaked off in long strips. The porridge itself, too, contained more lumps, hairs and unexplained black things than one would have thought possible, unless someone were putting them there on purpose. It was never safe to start on that porridge without investigating it first. And there was the slimy water of the plunge bath—it was twelve or fifteen feet long, the whole school was supposed to go into it every morning, and I doubt whether the water was changed at all frequently—and the always-damp towels with their cheesy smell. . . . And the sweaty smell of the changing room with its greasy basins, and, given on this, the row of filthy, dilapidated lavatories, which had no fastenings of any kind on the doors, so that whenever you were sitting there someone was sure to come crashing in. It is not easy for me to think of my school days without seeming to breathe in a whiff of something cold and evil-smelling—a sort of compound of sweaty stockings, dirty towels, fecal smells blowing along corridors, forks with old food between the prongs, neck-of-mutton stew, and the banging doors of the lavatories and the echoing chamber-pots in the dormitories.[31]

There are still other sources of physical contamination, as an interviewee suggests in describing a concentration camp hospital:

> We were lying two in each bed. And it was very unpleasant. For example, if a man died he would not be removed before twenty-four hours had elapsed because the block trusty wanted, of course, to get the bread ration and the soup which was allotted to this person. For this reason the dead person would be reported dead twenty-four hours later so that his ration would still be allotted. And so we had to lie all that time in bed together with the dead person.[32]

[30] For example, Johnson and Dodds, *op. cit.*, p. 75; Heckstall-Smith, *op. cit.*, p. 15.

[31] George Orwell, "Such, Such Were the Joys," *Partisan Review*, XIX (September–October 1952), p. 523.

[32] David P. Boder, *I Did Not Interview the Dead* (Urbana: University of Illinois Press, 1949), p. 50.

We were on the middle level. And that was a very gruesome situation, especially at night. First of all, the dead men were badly emaciated and they looked terrible. In most cases they would soil themselves at the moment of death and that was not a very esthetic event. I saw such cases very frequently in the lager, in the sick people's barracks. People who died from phlegmonous, suppurative wounds, with their beds overflowing from pus would be lying together with somebody whose illness was possibly more benign, who had possibly just a small wound which now would become infected.[33]

The contamination of lying near the dying has also been reported in mental hospital reports,[34] and surgical contamination has been cited in prison documents:

Surgical instruments and bandages in the dressing-room lie exposed to the air and dust. George, attending for the treatment, by a medical orderly, of a boil on his neck, had it lanced with a scalpel that had been used a moment before on a man's foot, and had not been sterilised in the meantime.[35]

Finally, in some total institutions the inmate is obliged to take oral or intravenous medications, whether desired or not, and to eat his food, however unpalatable. When an inmate refuses to eat, there may be forcible contamination of his insides by "forced-feeding."

I have suggested that the inmate undergoes mortification of the self by contaminative exposure of a physical or surface kind, but this must be amplified: for when the agency of contamination is another human being, then the inmate is in addition contaminated by forced interpersonal contact and, in consequence, a forced social relationship. Similarly, when the inmate loses control over who observes him in his predicament, or who knows about his past, he is being contaminated by a forced relationship to these people—for it is through such perception and knowledge that relations are expressed.

The model for interpersonal contamination in our society is

---

[33] *Idem.*
[34] Johnson and Dodds, *op. cit.*, p. 16.
[35] Dendrickson and Thomas, *op. cit.*, p. 122.

presumably rape, but, while sexual molestation certainly occurs in total institutions, there are many other less dramatic examples. Upon admission, one's on-person possessions are pawed and fingered by an official as he itemizes and prepares them for storage. The inmate himself may be frisked and searched to the extent—often reported in the literature—of a rectal examination.[36] Later in his stay he may be required to undergo searchings of his person and of his sleeping-quarters, either routinely or when trouble arises. In all these cases it is the searcher as well as the search that penetrates the private reserve of the individual and violates the territories of his self. Even routine inspections can have this effect, as Lawrence suggests:

In the old days men had weekly to strip off boots and socks, and expose their feet for an officer's inspection. An ex-boy'd kick you in the mouth, as you bent down to look. So with the bath-rolls, a certificate from your N.C.O. that you'd had a bath during the week. One bath! And with the kit inspections, and room inspections, and equipment inspections, all excuses for the dogmatists among the officers to blunder, and for the nosy-parkers to make beasts of themselves. Oh, you require the gentlest touch to interfere with a poor man's person, and not give offence.[37]

Further, the practice of mixing age, ethnic, and racial groups in prisons and mental hospitals can lead an inmate to feel he is being contaminated by contact with undesirable fellow-inmates. A prisoner, describing his admission to prison, provides an example:

Another warder came up with a pair of handcuffs and coupled me to the little Jew, who moaned softly to himself in Yiddish.[38]

Suddenly, the awful thought occurred to me that I might have to share a cell with the little Jew and I was seized with panic. The thought obsessed me to the exclusion of all else.[39]

[36] For example, Lowell Naeve, *A Field of Broken Stones* (Glen Gardner, N.J.: Libertarian Press, 1950), p. 17; Kogon, *op. cit.*, p. 67; Holley Cantine and Dachine Rainer, *Prison Etiquette* (Bearsville, N.Y.: Retort Press, 1950), p. 46.

[37] Lawrence, *op. cit.*, p. 196.

[38] Heckstall-Smith, *op. cit.*, p. 14.

[39] *Ibid.*, p. 17.

Obviously, group-living will necessitate mutual contact and exposure among inmates. At the extreme, as in cells for Chinese political prisoners, mutual contact may be very great:

At some stage in his imprisonment the prisoner can expect to find himself placed in a cell with about eight other prisoners. If he was initially isolated and interrogated, this may be shortly after his first "confession" is accepted; but many prisoners are placed in group cells from the outset of their imprisonment. The cell is usually barren, and scarcely large enough to hold the group it contains. There may be a sleeping platform, but all of the prisoners sleep on the floor; and when all lie down, every inch of floor space may be taken up. The atmosphere is extremely intimate. Privacy is entirely nonexistent.[40]

Lawrence provides a military illustration in discussing his difficulties in merging with fellow-airmen in the barracks hut:

You see, I cannot play at anything with anyone: and a native shyness shuts me out from their freemasonry of————and blinding, pinching, borrowing, and talking dirty: this despite my sympathy for the abandon of functional frankness in which they wallow. Inevitably, in our crowded lodging, we must communicate just those physical modesties which polite life keeps veiled. Sexual activity's a naive boast, and any abnormalities of appetite or organ are curiously displayed. The Powers encourage this behavior. All latrines in camp have lost their doors. "Make the little ————s sleep and ———— and eat together," grinned old Jock Mackay, senior instructor, "and we'll have 'em drilling together, naturally."[41]

One routine instance of this contaminative contact is the naming system for inmates. Staff and fellow-inmates automatically assume the right to employ an intimate form of address or a truncated formal one: for a middle class person, at least, this denies the right to hold himself off from others through a formal style of address.[42] When the individual has to eat food he considers alien and polluted, this contamination sometimes derives from other persons' connection with the

[40] Hinkle and Wolff, *op. cit.*, p. 156.
[41] Lawrence, *op. cit.*, p. 91.
[42] For example, see Hassler, *op. cit.*, p. 104.

food, as is nicely illustrated in the penance of "begging soup" practiced in some nunneries:

> . . . she placed her pottery bowl on the left of the Mother Superior, knelt, clasped her hands and waited until two spoonfuls of soup had been put into her beggar's bowl, then on to the next oldest and the next, until the bowl was filled. . . . When at last her bowl was filled, she returned to her place and swallowed the soup, as she knew she must, down to the last drop. She tried not to think how it had been tossed into her bowl from a dozen other bowls that had already been eaten from.[43]

Another kind of contaminative exposure is that which brings an outsider into contact with the individual's close relationship to significant others. For example, an inmate may have his personal mail read and censored, and even made fun of to his face.[44] Another example is the enforced public character of visits, as reports from prisons suggest:

> But what a sadistic kind of arrangement they have for these visits! One hour a month—or two half-hours—in a big room with perhaps a score of other couples, with guards prowling about to make sure you exchange neither the plans nor the implements of escape! We met across a six-foot-wide table, down the middle of which a sort of bundling-board six inches high presumably prevents even our germs from intermingling. We were permitted one sanitary handshake at the beginning of the visit and one at the end; for the rest of the time we could only sit and look at each other while we called across that vast expanse![45]

> Visits take place in a room by the main gate. There is a wooden table, at one side of which sits the prisoner and at the other side his visitors. The warder sits at the head; he hears every word that is spoken, watches every gesture and nuance of expression. There is no privacy at all—and this when a man is meeting his wife whom he may not have seen for years. Nor is any contact allowed between prisoner and visitor, and, of course, no articles are allowed to change hands.[46]

[43] Hulme, op. cit., pp. 52–53.
[44] Dendrickson and Thomas, *op. cit.*, p. 128.
[45] Hassler, *op. cit.*, pp. 62–63.
[46] Dendrickson and Thomas, *op. cit.*, p. 175.

A more thoroughgoing version of this type of contaminative exposure occurs in institutionally-arranged confessions. When a significant other must be denounced, and especially when this other is physically present, confession of the relationship to outsiders can mean an intense exposure and contamination of self. A description of practices in a nunnery provides an illustration:

The bravest of the emotionally vulnerable were the sisters who stood up together in the culpa and proclaimed each other—for having gone out of their way to be near to one another, or perhaps for having talked together in recreation in a way that excluded others. Their tormented but clearly spoken disclosures of a nascent affinity gave it the *coup de grâce* which they themselves might not have been able to do, for the entire community would henceforth see to it that these two would be kept far apart. The pair would be helped to detach themselves from one of those spontaneous personal attachments which often sprang to life in the body of the community as unexpectedly as wildflowers appeared, now and again, in the formal geometric patterns of the cloister gardens.[47]

A parallel example can be found in highly professionalized mental hospitals devoted to intensive milieu therapy, where patient-pairs conducting an affair may be obliged to discuss their relationship during group meetings.

In total institutions, exposure of one's relationships can occur in even more drastic forms, for there may be occasions when an individual must witness a physical assault upon someone to whom he has ties, and suffer the permanent mortification of having taken no action. Thus we learn of a mental hospital:

This knowledge [of shock therapy] is based on the fact that some of the patients in Ward 30 have assisted the shock team in the administration of therapy to patients, holding them down, and helping to strap them in bed, or watching them after they have quieted. The administration of shock on the ward is often carried out in full sight of a group of interested onlookers. The patient's convulsions often resemble those of an accident victim in death agony and are accompanied by choking gasps and at times by a foaming overflow of saliva from the mouth. The patient slowly recovers without mem-

[47] Hulme, *op. cit.*, pp. 50–51.

ory of the occurrence, but he has served the others as a frightful spectacle of what may be done to them.[48]

Melville's report on flogging aboard a nineteenth century man-of-war provides another example:

However much you may desire to absent yourself from the scene that ensues, yet behold it you must; or, at least, stand near it you must; for the regulations enjoin the attendance of almost the entire ship's company, from the corpulent captain himself to the smallest boy who strikes the bell.[49]

And the inevitableness of his own presence at the scene: the strong arm that drags him in view of the scourge, and holds him there till all is over: forcing upon his loathing eye and soul the sufferings and groans of men who have familiarly consorted with him, eaten with him, battled out watches with him—men of his own type and badge —all this conveys a terrible hint of the omnipotent authority under which he lives.[50]

Lawrence offers a military example:

Tonight's crash of the stick on the hut door at roll call was terrific; and the door s¹ammed back nearly off its hinges. Into the light strode Baker, V.C., a corporal who assumed great licence in the camp because of his war decoration. He marched down my side of the hut, checking the beds. Little Nobby, taken by surprise, had one boot on and another off. Corporal Baker stopped. "What's the matter with YOU?" "I was knocking out a nail which hurts my foot." "Put your boot on at once. Your name?" He passed on to the end door and there whirled around, snorting, "Clarke." Nobby properly cried, "Corporal," and limped down the alley at a run (we must always run when called) to bring up stiffly at attention before him. A pause, and then curtly, "Get back to your bed."
Still the Corporal waited and so must we, lined up by our beds. Again, sharply, "Clarke." The performance was repeated, over and over, while the four files of us looked on, bound fast by shame and discipline. We were men, and a man over there was degrading himself and his species, in degrading another. Baker was lusting for

48 Ivan Belknap, *Human Problems of a State Mental Hospital* (New York: McGraw-Hill, 1956), p. 194.
49 Herman Melville, *White Jacket* (New York: Grove Press, n.d.), p. 135.
50 *Idem.*

trouble and hoped to provoke one of us into some act or word on which to base a charge.[51]

The extreme of this kind of *experiential mortification* is found of course in the concentration camp literature:

A Jew from Breslau named Silbermann had to stand by idly as SS Sergeant Hoppe brutally tortured his brother to death. Silbermann went mad at the sight, and late at night he precipitated a panic with his frantic cries that the barracks was on fire.[52]

I have considered some of the more elementary and direct assaults upon the self—various forms of disfigurement and defilement through which the symbolic meaning of events in the inmate's immediate presence dramatically fails to corroborate his prior conception of self. I would like now to consider a source of mortification that is less direct in its effect, with a significance for the individual that is less easy to assess: a disruption of the usual relationship between the individual actor and his acts.

The first disruption to consider here is *looping*: an agency that creates a defensive response on the part of the inmate takes this very response as the target of its next attack. The individual finds that his protective response to an assault upon self is collapsed into the situation; he cannot defend himself in the usual way by establishing distance between the mortifying situation and himself.

Deference patterns in total institutions provide one illustration of the looping effect. In civil society, when an individual must accept circumstances and commands that affront his conception of self, he is allowed a margin of face-saving reactive expression—sullenness, failure to offer usual signs of deference, *sotto voce* profaning asides, or fugitive expressions of contempt, irony, and derision. Compliance, then, is likely to be associated with an expressed attitude to one's compliance which is not itself subject to the same degree of pressure for conformity. Although such self-protective expressive response to humiliating demands does occur in total institutions, staff may directly penalize inmates for such expressive activity, citing sullenness or

[51] Lawrence, *op. cit.*, p. 62.
[52] Kogon, *op. cit.*, p. 160.

insolence explicitly as grounds for further punishment. Thus, in describing the contamination of self resulting from having to drink soup from a beggar's bowl, Kathryn Hulme says that she:

. . . blanked out from her facial expression the revolt that rose up in her fastidious soul as she drank her dregs. One look of rebellion, she knew, would be enough to invite a repetition of the awful abasement which she was sure she could never go through again, not even for the sake of the Blessed Lord Himself.[53]

The desegregating process in total institutions creates other instances of looping. In the normal course of affairs in civil society, audience and role segregation keep one's avowals and implicit claims regarding self, made in one physical sense of activity, from being tested against conduct in other settings.[54] In total institutions, spheres of life are desegregated, so that an inmate's conduct in one scene of activity is thrown up to him by staff as a comment and check upon his conduct in another context. Thus a mental patient, in an effort to present himself in a well-oriented, unantagonistic manner during a diagnostic or treatment conference may be directly embarrassed by evidence introduced concerning his apathy during recreation, or by showing him the bitter comments he made in a letter to a sibling— a letter which the recipient has forwarded to the hospital administrator, to be added to the patient's dossier and brought along to the conference.

Psychiatric establishments of the advanced type play a special role in looping, since didactic feedback may there be erected into a basic therapeutic doctrine. A "permissive" atmosphere is felt to encourage the inmate to "project" or "act out" his typical difficulties in living, which can then be brought to his attention during group therapy sessions.[55]

---

[53] Hulme, *op. cit.*, p. 53.

[54] In civil society, crimes and certain other forms of deviance affect the way in which the offender is received in all areas of life, but this breakdown of spheres applies mainly to offenders, not to the bulk of the population that does not offend in these ways or offends without being caught.

[55] A clear statement may be found in R. Rapoport and E. Skellern, "Some Therapeutic Functions of Administrative Disturbance," *Administrative Science Quarterly*, II (1957), pp. 84–85.

Through the process of looping, then, the inmate's reaction to his own situation is collapsed back into this situation itself, and he is not allowed to retain the usual segregation of these phases of action. A second assault upon the inmate's status as an actor may now be cited, one that has been loosely described under the categories of regimentation and tyrannization.

In civil society, by the time the individual is an adult he has incorporated socially acceptable standards for the performance of most of his activity so that the issue of the correctness of his action arises only at certain points, as when his productivity is judged. Beyond this, he is allowed to go at his own pace.[56] He need not constantly look over his shoulder to see if criticism and other sanctions are coming. In addition, many actions will be defined as matters of personal taste, with choice from a range of possibilities specifically allowed. For much activity, then, the judgment and action of authority is held off and one is on one's own. Under such circumstances, one can schedule activity so as to fit actions into one another to one's over-all profit—a kind of "personal economy of action," as when an individual postpones eating for a few minutes in order to finish a task, or lays aside a task a little early in order to join a friend for dinner, or maintains a side-activity while focusing on a main one. For a person who joins a total institution, however, minute segments of his line of activity may be subjected to regulations and judgment by staff; the individual's life is penetrated by the constant, sanctioning interaction with staff, especially during the initial period of stay before the inmate accepts the regulations unthinkingly. Each specification robs the individual of an opportunity to balance his needs and objectives in a personally efficient way, and opens up his line of action to sanctions. Thus the autonomy of the act itself is violated.

Although this process of social control is in effect in all or-

[56] The span of time over which an employee works at his own discretion without supervision can in fact be taken as a measure of his pay and status in an organization. See Elliott Jacques, *The Measurement of Responsibility: A Study of Work, Payment, and Individual Capacity* (Cambridge: Harvard University Press, 1956). And just as "time-span of responsibility" is an index of position, so a long span of freedom from inspection is a reward of position.

ganized society, we tend to forget how detailed and act-controlling it can become in total institutions. The routine reported for one jail for youthful offenders provides a striking example:

At 5:30 we were wakened and had to jump out of bed and stand at attention. When the guard shouted "One!" you removed your night shirt; at "Two!" you folded it; at "Three!" you made your bed. (Only two minutes to make the bed in a difficult and complicated manner.) All the while three monitors would shout at us: "Hurry it up!" and "Make it snappy!"

We also dressed by numbers: shirts on at "One!"; pants at "Two!"; socks at "Three!"; shoes at "Four!" Any noise, like dropping a shoe or even scraping it along the floor, was enough to send you to the line.

. . . Once downstairs everyone faced the wall at strict attention, hands at side, thumbs even with trouser seams, head up, shoulders back, stomach in, heels together, eyes straight ahead, no scratching or putting hands to face or head, no moving even the fingers.[57]

A jail for adults provides another example:

The silence system was enforced. No talking outside the cell, at meals or at work.

No pictures were allowed in the cell. No gazing about at meals. Bread crusts were allowed to be left only on the left side of the plate. Inmates were required to stand at attention, cap in hand, until any official, visitor or guard moved beyond sight.[58]

And a concentration camp:

In the barracks a wealth of new and confusing impressions overwhelmed the prisoners. Making up beds was a particular source of SS chicanery. Shapeless and matted straw pallets had to be made as even as a board, the pattern of the sheets parallel to the edges, head bolsters set up at right angles.[59]

The SS seized on the most trifling offenses as occasions for punishment: keeping hands in pockets in cold weather; turning up the

[57] Hassler, *op. cit.*, p. 155, quoting Robert McCreery.

[58] T. E. Gaddis, *Birdman of Alcatraz* (New York: New American Library, 1958), p. 25. For a similar rule of silence in a British prison, see Frank Norman, *Bang to Rights* (London: Secker and Warburg, 1958), p. 27.

[59] Kogon, *op. cit.*, p. 68.

coat collar in rain or wind; missing buttons; the tiniest tear or speck of dirt on the clothing; unshined shoes . . . ; shoes that were too well shined—indicating that the wearer was shirking work; failure to salute, including so-called "sloppy posture"; . . . The slightest deviation in dressing ranks and files, or arranging the prisoners in the order of size, or any swaying, coughing, sneezing—any of these might provoke a savage outburst from the SS.[60]

From the military comes an example of the specifications possible in kit-laying:

Now the tunic, so folded that the belt made it a straight edge. Covering it, the breeches, squared to the exact area of the tunic, with four concertina-folds facing forward. Towels were doubled once, twice, thrice, and flanked the blue tower. In front of the blue sat a rectangular cardigan. To each side a rolled puttee. Shirts were packed and laid in pairs like flannel bricks. Before them, pants. Between them, neat balls of socks, wedged in. Our holdalls were stretched wide, with knife, fork, spoon, razor, comb, toothbrush, lather brush, button-stick, in that order, ranged across them.[61]

Similarly, an ex-nun speaks of having to learn to keep her hands still[62] and hidden and to accept the fact that only six specified items were permitted in one's pockets.[63] An ex-mental patient speaks of the humiliation of being doled out limited toilet paper at each request.[64]

As suggested earlier, one of the most telling ways in which one's economy of action can be disrupted is the obligation to request permission or supplies for minor activities that one can execute on one's own on the outside, such as smoking, shaving, going to the toilet, telephoning, spending money, or mailing letters. This obligation not only puts the individual in a submissive or suppliant role "unnatural" for an adult but also opens up his line of action to interceptions by staff. Instead of having

[60] *Ibid.*, pp. 99–100.
[61] Lawrence, *op. cit.*, p. 83. In this connection see the comments by M. Brewster Smith on the concept of "chicken," in Samuel Stouffer *et al.*, *The American Soldier* (4 vols.; Princeton: Princeton University Press, 1949), Vol. I, p. 390.
[62] Hulme, *op. cit.*, p. 3.
[63] *Ibid.*, p. 39.
[64] Ward, *op. cit.*, p. 23.

his request immediately and automatically granted, the inmate may be teased, denied, questioned at length, not noticed, or, as an ex-mental patient suggests, merely put off:

> Probably anyone who has never been in a similarly helpless position cannot realize the humiliation to anyone able-bodied yet lacking authority to do the simplest offices for herself of having to beg repeatedly for even such small necessities as clean linen or a light for her cigarette from nurses who constantly brush her aside with, "I'll give it to you in a minute, dear," and go off leaving her unsupplied. Even the canteen staff seemed to share the opinion that civility was wasted upon lunatics, and would keep a patient waiting indefinitely, while they gossiped with their friends.[65]

I have suggested that authority in total institutions is directed to a multitude of items of conduct—dress, deportment, manners—that constantly occur and constantly come up for judgment. The inmate cannot easily escape from the press of judgmental officials and from the enveloping tissue of constraint. A total institution, then, is like a finishing school, but one that has many refinements and is little refined.

I would like to comment on two aspects of this tendency toward a multiplication of actively enforced rulings. First, these rulings are often geared in with an obligation to perform the regulated activity in unison with blocks of fellow-inmates. This is what is sometimes called regimentation.

Secondly, these diffuse rulings occur in an authority system of the *echelon* kind; *any* member of the staff class has certain rights to discipline *any* member of the inmate class, thereby markedly increasing the probability of sanction. (This arrangement, it may be noted, is similar to the one that gives any adult in some small American towns certain rights to correct, and demand small services from, any child not in the immediate presence of his parents.) On the outside, the adult in our society is typically under the authority of a *single* immediate superior in connection with his work, or under authority of one spouse in connection with domestic duties; the only echelon authority he must face—the police—is typically not constantly

[65] Johnson and Dodds, *op. cit.*, p. 39.

or relevantly present, except perhaps in the case of traffic-law enforcement.

Given echelon authority and regulations that are diffuse, novel, and strictly enforced, we may expect inmates, especially new ones, to live with chronic anxiety about breaking the rules and in fear of the consequence of breaking them—physical injury or death in a concentration camp, being "washed out" in an officer's training camp, or merely demotion in a mental hospital:

Yet, even in the apparent liberty and friendliness of an "open" ward, I still found a background of threats that made me feel something between a prisoner and a pauper. The smallest offence, from a nervous symptom to displeasing a sister personally, was met by the suggestion of removing the offender to a closed ward. The idea of a return to "J" ward, if I did not eat my food, was brandished at me so constantly that it became an obsession and even such meals as I was able to swallow disagreed with me physically, while other patients were impelled to do unnecessary or uncongenial work by a similar fear.[66]

In total institutions, then, staying out of trouble is likely to require persistent conscious effort. The inmate may therefore forego certain levels of sociability with his fellows to avoid possible incidents.

In concluding this description of the processes of mortification, three general issues must be raised.

First, total institutions disrupt or defile precisely those actions that in civil society seem to have the special role of attesting to the actor and to those in his presence that he has some command over his world—that he is a person with "adult" self-determination, autonomy, and freedom of action. A failure to retain this kind of adult executive competency, or at least the symbols of it, can produce in the inmate the terror of feeling radically demoted in the age-grading system.[67]

A margin of self-selected expressive behavior—whether of antagonism, affection, or unconcern—is one symbol of self-determination. This evidence of one's autonomy is weakened

[66] *Ibid.*, p. 36.
[67] *Cf.* Sykes, *op. cit.*, pp. 73–76, "The Deprivation of Autonomy."

by such specific obligations as having to write one letter home a week, or having to refrain from expressing sullenness. It is further weakened when this margin of behavior is used as evidence concerning the state of one's psychiatric, religious, or political conscience.

There are certain bodily comforts significant to the individual that tend to be lost upon entrance into a total institution—for example, a soft bed,[68] or quietness at night.[69] Loss of this set of comforts is apt to reflect a loss of self-determination, too, for the individual tends to ensure these comforts the moment he has resources to expend.[70]

Loss of self-determination seems to have been ceremonialized in concentration camps; thus we have atrocity tales of prisoners being forced to roll in the mud,[71] stand on their heads in the snow, work at ludicrously useless tasks, swear at themselves[72] or, in the case of Jewish prisoners, sing anti-Semitic songs.[73] A milder version is found in mental hospitals where attendants have been observed forcing a patient who wanted a cigarette to say "pretty please," or to jump for it. In all such cases the inmate is made to display a giving up of his will. Less ceremonialized, but just as extreme, is the embarrassment to one's autonomy that comes from being locked in a ward, placed in a tight wet-pack, or tied up in a camisole, and thereby denied the liberty of making small adjustive movements.

Another clear-cut expression of personal inefficacy in total institutions has to do with inmates' use of speech. One implication of using words to convey decisions about action is that the recipient of an order is seen capable of receiving a message and acting under his own power to complete the suggestion or command. Executing the act himself, he can sustain some vestige

<hr>

68 Hulme, *op. cit.*, p. 18; Orwell, *op. cit.*, p. 521.

69 Hassler, *op. cit.*, p. 78; Johnson and Dodds, *op. cit.*, p. 17.

70 This is one source of mortification that civilians practice on themselves during camping vacations, perhaps on the assumption that a new sense of self can be obtained by voluntarily foregoing some of one's previous self-impregnated comforts.

71 Kogon, *op. cit.*, p. 66.

72 *Ibid.*, p. 61.

73 *Ibid.*, p. 78.

of the notion that he is self-determining. Responding to the question in his own words, he can sustain the notion that he is somebody to be considered, however slightly. And since it is only words that pass between himself and the others, he succeeds in retaining at least physical distance from them, however unpalatable the command or statement.

The inmate in a total institution can find himself denied this kind of protective distance and self-action. Especially in mental hospitals and political training prisons, the statements he makes may be discounted as mere symptoms, and the non-verbal aspects of his reply attended to.[74] Often he is considered to be of insufficient ritual weight to be given even minor greetings, let alone listened to.[75] Or the inmate may find that a kind of rhetorical use of language occurs: questions such as, "Have you washed yet?" or "Have you got both socks on?" may be accompanied by a simultaneous searching action by staff which physically discloses the facts, making their verbal questions superfluous. And instead of being told to move in a particular direction at a particular rate, he may find himself pushed along by the guard, or pulled (in the case of overalled mental patients), or frog-marched. And finally, as will be discussed later, the inmate may find that a dual language exists, with the disciplinary facts of his life given a translated ideal-phrasing by staff that mocks the normal use of language.

The second general consideration is the rationale that is employed for assaults upon the self. This issue tends to place total institutions and their inmates into three different groupings.

In religious institutions, the implications environmental arrangements have for self are explicitly recognized:

That is the meaning of the contemplative life, and the sense of all the apparently meaningless little rules and observances and fasts and obediences and penances and humiliations and labors that go to make up the routine of existence in a contemplative monastery:

[74] See Alfred H. Stanton and Morris S. Schwartz, *The Mental Hospital* (New York: Basic Books, 1954), pp. 200, 203, 205–6.

[75] For an example of this nonperson treatment, see Johnson and Dodds, *op. cit.*, p. 122.

they all serve to remind us of what we are and Who God is—that we may get sick of the sight of ourselves and turn to Him: and in the end, we will find Him in ourselves, in our own purified natures which have become the mirror of His tremendous Goodness and of His endless love. . . .[76]

The inmates, as well as the staff, actively seek out these curtailments of the self, so that mortification is complemented by self-mortification, restrictions by renunciations, beatings by self-flagellations, inquisition by confession. Because religious establishments are explicitly concerned with the processes of mortification, they have a special value for sociological study.

In concentration camps, and to a lesser extent, prisons, some mortifications seem to be arranged solely or mainly for their mortifying power, as when a prisoner is urinated on, but here the inmate does not embrace and facilitate his own destruction of self.

In many of the remaining total institutions, mortifications are officially rationalized on other grounds, such as sanitation in connection with latrine duty, responsibility for life in connection with forced pill-taking, combat capacity in connection with Army rules for personal appearance, "security" in connection with restrictive prison regulations.

In total institutions of all three varieties, however, the various rationales for mortifying the self are very often merely rationalizations, generated by efforts to manage the daily activity of a large number of persons in a small space with a small expenditure of resources. Further, curtailments of the self occur in all three, even in the case where the inmate is willing and the management has ideal concerns for his well-being.

Two issues have been considered: the inmate's sense of personal inefficacy, and the relation of his own desires to the ideal interests of the establishment. The connection between these two issues is variable. Persons can voluntarily elect to enter a total institution and cease thereafter, to their regret, to be able to make such important decisions; in other cases, notably the religious, inmates may begin with and sustain a willful desire to

[76] Merton, *op. cit.*, p. 372.

be stripped and cleansed of personal will. Total institutions are fateful for the inmate's civilian self, although the attachment of the inmate to this civilian self can vary considerably.

The processes of mortification I have been considering have to do with the implications for self that persons oriented to a particular expressive idiom might draw from an individual's appearance, conduct, and general situation. In this context I want to consider a third and final issue: the relation between this symbolic-interaction framework for considering the fate of the self and the conventional psychophysiological one centered around the concept of stress.

The basic facts about self in this report are phrased in a sociological perspective, always leading back to a description of the institutional arrangements which directly delineate the personal prerogatives of a member. Of course, a psychological assumption is also implied; cognitive processes are invariably involved, for the social arrangements must be "read" by the individual and by others for the image of himself that they imply. But, as I have argued, the relation of this cognitive process to other psychological processes is quite variable: according to the general expressive idiom of our society, having one's head shaved is easily perceived as a curtailment of the self, but while this mortification may enrage a mental patient, it may please a monk.

Mortification or curtailment of the self is very likely to involve acute psychological stress for the individual; but for an individual sick with his world or guilt-ridden in it, mortification may bring psychological relief. Further, the psychological stress often created by assaults on the self can also be produced by matters perceived as unrelated to the territories of the self—such as loss of sleep, insufficient food, or protracted decision-making. So, too, a high level of anxiety or the unavailability of fantasy materials, such as movies and books, may greatly increase the psychological effect of a violation of the self-boundaries, but in themselves these facilitating factors have nothing to do with the mortification of the self. Empirically, then, the study of stress and of encroachments on the self seem to be tied together; but analytically, two different frameworks are involved.

THE URGE
TO PUNISH

Henry Weihofen

In persons charged with the commission of criminal offenses, how
should the nature and degree of mental disturbance be assessed
by law? Henry Weihofen, student of law and criminology, ad-
dresses himself to this question in the following selection. He
considers new approaches to the problem of mental irresponsibility for crime and relates these to the highly controversial
question of the abolition of capital punishment.

Briefly, the series of decisions and the changes in attitudes concerning the responsibility of offenders for their criminal acts derive from the free moral agent concept. Here, *mens rea* was
presumed: the guilty mind, the criminal intent, the purposeful
act of an individual seeking to commit harm to another or to
society. There followed, in the early part of the eighteenth century, the "wild beast" test, which exempted a person from punishment if and only if he were totally deprived of his understanding and memory of the act, and had no more knowledge of what
he was doing than "an infant, a brute, or a wild beast."

Source: Henry Weihofen, *The Urge to Punish* (New York: Farrar,
Straus & Giroux, 1956), pp. 130–170. Copyright © 1956 by Henry
Weihofen. Reprinted by permission of Farrar, Straus & Giroux, Inc. This
selection was the final lecture of the Fourth Annual Isaac Ray Award
lectures, which the author gave at Temple University in 1954.

The development of criminal law continued from this point to the famed M'Naghten Rules (which a historian would more accurately call the Macnaghten Rules, but the former spelling has come into general usage). These permitted punishment if the transgressor knew that he was acting contrary to the law; furthermore, under M'Naghten, there was a presumption of sanity, with the burden of proof on the defense to establish that the accused had a defect or a diseased mind, so as to be unable to know the nature and quality of his act and the fact that it was wrong to commit it.

Although the M'Naghten Rules were laid down in 1843, they were antedated by Isaac Ray's surprisingly modern formulation, first set forth in 1838, restated in 1850, adopted by the American Psychiatric Association in 1864, and by the New Hampshire Supreme Court in 1871, and described here by Weihofen; in essence, Ray was pleading that insane persons should not be held responsible for their criminal acts, unless the acts are proved not to have been a direct or an indirect result of the insanity.

Still another test was introduced in America starting in 1884, when in several states "irresistible impulse" became the deciding factor; by this was meant that a person must not only be capable of *knowing* right from wrong, but also must be capable of *doing* that which is right and *abstaining* from acts that he knows to be wrong. It is interesting that a formulation of this type, so close to modern psychiatric concepts of compulsiveness, dates back almost a century.

During the period following World War II, many changes in law were proposed or made. In 1954, in the Durham case, a clear break was made with M'Naghten, when United States District Court Judge David Bazelon stated: "An accused is not criminally responsible if his unlawful act was a product of a mental disease or mental defect." The Model Penal Code of the American Law Institute calls for a denial of responsibility if in the accused there is "lack of substantial capacity *either* to appreciate the criminality of his conduct or to conform his conduct to requirements of law." In England, a 1953 Royal Commission Report left it to the jury to decide whether, at the time of the criminal act, the accused was suffering from disease of the mind or mental deficiency to such a degree that he ought to be held criminally responsible. Maryland, New York, and California, among other jurisdictions, have wrestled recently with this complex psycho-legal problem, without expanding these basic approaches.

The quest for a medically and legally satisfactory criterion for criminal responsibility is based fundamentally on our preoccupation with *punishing* offenders. Since it would be objectionable to punish one who was not blameworthy (for example, one who was so mentally diseased or deficient as to be incapable of *mens rea* or to not know that what he was doing was morally and legally wrong), we must therefore absolve those whose acts, no matter how dangerous to society, were committed while not "responsible."

The editors suggest another and quite different approach. It is time we discarded retributive punishment as society's response to crime and confined our legal determination to the question, "Did the accused commit the act charged in the indictment?" We could then more intelligently address ourselves to the really important issue: What mode of treatment, what system of supervision and support, is best calculated to correct, cure, or rehabilitate this offender, while at the same time protecting society from possible future misconduct?

Our interest in those who commit socially dangerous or proscribed acts should be therapeutic. All of our determinations and procedures should be designed to reduce the possibility of recurrence of criminal acts. This should be the case whether the accused is normal or insane, intelligent or defective, drunk or drugged, free moral agent or environmentally pressured and shaped, uncontrollably hedonistic or irresistibly impulsive. To turn loose the murderer, rapist, thief, or other assailant on the grounds that he was not "criminally responsible" for his act under any of the discarded, accepted, or proposed rules is as great a crime against the community as the conviction and punishment of an innocent man is against justice.

Most of the criticisms of the law governing mental disorder as a defense in criminal law . . . have been repeated for decades. Why then has so little been done about them?

Here, as is true of other defects and shortcomings in our criminal law principles and practices, inaction has probably been due not so much to logical rejection of proposed reforms as to irrational preconceptions and prejudices.

It is not only criminals who are motivated by irrational and emotional impulsions. The same is true also of lawyers and judges, butchers and bakers. And it is especially true on such a subject as punishment of criminals. This is a matter on which we are all inclined to have deep feelings. When a reprehensible crime is committed, strong emotional reactions take place in all of us. Some people will be impelled to go out at once and work off their tensions in a lynching orgy. Even the calmest, most law-abiding of us is likely to be deeply stirred. All our ingrained concepts of morality and "justice" come into play, all our ancient tribal fears of anything that threatens the security of the group. It is one of the marks of a civilized culture that it has devised legal procedures that minimize the impact of emotional reactions and strive for calm and rational disposition. But law-yers, judges and jurors are still human, and objective, rational inquiry is made difficult by the very irrationality of the human mind itself.

Many of the judicial explanations for refusing to relax the traditional tests are so obviously baseless that they can only be taken as emotional reactions rather than as reasons. How else can one explain judicial pronouncements that liberalizing the right and-wrong test would be dangerous to society, would render prosecution for crime impossible, and in effect would break down the fabric of civilization?[1]

This problem, of course, is not peculiar to our field. All social science suffers from it. All social science research is likely to have its data colored and its propositions distorted by fear and by prejudice, for religious dogma, ethical concepts, social outlook and economic interests are likely to be deeply involved. These may have more unconscious than conscious impact, and the unconscious is the more dangerous. Consciously we want to be rational. We prefer to think of ourselves as governed by reason

[1] See, for examples of such judicial prophecies of doom, *State* v. *Buck*, 205 Iowa 1028, 219 N.W. 17 (1928); *Smith* v. *State*, 95 Miss. 768, 49 So. 836 (1909); *State* v. *Williamson*, 106 Mo. 173, 17 S. W. 172 (1891); *Oborn* v. *State*, 143 Wis. 249, 126 N.W. 737 (1910).

rather than as creatures swept by irrational emotions or sluggishly adhering to the old rules because they protect us against the painful sensation of doubt and the still more painful task of rethinking and reexamining old solutions.

Socrates' admonition, "Know thyself," calls for emotional maturity and psychological insight. We need more of both before we fully understand why we treat criminals as we do, and why we hold so desperately to the M'Naghten Rule.

It is only in recent times that we have dared to suspect that even judicial opinion may be subject to this tendency to rationalize, to suggest that the reasons judges set forth for their conclusions may not actually be the premises which led to the conclusion, but that the conclusion may have come first, as a nonrational emotional reaction, or as an unarticulated "hunch," with the reasons being contrived afterward to bolster the decision already reached. This subjecting of the judicial process to psychological scrutiny is no reflection on the bench. It is rather a sign of growing cultural maturity that we are willing to recognize the existence of irrational processes, because only if we honestly face the fact of their existence can we hope to limit their effects.

Let us take a look at some of the arguments that have been advanced for refusing to relax the traditional tests of insanity, and in particular, for refusing to accept the New Hampshire Durham case rule. I have already discussed such arguments as that the traditional test is clear and certain whereas the new proposal is allegedly too loose and uncertain, and the converse argument that the traditional test is so flexible that it can be stretched to cover every proper case. Here I want to consider some other arguments, arguments that rest on a psychological attitude, the all-too-human urge to punish. The arguments take various forms.

It is argued that the new test would, because of its liberality or its looseness, result in the release of numerous dangerous criminals against whom the public should be protected, that it would encourage malingering, and that it would flout the public demand for retributive "justice." When the Durham case was decided, the United States Attorney for the District of Columbia was reported as fearing "that the new rule will greatly increase the number of insanity pleas in criminal cases, multiply the work of psychiatrists, bog down prosecutions and bring about the release of criminals from whom the public should be protected."[2]

More than a year has now passed since the Durham decision [1954]. I recently inquired how the rule was working. The chairman of the committee on mental disorder as a criminal defense of the Council on Law Enforcement of the District of Columbia replied:

I think it is safe to say that the fears expressed at the time the Durham decision was announced, to the effect that the number of insanity pleas in criminal cases would be greatly increased, have not materialized. I have kept in rather constant contact with the local United States Attorney's office in connection with this matter, and I am sure that they now feel that their original fears were unfounded.

I think it also safe to say that the fears at first entertained that more criminals would be acquitted on the ground of insanity have likewise not materialized. The findings of "not guilty by reason of insanity" do not certainly appear to have increased and I think it is more than possible that the number, percentagewise, has decreased.[3]

The only other jurisdiction that has accepted this rule, New Hampshire, certainly has not been plagued with an undue number of insanity pleas. There are few statistics, but I have made as careful an inquiry as I could about the operation of the law in that state. Judge Amos N. Blandin, Jr. of the New Hampshire Supreme Court canvassed the judges and prosecuting attorneys of the state for me, and Professor Arthur E. Prell, sociologist of the University of New Hampshire, canvassed the psychiatrists and sociologists. There seems to be complete satisfaction with the operation of the rule on the part of all concerned. I do not pretend that this was a scientifically valid study. New Hampshire is too small, too free from crime—unfortunately for research purposes—and also too free from statistical

[2] Washington (D.C.) *Evening Star,* Oct. 7, 1954, p. A-24, col. 1.
[3] Letter to the author from Mr. George L. Hart, Jr., Oct. 3, 1955.

records, to permit statistically valid conclusions. But it certainly can be said that the available evidence does not in the least support the idea that the New Hampshire rule has resulted in undue pleas of insanity. No criminal case involving the rule governing mental irresponsibility has been appealed to the state Supreme Court since 1871. In no other state have there been so few cases.

As for releasing too many dangerous persons into the community, we must remember that a person acquitted of crime by reason of insanity is not released; he is sent to a mental hospital. And the statistics show that persons so committed are kept confined *longer* than they would have been if they had been convicted of the crime charged.[4] It is true that if the new rule is construed to include psychopaths, we may find cases where a psychopath is acquitted because of his disorder, sent to a mental hospital, and shortly thereafter released because he is not psychotic. But the way to meet this problem is not by keeping a narrow general test of irresponsibility. Instead, it should be met by providing that persons so committed should not be released until they are *no longer dangerous*, or, better yet, by legislation dealing directly with the problem of the psychopaths.

As for malingering, the short answer is that the medical problem of detecting malingerers has practically nothing to do with the legal test of irresponsibility. That problem will be no more and no less difficult under the Durham case rule than under the right-and-wrong or any other. Dr. Ray said long ago, "The supposed insurmountable difficulty of distinguishing between feigned and real insanity has conduced, probably more than all other causes together, to bind the legal profession to the most rigid construction and application of the common law relative to this disease, and is always put forward in objection

---

[4] "Dr. William Alanson White made a study many years ago showing that, on the average, perpetrators of homicide committed to institutions for the insane spent more time in confinement than those sentenced to penal institutions." Simon E. Sobeloff, "Insanity and the Criminal Law: From McNaghten to Durham, and Beyond," *American Bar Association Journal*, XLI (September, 1955), pp. 793, 878; reprinted in *Maryland Law Review*, XV (1955), pp. 93, 108.

to the more humane doctrines that have been inculcated in the présent work."[5]

Even in 1838, Dr. Ray was able to devote a whole chapter, of thirty pages, in his *Medical Jurisprudence* to explaining how simulated insanity might be distinguished from the genuine. Most of what he said is still quite sound, and a lot of knowledge has been added since. Yet probably the majority of judges today are almost as ignorant of these means for distinguishing as they were then. Most judges who fear that liberalizing the test would facilitate malingering would be reassured by reading that chapter. For further assurance, they might read about newer discoveries that psychoanalysis and other techniques have added, as well as new mechanical methods such as the EEG and the lie detector, truth serums, etc. Dr. Henry Davidson's short chapter on the subject, in his *Forensic Psychiatry*, should dispose of any exaggerated fears on this score.

More basic is the argument that the "instinctive sense of justice" of the community will be offended if we adopt a rule that fails to mete out punishment where punishment seems to the public to be deserved. As Dr. Franz Alexander has argued, when a defendant escapes who, people think, deserves punishment, they may lose faith in the social structure and may relax their own inhibitions.[6] "If he escapes his just deserts," they may tend to think, "why should I continue to obey the law?" The public is willing to recognize the mentally irresponsible as a class that should be exempted from punishment, since it is futile to threaten and punish people who cannot be "cured or taught a lesson" by such sanctions. But the exception must be narrowly restricted. Professor Herbert Wechsler has well stated this argument: "The category must be so extreme that to the ordinary man, burdened by passion and beset by large temptations, the exculpation of the irresponsible bespeaks no weakness in the law. He does not identify himself and them: they are a world

[5] Isaac Ray, *A Treatise on the Medical Jurisprudence of Insanity* (Boston: Little and Brown, 1838), p. 349, sec. 341.

[6] See Franz Alexander and Hugo Staub, *The Criminal, the Judge and the Public* (London: G. Allen & Unwin, 1931, translated by Gregory Zilboorg), p. 207 *et seq.*

apart. . . . Beyond such extreme incapacities however, the exception cannot go. This, to be sure, is not poetic justice. It is public justice, which in the interest of the common good prescribes a standard all must subscribe to who can, those whose nature or nurture leads them to conform with difficulty no less than those who find compliance easy."[7]

Eminent jurists have told us that we must be careful to heed and respect this public demand for punitive "justice." Public "qualms at the prospect of a softening of retribution," we are told, "deserve attention, and should, so far as is compatible with advance rather than regression in the penal field, be relieved."[8] "The first requirement of a sound body of law," said Mr. Justice Holmes, "is that it should correspond with the actual feelings and demands of the community, whether right or wrong."[9] Perhaps the strongest such statement is the famous remark of Sir James Stephen, who said: "I think it highly desirable that criminals should be hated, that the punishment inflicted on them should be so contrived as to give expression to that hatred, and to justify it so far as the public provision of means for expressing and gratifying a healthy natural sentiment can justify and encourage it"[10]

But let us take a look at this "instinctive sense of justice" the public is supposed to feel so keenly, and that we are so anxious to mollify. "Justice" is a noble word, and the use of it implies we have here a noble sentiment.

But psychiatrists have been holding up the mirror to this sentiment, and the picture they see is not so pretty. The urge to punish wrongdoers is not always an impersonal demand that the law keep its promises. Often it is an outlet for our own antisocial

[7] Herbert Wechsler, "The Criteria of Criminal Responsibility," *University of Chicago Law Review*, XXII (1955), pp. 367, 374–75.

[8] George H. Dession, "Justice after Conviction," *Connecticut Bar Journal*, XXV (September, 1951), pp. 215, 221–22.

[9] Oliver Wendell Holmes, *The Common Law* (1881), p. 41; new edition, ed. by Mark De Wolfe Howe (Cambridge: Belknap Press of Harvard University Press, 1963).

[10] James Stephen, *A History of the Criminal Law of England*, Vol. 2 (London: Macmillan & Co., 1883), pp. 81–82.

aggressiveness which we have more or less effectively but guiltily repressed. "It is a weapon in our own struggle against trends and drives which we do not admit to consciousness. We should be continuously aware that over-assertion of a prosecuting, punishing, attitude toward lawbreakers reveals the intensity of our inner struggle and the instability of our own emotional equilibrium."[11] "Distrust," said Nietzsche, "all in whom the impulse to punish is strong." No one is more ferocious in demanding that the murderer or the rapist "pay" for his crime than the man who has felt strong impulses in the same direction. No one is more bitter in condemning the "loose" woman than the "good" women who have on occasion guiltily enjoyed some purple dreams themselves. It is never he who is without sin who casts the first stone.

Along with the stone, we cast our own sins onto the criminal. In this way we relieve our own sense of guilt without actually having to suffer the punishment—a convenient and even pleasant device, for it not only relieves us of sin, but makes us feel actually virtuous. A criminal trial, like a prize fight, is a public performance in which the spectators work off in a socially acceptable way aggressive impulses of much the same kind that the man on trial worked off in a socially unacceptable way.

We even piously quote Scripture to justify our vindictiveness: "An eye for an eye and a tooth for a tooth." But what that says, as the Archbishop of Canterbury pointed out, was that one must not exact *more* than an eye for an eye. "It was not an exhortation that you should exact an equivalent, but it said that if somebody knocked your tooth out, morality requires that you do no more than knock one of his out. It is a restraint on the passions of mankind . . . no Christian law says you must exact equivalent penalty. Indeed, Christianity works on the other principle, that whatever the crime, you should seek to remedy it by the operation of redemption and love."[12]

The phenomenon is perhaps analogous to Aldous Huxley's

[11] Marcel Frym, "Past and Future of Criminal Rehabilitation," *Journal of Public Law*, III (1955), pp. 451, 460.

[12] Testimony before the Royal Commission on Capital Punishment, Minutes of Evidence, p. 338, par. 4128 (1950).

theory of why war was more popular in the days when it was less dangerous to civilians. Those back home identified with their armies, and shared in their glories.[13] So today the individual who reads about an atrocious crime in the newspaper identifies with society, makes the crime a personal affront to himself, and demands strong-arm retaliation.

This strong but largely unconscious impulse to punish in others the tendencies that we deny or repress in ourselves may provide a partial explanation for the hostility that psychiatrists sometimes feel to their testimony. "A peculiar feature of psychiatric evidence is that it is directed not to the external facts of the case but to facts relevant to the accused's moral responsibility, and it is therefore in its very nature apt to create an emotional disturbance in the minds of the jury."[14] Especially in cases of violent or sexual crimes, the emotionally disturbing conflict between feelings of guilty identification and of righteous indignation will be strong. The result is likely to be powerful feelings of criticism and hostility against those who present such disturbing evidence.

As for Stephen's notion that hatred of criminals is a "healthy natural sentiment" that should be encouraged, we may concede that it is natural, human nature being something less than Christlike, but modern psychology would hardly call it healthy. Hatred is not health. It is a poison. It will cripple and even kill the individual or the society that feeds on it. The function of law is to hold the brute forces of hate and vindictiveness in check—not to encourage them. The history of law is the story of the slow—painfully slow—steps by which society, one short step at a time, restricted this and that manifestation of these forces. They yielded each step only slowly and after long and stubborn opposition. If we open the door to them, it will be hard to close again. The Nazi regime was an outstandingly terrible example of the dangers that engulf a society where official sanction is given to the brute forces of hatred.

[13] See Walter Lindesay Neustatter, *Psychological Disorder and Crime* (London: C. Johnson, 1953), p. 223.

[14] Glanville Williams, "The Royal Commission and the Defence of Insanity," *Current Legal Problems*, VII (1954), pp. 16, 25.

The primitive and irrational nature of the urge to punish is demonstrated by the fact that it is murder and sex crimes that bring our blood to the boiling point. But the real threat to social well-being and security in our society does not arise out of these anachronistic and atavistic acts of a few abnormal individuals. Our real crime problem is the white collar crime and organized racketeering that costs us annually at least ten times as much as all the old-fashioned crimes of violence put together. And before anyone charges me with equating mere money losses with crimes against life and person, let me say that there is a personal tragedy also when a small businessman is hounded to bankruptcy and suicide by racketeers. It is merely primitive impulse that causes us to bay for the blood of murderers and rapists, but accept with philosophic equanimity the existence of thousands of racketeers, swindlers, fraudulent promoters and clever operators in high places, who cost the nation billions in losses every year.

The danger is that the irrational urge to do something emotionally satisfying will brush aside calmer efforts to do something constructive. "Aggressiveness, a heritage from the past based on fear, ignorance, and frustration, is becoming an increasingly heavy burden for civilized man to bear. How to substitute for it cooperation and harmonious interpersonal relationships is a problem which increasing knowledge of mental health may help to solve. I need not emphasize how urgent it has become to prevent 'the old savage in the new civilization' from wrecking our plans for building up a peaceful world society."[15]

And it seems to me an abdication of the leadership that the public has a right to expect of the legal profession abjectly to accept this primitive aggressiveness as inevitable and unchangeable.

It is of course a difficult question how far law can outrun public sentiment. The Negro problem is an illustration of how hard it is to change deep-rooted social customs and habits by

[15] Frank G. Boudreau, "Mental Health, The New Public Health Frontier," *The Annals of the American Academy of Political and Social Science,* 286 (March, 1953), pp. 1, 4.

legal fiat. For decades, the Supreme Court dodged the responsibility of making the Civil War amendments really effective and compelling the southern states to give Negroes political equality. The court apparently agreed with Carter, that "the attempt to compel a community of men to do right by legislative command, when they do not think it to be right, is tyranny."[16] Charles Warren agreed that the court couldn't have done more with a problem so packed with emotional and sectional dynamite.[17]

But others thought that the court failed to seize an opportunity to exert a great moral and educative influence. And in recent years, the court has shown a greater willingness to exert leadership, with results still to be seen. The court has been confronted with the same problem of choice between following and leading public opinion in the field of civil liberties. The difference in viewpoints is brought into high relief in two recent little books. One is *The Supreme Court in the American System of Government*, by the late Mr. Justice Robert H. Jackson; the other is *National Security and Individual Freedom*, by John Lord O'Brian. Mr. Justice Jackson had been selected to deliver the Godkin lectures at Harvard University. He prepared the lectures but died before he could deliver them. His book contains these undelivered lectures. On his death, John Lord O'Brian was asked to step into the breach, and his book contains the lectures that he did deliver. On this matter of leadership versus followership the two reveal an interesting and important difference in emphasis. Jackson's emphasis is on what the court cannot do. "Any court," he wrote, "which undertakes by its legal processes to enforce civil liberties needs the support of an enlightened and vigorous public opinion. . . . I do not think the American public is enlightened on this subject."

O'Brian on the other hand takes the view that the public needs and should be provided leadership toward understanding, instead of being merely passively followed, and he deplores the

---

[16] James Coolidge Carter, *Law: Its Origin, Growth and Function* (New York: G. P. Putnam's Sons, 1907), p. 217.

[17] Charles Warren, *The Supreme Court in United States History* (Boston: Little, Brown, rev. ed., 1926), pp. 608, 616–18.

"scarcity of leaders courageous and outspoken in the cause of individual freedom."

There is of course essential truth in both positions, but I stand with O'Brian in feeling that the emphasis belongs on the need for leadership, in civil liberties and in penal philosophy. The human thirst for vengeance, the human instincts of hate and fear, need no encouragement from the law. So long as they exist, we must of course take them into account, but we need not reinforce them and give them dignity by legal endorsement.

I even venture to guess that the public thirst for vengeance is not as great as courts have seemed to fear. Law and order will not collapse if we frankly repudiate blind vengeance. Public opinion today is different from what it was in Stephen's day— and the dominant opinion was probably not as bloodthirsty in Stephen's day as his statement assumed. For the past two or three centuries, public opinion has generally been less retributive than the law itself. It was public opinion that forced the law to become more humanitarian. In the eighteenth century, juries simply refused to follow the law that called for capital punishment for grand larceny. They either acquitted, or found defendants guilty of stealing goods of the value of 39 shillings (40 shillings made it capital)—regardless of the value of the goods they were proved to have stolen or that they confessed to stealing. It was juries who ended witchcraft prosecutions, and who caused the bankers to plead for abolition of the death penalty for forgery. Not only juries, but witnesses and even victims refused to cooperate.

Today, I believe public opinion is still in advance of the law. Increased impersonality in our civilization has been added to other factors feeding this trend. From reading our criminal codes, one would get the impression that death is the standard punishment for first degree murder. In fact, the death penalty is extremely rare. Juries simply will not impose it in most cases. If death is the mandatory punishment they will not convict of that degree. That is why state after state has had to give up the mandatory death penalty.

If the legal profession is not to take the lead in the movement toward a less bloody and vengeful law, it should at least not stand in the way. If judges and lawyers cannot or will not speak up for the side of reason and understanding, it is at least time that they stop talking like apologists for the forces of hate and fear.

Understanding and love instead of hate are enjoined upon us not only by the teachings of religion but also by the teachings of psychology. We can put to death only creatures whom hatred and fear have convinced us are inhuman monsters. In war, we whip ourselves up a conviction—for the duration—that every man, woman and child in the enemy nation is a japrat, a hun, a beast. Only so can we rain bombs upon them, and live with ourselves. We could not do so to human beings like ourselves.

The injunction that we love those who hate us, that we return good for evil, is not easy to obey—as two thousand years of professed Christianity have shown. Criminals and psychopaths are likely to be unlovely and unlovable personalities. It takes profound understanding not to become discouraged and even angry with the delinquent who responds to your efforts at kindness by acting *worse* than ever. Yet this is often the most promising case. This negative response may signal a transitory phase, in which he is testing you out, to see whether your gestures of kindness are genuine, or—what his whole past life has led him to expect—insincere, phony, and probably with an ulterior "angle." With understanding and with infinite patience, this hostile attitude can be overcome. This is the kind of work that probation officers and other social workers are doing day in and day out. It is infinitely more constructive, for the person and for society, than all the impregnable prisons, and all the gallows, the electric chairs and the gas chambers in the world.

I do not mean to suggest that irrational and emotional reactions are the only motivations behind criminal punishment and that there are no rational arguments for punishment. Punishment calmly devised and administered without hate probably performs a needed function. The psychiatrist would say that by developing a superego leading to displacement and sublimation of elemental impulses, punishment is an important factor in personality development and in the progress of civilization. What I do say is that the rational arguments are not the only reasons for what we do to criminals; the irrational elements play a much bigger role than we admit or perhaps even consciously realize. And if we will come to understand the motivations that lie behind the way human beings behave—wrongdoer and righteous both—we shall be increasingly able to supplant an emotionally charged, moralizing approach to the problem of crime with a more scientific emphasis on social dangerousness, deterrability and treatability.

. . . Consider . . . in particular the punishment of death. The question of whether the defendant was "insane" at the time of the crime would lose much of its consequence if we would take a step that I believe we ought to take for a lot of additional reasons. That is to abolish the death penalty.

The insanity defense is almost never raised except in murder cases. A defendant charged with anything less than a capital offense usually prefers to take his chances on receiving a prison sentence, which will run for only a limited number of years, rather than enter an insanity plea, which if successful will get him committed to a mental institution indefinitely. At least the doubtful cases and the cases of outright malingering would pretty certainly be reduced if the only difference between acquittal by reason of insanity and conviction were commitment to a mental hospital, instead of a prison—or not even that, in states where persons so acquitted are nevertheless sent to the *prison*, but confined in a psychiatric ward.

Absent the death penalty, if by mistake a defendant who was actually irresponsible were found guilty, the only practical effect would be that he would be sent to the prison instead of the hospital. And life in a modern prison is not so incomparably worse than in a mental institution that that would be a shocking injustice—especially since after he got to the prison, if he were found to be disordered, he could be transferred to the hospital. On expiration of his sentence, if still not safe to be released, he could be detained on civil commitment.

Of course, he would suffer the stigma of criminal "guilt," instead of being acquitted on the ground of insanity. But that is a distinction that looms larger in the minds of moral philosophers than it probably does for the general run of defendants. When "Three Finger" Jack McGurk is indicted for an offense for which he fears he might burn, his main concern is to avoid that melancholy end. If there seems to be no other way to avoid it, he may plead insanity. But if the death penalty were abolished, he probably wouldn't: he'd prefer to be found guilty and given a fixed sentence rather than seek a commitment to a mental hospital which might last for life. Of course the prison sentence might be for life too. But prison life holds fewer unknown terrors than life in an "insane asylum." Nor are those terrors all imaginary. At the hospital he may find himself strapped to a table and subjected to the painful and terrifying convulsions of electric shock or insulin shock therapy. In some states he may be sterilized. If the hospital after commitment makes a really comprehensive "criminal investigation of his unconscious," laying naked his entire personality, stripping his act of any possible glamor and perhaps even of rationality, the experience will be uncomfortable. Until he can be taught to appreciate this approach, the average criminal will prefer the prison routine, which a smart crook can live with without any disturbance to his personality—which is to say without any reform of his personality.

It is time we Americans realized that we have probably the most ferocious penal policy in the whole civilized world. Most other civilized countries have not only abolished the death penalty, but have also reduced prison sentences far below the terms we hand out here.[18] Some 36 jurisdictions throughout the world have abolished the death penalty entirely, in Europe, in South America, in Asia. Of all of the democracies of Western Europe, only England (since this was written the House of Commons on February 16, 1956, adopted a resolution looking to the prompt abolition of capital punishment) and France retain it, and England has been seriously debating abolition.

[18] It is sometimes argued that our long prison sentences must be viewed in light of the fact that a person may be paroled before full term is served. This is true, but most other countries also have parole or provisions for earlier release, pardon, etc. In Sweden a limited number, including murderers, are actually allowed to go out and earn ordinary wages in the market outside the prisons.

Holland has not executed any criminals since 1860, Belgium since 1863, Norway, 1875, and Denmark, 1892. In some of those countries, the death penalty is still on the statute books, but it is never used. Soviet Russia has restricted the death penalty largely if not wholly to offenders regarded as serious enemies of the state, a concept analogous to treason, though considerably broader.

In South America, the eight countries that comprise 80 per cent or more of the population and of the land area of that continent have abolished capital punishment as a civil sanction. Cuba, Puerto Rico, Costa Rica and most of Mexico have done the same. In this country, six states have no death penalty.[19]

And the experience of these jurisdictions gives no evidence that abolition leads to more crime. Of the eight states having the lowest murder rate in the United States, five have no death penalty. The state with the very lowest murder rate is Maine, which abolished capital punishment in 1870. The state with the highest murder rate is Georgia. It is also the state that itself does more killing than any other, with 280 executions in twenty years as against 270 for the four times more populous New York, and 124 for the three times more populous state of Pennsylvania.[20]

If the death penalty is a deterrent, its greatest effect should be shown through executions that are well publicized. Some years ago, a study was made under the supervision of Professor Thorsten Sellin of the University of Pennsylvania, of the preventive value of such executions. Five executions were found which had received great notoriety, and which had occurred over a period of five years. On the assumption that deterrence should manifest itself by a decline or at least a temporary drop

[19] Lee Emerson Deets, "Changes in Capital Punishment Policy Since 1939," *Journal of Criminal Law and Criminology*, XXXVIII (1948), p. 584; Frank E. Hartung, "Trends in the Use of Capital Punishment," *The Annals*, 284 (November, 1952), p. 8; Viscount Samuel, testimony before the Royal Commission on Capital Punishment, Minutes of Evidence, March 3, 1950, p. 380.

[20] Hartung, *op. cit.*, p. 14; George P. Vold, "Extent and Trend of Capital Crimes in the United States," *The Annals*, 284 (November, 1952), pp. 1, 3.

in homicides, tables were prepared showing the number of homicides committed during the sixty-day period immediately following each of these executions, as compared with the sixty-day period immediately preceding. It was found that "there were a total of 105 days *free from homicides* during the sixty-day periods before the executions and 74 in the periods after the executions. There were a total of ninety-one homicides in the 'before execution' periods and 113 in the 'after' periods."[21]

From all the statistical studies that have been made, "it seems clear that the presence or absence of the death penalty makes no particular difference in the amount of murder in a given state. Its murder rate will be closely parallel to that of adjoining states, where conditions of life and social-cultural attitudes are similar."[22] Murder is a complex sociological phenomenon, and is not controllable by simply imposing severe punishment. This is so true that students of the problems of homicide rarely discuss the death penalty. They do not consider it a factor worth mentioning.[23]

One prison warden has said that in his twenty years in that profession, he has never seen a single criminal who would have refrained from using a gun because of any idea that he might get the death sentence. "The criminal's fear of the gallows," he said, "is a fairy story built up by well-meaning people to deter others. We could build up just as effective a hoax about the horrors of life imprisonment if it were our wish."[24]

[21] Thorsten Sellin, Memorandum submitted to the Royal Commission on Capital Punishment, Minutes of Evidence, February 1, 1951, p. 656.

[22] Vold, *op. cit.*, p. 4.

[23] "Even in personality studies of murderers it is rare to find any mention of the role which the potential threat of execution is assumed to play. It is only those who are primarily concerned with the social policy of penal treatment who in considering the death penalty wonder what purpose it may serve. The behavioral scientist has apparently written off this problem as of no significance. He has found that murder is a type of conduct which at least in well-ordered countries is as irrational as the penalty which threatens it." Sellin, *op. cit.*, note 21, par. 84.

[24] Testimony of Warden Hugh Christie of Okalla Prison Farm, South Burnaby, British Columbia, before the Committee on Capital and Corporal Punishment and Lotteries (Canada), Minutes of Proceedings and Evidence, No. 14, May 18, 1954, p. 590.

The stable, normal person is held back from committing murder by moral feelings that have been developed in him since early childhood. Legal sanctions—whether capital or other —are only a secondary and for most persons quite unnecessary reinforcement of the moral prohibition. It takes an abnormal mind to commit a killing. This is worth emphasizing. In detective stories, any person who had a motive and opportunity is a suspect, and the actual killer always turns out to be someone who, except for this one excursion into murder, has led an exemplary life. That isn't the way it happens in real life. A person who has lived a decent, balanced life doesn't suddenly murder his Uncle Jonathan in order to inherit his estate. In cases where something of the sort seemed to have happened, investigation will show that the murderer had long been that kind of person.

Whereas the law—like the detective story writer—tends to regard the criminal as a man who at a given point in time intentionally and of his free will decided to commit a wrongful act, the psychologist sees the act as the culmination of an enormous variety of forces extending far back into the past. Murderous impulses often go back to early impulses of suicide, sadism or masochism.[25] We all bear certain emotional scars from our early childhood, some much worse than others. Some of these early influences, which Sheldon and Eleanor Glueck deem weighty enough to be used as social predictive factors for predicting delinquency, are:

[25] "Psychoanalytic theory sees both suicide and homicide as extreme forms of aggression, the one directed against the self, the other directed against another person. Suicide is seen as a function of an aggressively strict and punishing 'superego' or internalizing restraining mechanism of the personality which prohibits the outward expression of aggression." Andrew F. Henry and James F. Short, Jr., *Suicide and Homicide* (Glencoe, Ill.: Free Press, 1954), p. 13. There are about twice as many suicides in the United States as murders. In England in 1946–48, aside from cases of infanticide, of 301 known murderers, 35 per cent actually committed suicide before arrest. This suggests that the suicidal tendency is strong in murderers. Royal Commission on Capital Punishment, Minutes of Evidence, pp. 532–33, par. 4646, testimony of Dr. William H. Gillespie of the Institute of Psycho-Analysis.

1. Discipline of boy by father.
2. Supervision of boy by mother.
3. Affection of father for boy.
4. Affection of mother for boy.
5. Cohesiveness of family.[26]

A high percentage of murderers are not only emotionally scarred and twisted, but are actually psychotic. In England, of the patients in Broadmoor, the institution for the criminally insane, over 50 per cent are murder cases, and another 20 to 25 per cent are persons who attempted murder. Of persons suspected of murder, in 1946–47, 35 per cent attempted suicide before arrest. Some 22 per cent actually do commit suicide. Of those brought to trial, over 50 per cent are found either too mentally disordered to stand trial, or if tried, are found guilty but insane. Another 4 per cent are subsequently certified as insane.[27] These figures indicate that mental disorder is the predominant factor in murder. Studies in this country tend to support the same conclusion. In fact, Bernard C. Glueck, Jr. has said, "It is my personal opinion, based on the examination of men in the death house at Sing Sing, that no person in our society is in a normal state of mind when he commits a murder."[28]

The argument that abolishing the death penalty would encourage a terrible crime wave is an old one. It has been raised every time we abolished the death penalty for each of the scores, and even hundreds, of other crimes formerly so punishable.[29]

[26] Robert W. Whelan, "An Experiment in Predicting Delinquency," *Journal of Criminal Law and Criminology*, XLV (1954), p. 432.

[27] Testimony of Dr. J. S. Hopwood, Medical Superintendent of Broadmoor Institution, before the Royal Commission, Minutes of Evidence, pp. 359, 361, par. 4344, 7406 (1950). See also testimony of Dr. Gillespie, *op. cit.*, p. 553, par. 7646.

[28] Bernard C. Glueck, Jr., "Changing Concepts in Forensic Psychiatry," *Journal of Criminal Law and Criminology*, XLV (1954), pp. 123, 130–31. See also Edward Podolsky, "Mind of the Murderer," *ibid.*, p. 48.

[29] "England had 17 capital crimes in the early part of the fifteenth century. This number was rapidly increased about the first quarter of the seventeenth century, reaching a peak, according to Radzinowicz, of some 350 capital crimes by 1780! Practically all the capital crimes added after 1500 were offenses against property, most of these crimes being trivial. This number was drastically reduced in the nineteenth century: to about 220 by

The pattern is always the same. A movement to abolish capital punishment for a given crime is met by dire forebodings, mainly from the judges, that abolition would result in a dangerous increase in the crime in question. Then, after abolition, there is a remarkable absence of any such increase.

In 1810, Sir Samuel Romilly introduced a bill into the House of Commons to abolish capital punishment for the theft of five shillings or over from a shop. Chief Justice Lord Ellenborough opposed the bill. He said: "I trust your lordships will pause before you assent to an experiment pregnant with danger to the security of property, and before you repeal a statute which has so long been held necessary for public security. I am convinced with the rest of the Judges, public expediency requires there should be no remission of the terror denounced against this description of offenders. Such will be the consequences of the repeal of this statute that I am certain depredations to an unlimited extent would be immediately committed." Lord Ellenborough spoke for all his colleagues on the bench. Not a single judge or magistrate supported the bill. It failed to pass.

In 1814, Romilly tried to persuade Parliament to substitute as the penalty for treason simple hanging instead of the then penalty of hanging, being cut down while still alive, disembowelled, decapitated and quartered. That, notice, was less than a century and a half ago. Parliament refused to pass the bill. Apparently they concurred in the statement of one of the members that the bill was a "mischievous attempt 'to unsettle public opinion with respect to the enormity of these atrocious offenses.' "[30]

Eventually both of these reforms were enacted. "Depredations of an unlimited extent" were not immediately committed. Public opinion was not unsettled. None of the predictions of dire consequences came true. But the same kind of predictions

---

1825, to about 17 in 1839 and to 4 in 1861. This number was further reduced by the time capital punishment was suspended by the Parliament in 1948 [for a trial period]." Hartung, *op. cit.*, note 19, p. 11.

[30] "The Abolition of Capital Punishment: A Symposium," *Canadian Bar Review*, XXXII (May, 1954), pp. 485, 492; Eric Ray Calvert, *Capital Punishment in the Twentieth Century* (London: G. P. Putnam's Sons, 1927), p. 7.

continued to be made, by the same kind of armchair criminologists.

Mr. Justice Frankfurter has said of members of the legal profession that "the most eminent among them, for a hundred years, have testified with complete confidence that something is impossible which, once it is introduced, is found to be very easy of administration. The history of legal procedure is the history of rejection of reasonable and civilized standards in the administration of law by most eminent judges and leading practitioners."[31]

Investiture in high office, as judge, legislator or prosecutor, does not magically endow a man with scholarly training and competence in criminology. It is necessary to say this because the public too often assumes the contrary. The honorable gentlemen's pronouncements are assumed to be the product of many years of experience and study, when in fact they may be based on a few not necessarily typical cases, or even on nothing whatever except emotional reflexes. Lord Ellenborough was Chief Justice of the King's Bench and a legal scholar. But his pronouncements on the necessity of retaining the death penalty expressed merely a personal predilection not based on any data whatever. Equally baseless assertions continue to be made by his professional descendants to this day.

Opponents of abolition are always quick to cite atrocious cases and ask what we would do about them. Only last year [1953], a judge of the Ontario Court of Appeal answered the advocates of abolition at a Toronto forum on the subject by asking: "What about men like O'Donnell who raped and strangled to death Ruth Taylor under conditions of indescribable horror. . . ? Or Hutson . . . who was convicted on the clearest possible evidence of murdering a little girl of three years by a brutal, bestial attack during which she was virtually disembowelled? Or the three monsters . . . who literally fried to death a schoolteacher who lived alone, in order to make her reveal the whereabouts of her life savings?"[32]

---

[31] Testimony before the Royal Commission on Capital Punishment, Minutes of Evidence, p. 582, par. 7990 (1950).

[32] "The Abolition of Capital Punishment: A Symposium," *op. cit.,* pp. 485, 492.

Recalling such cases raises the hackles and the blood pressure. But what do they prove about the wisdom of retaining or abolishing the death penalty? All these cases happened in the judge's own jurisdiction, which *retains* the death penalty. Obviously capital punishment for the first of these cases did not prevent commission of the second, or the third.

Across the line from the Canadian province of Ontario is the State of Michigan, which abolished capital punishment more than a hundred years ago. It has consistently had a smaller number of murders per hundred thousand of population than its neighboring states of Illinois, Indiana and Ohio.[33] It would be invalid to conclude from this that abolition reduces the incidence of crime. But it is valid and correct to conclude that the death penalty is not more of a deterrent than other forms of punishment that might be substituted for it.

With all deference to judges, it seems proper to say that the deterrent effect of any given punishment can be calculated, if at all, only by someone having "extensive acquaintance with psychological *norms*, with the effectiveness of distant anxiety as an inhibiting force, with the after-history of every variety of behavioristic disorder, to say nothing of an expert knowledge of statistics and of statistical method."[34]

Psychiatrists have paid relatively little attention to the validity or fallacy of the "deterrent" effect of the death penalty, and have largely been content to leave such investigations to the sociologists and penal reformers. Yet students of the mind should find interesting this phenomenon of the continued repetition of the stock arguments in favor of capital punishment, not only by the man in the street but by eminent lawyers and judges—in spite of the fact that there is no evidence to support them. Does this not suggest the propriety of a psychological examination into the existence of some unconscious roots to this urge to punish, some sadistic impulses perhaps, and perhaps some unconscious guilts.

Today we have pretty generally abolished the death penalty

[33] Vold, *op. cit.*; Karl F. Schuessler, "The Deterrent Influence of the Death Penalty," *The Annals*, 284 (November, 1952), pp. 54, 58.

[34] Edward Glover, "Psychiatric Aspects of the Report on Capital Punishment," *Modern Law Review*, XVII (1954), pp. 329–30.

for all crimes except murder. Why this one great exception? Why should a punishment that did not deter men from stealing sheep be any more effective to deter them from committing murder? Murder usually involves less calm premeditation, not more. Punishment or the threat of it is more likely to deter crimes where there is a conscious and deliberate motive for gain. It is least likely to deter crimes attributable to passion, and to embittered, frustrated or actually disordered personality.

Perhaps the reason is that we regard murder with peculiar horror, as the "crime of crimes." But that view of murder is certainly not universal. The anthropologists tell us that most people throughout most of recorded history have regarded various other crimes as more abhorrent and more socially dangerous than killing—incest, for example. And some of us today would be willing to agree with our primitive ancestors that there are worse crimes than murder. Is the person who at one crisis in his life commits a sudden killing worse than the one who makes it his daily business to peddle dope to teenagers? Introducing a person to the dope habit not only destroys him physically but morally as well, yet it is done deliberately and cold-bloodedly, by persons who know and who count on the fact that once the victim is "hooked" he will almost certainly never break the habit, but will be reduced to lying, stealing and almost every possible crime, to get the money to buy dope.

I am not proposing that we make dope peddling a capital offense. I am pointing out the incongruity of our retaining the death penalty for one crime although we have abolished it for most, of retaining it for a primitive and today not socially threatening form of crime, although we do not extend it to newer crimes which are a real threat to our social organization.

But even if we agree that murder is the most wicked of crimes, that seems relevant only for a retributive theory of justice, not one based on deterrence. Today we don't like to say that we inflict punishment merely for vengeance. We say that we are doing it to deter repetition of the offense, either by the offender or by others who might otherwise be tempted to follow his example. So far as deterrence is concerned, the question is not so much whether murder creates a higher degree of moral revulsion, but rather, whether murderers are less likely to be deterred by imprisonment or other measures and more likely to be deterred by the threat of death.

Most murderers are not hardened criminals. Most of them fall into two classes, the pathological and the passionate. I have already cited the statistics showing how high a proportion fall into the pathological group. And most of the rest are people who killed in some momentary fit of passion.

A study of 1,000 murders committed in New Jersey revealed that 67 per cent of them arose out of unpremeditated quarrels —with wives, mistresses, sex rivals or acquaintances. Even of the premeditated murders, most were also of wives, sweethearts, sex rivals. Only 18.8 per cent were committed during other crimes such as robbery, burglary, rape and kidnapping. Another 3.1 per cent were committed while resisting an officer.[35]

Murder is not typically the crime of the so-called criminal class. Much more often, it is an incident in miserable lives characterized by domestic quarrels, brawls, drinking and fighting. The killing is the unpremeditated and more or less accidental culmination of a long series of acts of violence. If the harshest penalty is ever needed as the strongest deterrent, it ought to be reserved for the professionals, the gangsters, the pickpockets, the safecrackers, the confidence men. Not for the murderers. Yet of the really hardened criminals, the professionals, who are most likely to weigh the odds before they act, we find very few convicted of murder.

Police officials often argue that the threat of capital punishment deters criminals from carrying lethal weapons, or at least deters them from using them against the police when in danger of being arrested. Abolishing the death penalty, it is said, would therefore result in more policemen being killed or wounded. But the statistics reveal no factual basis for this assumption. The number of policemen killed is slightly smaller, proportionately, in the states that have abolished the death penalty than in those that retain it.[36]

[35] Royal Commission on Capital Punishment, Report, p. 335.
[36] See Joint Committee of the Senate and House of Commons on Capital and Corporal Punishment and Lotteries (Canada), Appendix "F" of the Minutes of Proceedings and Evidence, No. 20 (1955), "Findings of U.S.A. Surveys on the Death Penalty and Police Safety," by Thorsten Sellin and Donald Campion.

Everyone who has made any study of the subject knows that it is not the severity of the punishment that is most important for deterrence; it is the certainty that punishment will actually result. The perfect penal system would be one that operates like a red hot stove; touch it and you get burned. It isn't necessary that the burn be fatal to induce people to keep their hands off. As Sir Walter Moberly said a few years ago, ". . . the most ferocious penalties are ineffective so long as prospective criminals believe they have a fair chance of escaping them. . . . If he commits a murder he may not be caught; if caught he may not be convicted; if convicted he may still be reprieved. . . . Thus it is *certainty* rather than *severity* of punishment which really deters. . . . An increase in the efficiency of the police force does more to prevent murder than the busiest hangman."[37] For capital crimes, juries are notoriously reluctant to convict. This *reduces* the certainty of punishment and in consequence, its deterrent effect.

There are other objections to capital punishment beside the lack of evidence that it is any more of a deterrent than any other forms of punishment. Being irrevocable, it allows no opportunity for reversing a wrong conviction of an innocent man. It places on the officials who have to take part in an execution a hateful duty that even the advocates of capital punishment would not want to perform themselves and do not even want to witness. The executioner for New York and Pennsylvania suggested a few years ago that the judges who hand down the sentence should be required to witness its execution. I doubt whether most judges would want that. Warden Lewis E. Lawes of Sing Sing said that during all his term no judge and no prosecutor ever asked to witness the execution of a man they had prosecuted and sentenced.[38] But if executing wrongdoers were as effective a deterrent as its apologists claim, we should encourage—perhaps compel—not only judges and prosecutors but everybody to witness the act. We have given up public executions because we know the sight does not deter. It brutalizes people and makes them more callous toward killing.

[37] Quoted in "The Abolition of Capital Punishment: A Symposium," *op. cit.*, p. 499.
[38] Hartung, *op. cit.*, note 19, pp. 17–18.

Capital punishment is defeatist, because, contrary to modern developments in penal reform it abandons the possibility of reforming the criminal and it has an adverse effect upon efforts to reform other prisoners in the institution at the time the execution takes place. These convicts, whom the prison regime is presumably trying to treat and to rehabilitate into society, identify with the condemned man, and they align themselves against the hateful, punishing society that takes his life. The whole principle of intimidation by fear appears actually to contribute to aggressive behavior in some persons. Capital punishment may serve as an actual incitement to crime in three types of cases:

1. The suicidal group. Some depressed patients take the attitude that death is a just punishment for their imagined sins, and murder is a means of securing it.

2. Those to whom the lure of danger has a strong appeal; possibly a large group. The danger of capital punishment may act as an actual incentive to acts like robbery with violence.

3. The exhibitionist group. The exhibitionist wishes "for a time successfully to pit his wits against the police, but that would not satisfy him unless he was in the end caught; because otherwise nobody would know how clever he had been in outwitting the law so long. So that we can't think the exhibitionist would be expected to give himself up after his first crime; but sooner or later he would so arrange things that he was found out and had the satisfaction of a spectacular trial."[39] These persons do not usually carry their activities to the point of committing crimes that may lead to the death penalty, although even that occurs at times.

The death penalty probably also increases the cost of criminal trials. I say probably because this is largely an unexplored question. But it is probably true that persons charged with capital crimes are less likely to plead guilty than they would be if the crime were not capital. And avoiding a drawn-out criminal trial by a plea of guilty saves the state several thousand dollars. The money so saved could be better used to pay the salaries of parole and probation officers in a constructive effort to prevent crime.

[39] Testimony before the Royal Commission on Capital Punishment, Minutes of Evidence, pp. 551, 553–54, par. 7624, 7664 (1950).

In 1931, after a Pennsylvania capital trial, a social worker in Reading said: "It cost the State of Pennsylvania $23,658 to prosecute, convict and electrocute Irene Schroeder at the Western Penitentiary. If one-twentieth of this sum had been spent ten years ago by any social workers on that 22-year-old girl, that electrocution would have been prevented."[40]

Another way capital punishment increases the costs of trial is by increasing the time needed to obtain a jury. Jurors . . . are reluctant to serve where they have to send a man to his death. In notorious cases, this may cause fantastic delays—several days spent in interrogating from one to two hundred veniremen before a jury is obtained. The effect that this kind of sifting out of those most reluctant to convict of capital crime may have upon verdicts is another unexplored field.

The death penalty may actually make convictions harder to obtain. It is always necessary to present a very convincing case to obtain a conviction where the penalty is death. When lesser penalties are possible, the rate of convictions rises rapidly. When forgery was a capital offense in England, juries in the eighteenth century began to revolt, and simply refused to convict. As a result, we had the anomalous situation of the banks appealing to Parliament (in vain) to abolish the death penalty.[41] That probably gives one explanation for the fact that, whereas in 1918 twelve states made the death penalty mandatory on conviction of a capital offense, today only Vermont does so.[42]

In spite of all the controversy concerning it, the death penalty is so rarely resorted to that it hardly figures as an actual penal practice. In the whole United States, there are today only a little over one hundred executions for murder per year, although there are about 7,000 murders per year; the rest are given prison

[40] Quoted in Herbert B. Ehrmann, "The Death Penalty and the Administration of Justice," *The Annals*, 284 (November, 1952), pp. 82–83n.

[41] Hartung, *op. cit.*, p. 11.

[42] Vermont Statutes, "Penalty," §8242, p. 1555 (1947); see also District of Columbia Code, "Punishment for murder in first and second degrees," §22–2404, p. 725, 1951 ed. (Washington, 1952). See Robert E. Knowlton, "Problems of Jury Discretion in Capital Cases," *University of Pennsylvania Law Review*, CI (June, 1953), p. 1099.

terms if they are convicted at all.[43] By dividing the crime into degrees and by giving the judge or the jury discretion in imposing sentence, we have in practice substantially reduced the number of capital sentences that otherwise would be passed. The same trend is going on everywhere else throughout the civilized world. Scotland in a period of fifty years had six hundred murders, yet only twenty-three executions, mainly because of the operation of the Scotch doctrine of diminished responsibility.[44] In England the device used is mainly that of the exercise of the prerogative of mercy. In other countries where the death penalty has not been abolished, it is falling into desuetude by administrative practice. In Belgium, for example, although the death penalty is still on the statute books, there has not actually been an execution since 1863. A sanction so rarely applied can hardly be regarded as an operative instrument of penal policy.[45]

Where it is applied, it is applied in a shockingly haphazard and discriminatory way. Of the few who are actually executed, almost all are poor, almost all are men, and a disproportionately high number are Negroes. Defendants of wealth or education

[43] There can of course be no statistics on the number of murders actually committed. As a matter of fact there are not even general statistics available as to the number of persons convicted per year of first degree murder. But in 1951, there were 6,820 cases of "murder and non-negligent manslaughter" known to the police. But only about 1600 to 1800 persons are sent to prison each year for murder, and, as said, only about 100 are executed. See Vold, op. cit., note 20, p. 6; Hartung, op. cit., note 19, p. 13.

[44] Royal Commission on Capital Punishment, Minutes of Evidence, Mar. 2, 1950, p. 351, par. 4209.

[45] "An average of one execution a year in a state of two million hardly suggests a constructive use of a rational instrument of penal policy unless we assume a selective process of incredible sensitivity and a subject who so far exceeds familiar ranges of pathological malformation, of dangerousness and of incorrigibility as to fall quite outside the human species." Dession, op. cit., pp. 215, 225. Sellin has said that the controversy over the death penalty is out of all proportion to its frequency of application. It is in fact "the rarest of all severe criminal punishments." Sellin, Memorandum submitted to the Royal Commission on Capital Punishment, Minutes of Evidence, Feb. 1, 1951, p. 647. That is why it is not a deterrent and "probably can never be made a deterrent. Its very life seems to depend on its rarity and, therefore, on its ineffectiveness as a deterrent." Thorsten Sellin, "Common Sense and the Death Penalty," Prison Journal, XII (October, 1932), p. 12.

practically never go to the gallows or the electric chair. Neither do women. Warden Lawes of Sing Sing escorted 150 persons to their death. Of them, 150 were poor; 149 were men.[46] During the twenty years from 1930 to 1950, there were 3,029 executions in the United States. Of these, 21 were women. And of these few, the majority were Negro women. In the southern states where capital punishment is retained for rape, it is used almost exclusively against Negroes. This is so flagrantly true that it was made the basis of an argument of discrimination by the NAACP in the notorious "Martinsville Rape Case" of 1950. The Association's brief on appeal cited figures, which have never been questioned, showing that although 809 white men had been convicted of rape since 1909, not one had been executed. During the same period 54 Negroes were executed on rape convictions.[47]

Thirty years ago, a House Committee recommended favorably on a bill to abolish the death penalty in the District of Columbia. It said:

As it is now applied the death penalty is nothing but an arbitrary discrimination against an occasional victim. It cannot even be said that it is reserved as a weapon of retributive justice for the most atrocious criminals. For it is not necessarily the most guilty who suffer it. Almost any criminal with wealth or influence can escape it but the poor and friendless convict, without means or power to fight his case from court to court or to exert pressure upon the pardoning executive, is the one singled out as a sacrifice to what is little more than a tradition.[48]

The bill did not pass. But what the committee said is at least as true today as it was then.

Warden Lewis E. Lawes said twenty years ago:

Capital punishment in the United States may be regarded as practically abolished through indifferent enforcement. But, by retaining the death penalty in its penal codes, it necessarily goes through

---

[46] Lewis E. Lawes, *Twenty Thousand Years in Sing Sing* (New York: R. Long & R. R. Smith, 1932), p. 302.

[47] Hartung, *op. cit.*

[48] House of Representatives, 69th Congress, first session, Report No. 876, sp. 14, 1926.

the theatricals of the threat of enforcement. These very theatricals lend glamor to the accused fighting for his life. The offense, no matter how heinous, is frequently disregarded in the new drama portrayed in the courtroom where prosecutors demand death for the prisoners and counsel pleads for mercy. These theatricals reach out beyond the courtroom and weaken law enforcement all along the line.[49]

They distort the administration of justice, producing unmerited acquittals in some cases and in others convictions not justified by an unemotional evaluation of the evidence.

But the main argument against capital punishment is not concerned with what it does or fails to do to criminals. It concerns what it does to the rest of us. Capital punishment does more harm in brutalizing and lowering the moral standard of the community as a whole than it does good by eliminating a few dangerous individuals.

It becomes for many people an absorbing and unhealthy fascination to follow the trial of a person on trial for his life. "Public interest of an almost prurient nature heightens under the influence of the modern media of mass communication. There seems to be released among us a perverted curiosity verging on mass sadism which crowds the trial courts and surrounds the place of execution. Unhappy and unpleasant emotions are stirred in most of us."[50]

As Mr. Justice Frankfurter said: "When life is at hazard in a trial, it sensationalizes the whole thing almost unwittingly; the effect on juries, the Bar, the public, the judiciary, I regard as very bad. I think scientifically the claim of deterrence is not worth much. Whatever proof there may be in my judgment does not outweigh the social loss due to the inherent sensationalism of a trial for life."[51] In England, Viscount Templewood said: "It makes people gloat over crime and I think, however

---

[49] Lawes, *op. cit.*, p. 336.

[50] A. M. Kirkpatrick, Executive Director, John Howard Society of Ontario, before the Joint Committee on Capital and Corporal Punishment and Lotteries (Canada), Minutes of Proceedings and Evidence, No. 14 (May 19, 1954), p. 607.

[51] Testimony before the Royal Commission on Capital Punishment, Minutes of Evidence, p. 580, par. 7967 (1950).

much you safeguard the actual carrying out of executions, they also pander to those morbid feelings that lie very near the surface in most of us and that would be much better repressed."[52]

... A sensational murder trial [was] held in Lancaster, Pennsylvania. A college student was charged with murdering a young woman. There hadn't been a death sentence in Lancaster County since 1922, but this case aroused all the old morbid curiosity and animosity. On the day of the opening of the trial the crowd began to form in the alley behind the court house as early as 6:00 A.M. By nine o'clock the lines stretched from the rear of the court house down the alley all the way to the next street and around the corner. A policeman later said there were at least five hundred people.

The crowd kept coming every day of the trial. In the morning, when the accused was brought in, and in the afternoon, when he was taken away, the crowd was so dense that police had difficulty getting through to the waiting vehicles. People shouted out words of encouragement or of condemnation. Some struggled to get a better look, others wanted to lay their hands on him. One woman brushed his sleeve with her fingertips. "I touched him," she said with her face bright, "that's enough for me—I touched him." On the last day some were weeping, some were praying, some were shouting.[53]

Part of the crowd interest may have been stimulated by the brutality of the crime and the implications of sexual attack. And part of it may have been spurred by the local press. The defendant's attorney, in later preparing an appeal, compiled a list of what he called inflammatory material taken from the three Lancaster papers. But that material wasn't particularly garish— nothing like the really lurid whipping up of morbid public curiosity that you have in other cities where some of the newspapers are much worse, as in New York, or where they're all worse, as in Los Angeles.

The basic value of our civilization is, in Albert Schweitzer's

---

[52] Viscount Templewood, testifying before the Royal Commission, *ibid.*, p. 629, par. 8556.
[53] Richard Gehman, *A Murder in Paradise* (New York: Rinehart, 1954), pp. 3, 4, 6.

phrase, Reverence for Life. Indeed, a good measure of any civilization is the extent to which this seminal concept is valued and implemented. If we want to inculcate respect for human life, we must not ourselves take life in the name of the law.

Official killing by the state makes killing respectable. It not merely dulls the sensibilities of people to cruelty and inhumanity, but actively stimulates cruelty. It negates the efforts of those who are working to stimulate the better instincts of men.

And let us not forget that in a democratic society the state is you and I. It is not an impersonal, inhuman machine that executes these persons. It is you and I who provide the money to erect the gallows or install the electric chair. It is you and I who pay the executioner to act as our representative. The execution of a condemned man is not a stage play, to be read about in the newspapers. It is a deliberated act in which every citizen participates.

And while Gallup polls have shown that about half of the people in the United States favor retaining capital punishment, it is interesting to observe that they don't like the idea of having anything to do with it themselves. We don't reveal the identity of the executioner because we know that he would be generally shunned by his neighbors if they knew his secret. One reason why execution by intravenous injection is not practical is that it would require a doctor to administer, and doctors want no part in the business. If we were honest with ourselves we would have to admit that we are ashamed of keeping capital punishment as a part of our penal system. In our hearts we agree with Viscount Templewood who said in his book, *The Shadow of the Gallows,* "The whole act from start to finish is repulsive and unworthy of a civilized community."

The driving force behind the movement for abolition has been democracy. Only Fascism halted the trend in countries like Italy, Austria and Germany. Democracy has fostered it, in Europe, in South America, in Australia—everywhere except in the United States.

Only in this country is there no organized political movement for abolition. No American state has abolished the death penalty since 1917. It isn't even the subject of political discussion here, as it is right now in England and in Canada. Here, it is a subject for high school debaters—nothing more. As long as abolition has no political champion, no organized voice in the forum of public discussion, we in America are failing to move along with the current of civilized thinking.

If and when we do renounce the illusory protection of the death penalty, we should not make the mistake of merely shifting our faith to imprisonment or any other negative sanction as a remedy for crime. Let us hope that abolition will lead us rather to provide more *preventive* law enforcement. As Thomas Fuller said more than two hundred years ago, "To punish and not prevent is to labor at the pump and leave open the leak." One way to get more preventive law enforcement is by increasing police efficiency. It was increased efficiency in enforcement that cut short the wave of kidnappings for ransom in the 1930's, rather than the adoption of laws authorizing the death penalty for this crime.[54] But the best way to prevent crime is to identify potential criminals and guide them away from an antisocial career before they carry that career to a tragic climax. It can be done. It is being done by agencies such as the Diagnostic Center

[54] "After 1931 about half the states in the Union introduced the death penalty for kidnapping for ransom, and the Federal Government also introduced the death penalty for that crime. . . . The first execution did not occur until years after the 'market' disappeared. I suspect that the reason why kidnapping for ransom disappeared as a behaviour was that all the machinery of law enforcement, from the Federal Bureau of Investigation down to the local policeman, was focused on its prevention. This was a business crime, and when the market disappeared, it was no longer a profitable venture. We saw the same thing happen in connection with automobile theft during the depression. While other thefts of various kinds increased, automobile thefts dropped during the depression to a very low degree. The stealing of automobiles for sale and exportation disappeared, because the buyer disappeared. . . . If a government were to apply similarly preventive methods to certain other types of criminality, they, too, would show a reduction. I do not think that murder ordinarily falls in that category. The psychological character of the crime is such that it would probably have no effect. Gang murders would, of course, disappear with the disappearance of gangs. Gangs could be broken up and made to disappear by effective police action, supported by the community, as anyone who knows anything about local conditions in the United States realizes." Prof. Thorsten Sellin, testifying before the Royal Commission on Capital Punishment, Minutes of Evidence, p. 673, par. 8885 (1951).

at Menlo Park, New Jersey, and the New York City Youth Board.[55]

With the help of insights that psychiatry and psychology are giving us into how the mainsprings of human behavior operate, we are learning much about how to bring up children to fit into the world. Perhaps we are also learning how to build a world fit for them to live in. With these insights, we are better armed for the task of molding a society that nurtures the healthy and fruitful growth of individual life, a society that holds inviolable the dignity of man and fosters love and understanding of one's fellow man rather than hostility and aggression—a society, in short, that respects life.

[55] The Diagnostic Center at Menlo Park, New Jersey, is an outstanding experiment in studying "problem children." A staff of specially trained psychiatrists, neurologists, clinical psychologists and social workers makes a thorough organic examination of the child. Standardized psychological and psychometric tests, interviews under sodium pentathol and projective creative art tests are also used. After a 90-day study, an extensive report is prepared, offering not only a diagnosis but also specific recommendations for future treatment and management of the delinquent. Marcel Frym, "Past and Future of Criminal Rehabilitation," *Journal of Public Law*, III (1954), pp. 451, 455.

The New York City Youth Board has been experimenting with the Glueck prediction techniques in two selected public schools in the Bronx, to see if they will make it possible to detect those first grade children who are likely to become delinquent later. At the same time, the board is also conducting experiments in delinquency treatment to test whether they are effective in preventing delinquency from developing in those children for whom delinquency is predicted by the Glueck techniques. Whelan, *op. cit.*, p. 432.

The Patuxent Institution in Maryland, which opened in 1955, is also engaged in an interesting experimental program for the treatment of "defective delinquents."

JUSTIFICATIONS FOR CRIMINAL PUNISHMENT

Herbert L. Packer

Herbert L. Packer, professor of law at Stanford University, deals, in the following selection, with a social problem, or rather a series of social problems, involving important legal, philosophical, and moral dimensions. Principally, the problem is that of trying to control antisocial behavior by imposing punishment on those convicted of violating society's laws; only slightly less complex is the problem of deciding what kinds of human conduct ought to be limited by criminal sanctions. Interrelated with these problems is the question of determining how effective punishments (or threats of punishments) have been in deterring offenders and preventing recidivism, especially in such offenses as prostitution, homosexuality, drug addiction, and gambling. "We can have as much or as little crime as we please," writes Professor Packer, "depending on what we choose to count as criminal."

Rationalizations or justifications for either a moralistic-judgmental-retributive approach to the offender or a utilitarian-pragmatic defense of the employment of punishment are not *theories*

Source: Herbert L. Packer, *The Limits of the Criminal Sanction* (Stanford, Calif.: Stanford University Press, 1968), pp. 35–61. Copyright © 1968 by Herbert L. Packer. Reprinted by permission of the publisher.

in the scientific sense, but rather oversimplified attempts to deal with the complex multiple issues that characterize our inherited ways of talking or thinking about punishment. But such justifications, to use the author's term, do address the questions of why, when, how, and to what extent (of severity) punishment may or should, morally, be used.

Professor Packer is not primarily concerned with the dilemma faced by those who feel compelled to choose between the moralistic and the utilitarian approaches to punishment; rather, he makes his major contribution in articulating his view that although prevention of crime is the primary purpose of criminal law, that purpose, like any other in society, does not exist in a vacuum. It has to be qualified by other social purposes, namely, the enhancement of freedom and the dispensation of justice, the effectuation of which requires that limits be placed on the original goal of crime prevention. Chief among these limits is the requirement that the finding of moral responsibility be a necessary though not wholly sufficient condition for determining criminal guilt and meting out punishment for it.

INTRODUCTION

Criminal punishment means simply any particular disposition or the range of permissible dispositions that the law authorizes (or appears to authorize) in cases of persons who have been judged through the distinctive processes of the criminal law to be guilty of crimes. Not all punishment is criminal punishment but all criminal punishment is punishment. Punitive damages imposed in a civil suit constitute punishment but not criminal punishment. The deportation of an alien, under our present legal arrangements, is punishment but not criminal punishment. Punishment is a concept; criminal punishment is a legal fact. This important distinction is obscured by loose references in judicial opinions to "punishment" when what is meant is "criminal punishment." For example the deportation of an alien for membership in the Communist Party under a statute that made such membership a ground for deportation after the alien's membership had terminated was upheld by the Supreme Court against the claim, among others, that it constituted ex post facto punishment in contravention of the constitutional prohibition.[1] The Court refused to characterize the deportation as punishment, or so they said. What they were refusing to call it was not punishment considered as a general concept, but rather a particular kind of punishment, criminal or perhaps quasi-criminal. If they had agreed that the deportation was quasi-criminal punishment, it would fall within the prohibition of the ex post facto clause. In legal usage, the term punishment ordinarily has this additional element.

The range of permissible punishments is at the present time very broad, ranging from death, at one extreme, to a suspended sentence at the other. Criminal punishment always includes but is not limited to a formal judgment of guilt. Typically, this judgment is entered when the trier of fact, judge or jury, determines that the defendant is guilty of the offense charged. In a sense this legal usage departs somewhat from common word usage. When Hermann Goering committed suicide in prison following his conviction of war crimes by the Nuremberg Tribunal, it was said of him that he had escaped punishment. It is true that he had escaped the full measure of punishment to which he was potentially subject by the Tribunal's sentence to death. But in contemplation of law, a significant part of his punishment had already occurred, in that he had been found guilty as charged. This idea is not totally foreign to common usage, as can be seen by the plea frequently voiced on behalf of a convicted defendant before sentencing that "he has already been punished enough." And indeed, if he is a respectable member of the community who wants the good opinion of his fellows and of society, he has in a relevant sense already suffered some punishment. Thus the formal announcement of a criminal conviction is itself a form of criminal punishment and one that in many cases may be at least as potent as any other likely to be imposed.

In my view, there are two and only two ultimate purposes to

[1] Galvan v. Press, 347 U.S. 522, 531 (1954).

be served by criminal punishment: the deserved infliction of suffering on evildoers and the prevention of crime. It is possible to distinguish a host of more specific purposes, but in the end all of them are simply intermediate modes of one or the other of the two ultimate purposes. These two purposes are almost universally thought of as being incompatible; and until recently, moral philosophers, who are the arbiters as well as the combatants in this struggle, have tended to assume that one or the other of these purposes must be justifiable to the exclusion of the other. My main point here is that, not simply as a description of existing reality but as a normative prescription for legal action, the institution of criminal punishment draws substance from both of these ultimate purposes; it would be socially damaging in the extreme to discard either. Before arguing this point, however, it may be desirable to elaborate somewhat the description of the two ultimate purposes of punishment.

RETRIBUTION

The retributive view rests on the idea that it is right for the wicked to be punished: because man is responsible for his actions, he ought to receive his just deserts. The view can take either of two main versions: the revenge theory or the expiation theory. Revenge as a justification for punishment is deeply ingrained in human experience, and goes back at least as far as the *lex talionis*: an eye for an eye, a tooth for a tooth, and, we might add, a life for a life. Its marks on the criminal process are similarly deep, the most conspicuous example today being the death penalty for murder. If, as F. H. Bradley has observed, the revenge morality represents the view of the man in the street, then punishment can be seen as a way of satisfying what is essentially a community blood lust. Thus it is an important sociological question whether this view is as widely held today as it was in Victorian England.

It was a distinguished Victorian judge and historian of criminal law, Sir James Fitzjames Stephen, who is known as the most eloquent exponent of the revenge theory, but curiously enough his views have utilitarian underpinnings. To him the punish-

ment of criminals was simply a desirable expression of the
hatred and fear aroused in the community by criminal acts. . . .
Stephen observed that punishment bears the same relation to
the appetite for revenge as marriage bears to the sexual appetite.
The figure is an arresting one, but it does not express a pure
revenge theory. Instead, it conveys a disguised utilitarian position: punishment is justifiable because it provides an orderly
outlet for emotions that, denied it, would express themselves in
socially less acceptable ways.

This is but one example of the ways in which an ostensibly
retributionist theory may have an implicit utilitarian connotation. We are somehow not content to say that criminals should
be punished because *we* hate them and want to hurt them. It
has to be because others hate them and would, were it not for
our prudence in providing them with this spectacle, stage a far
worse one of their own. This kind of hypocrisy is endemic in
arguments about the death penalty, but it does not seem to be
empirically verified. Lynchings do not, as this theory would
lead us to conclude, seem to increase in places that have abolished capital punishment.

The other principal version of the retributive view is that
only through suffering punishment can the criminal expiate his
sin. Atonement through suffering has been a major theme in
religious thought through the ages, and it doubtless plays a role
in thought about secular punishment as well. In this view the
emphasis is shifted from our demands on the criminal and becomes a question of demands that the criminal does or should
make on himself to reconcile himself to the social order. In the
absence of assurance that his sense of guilt is equal to the demands made upon it, we help to reinforce it by providing an external expression of guilt.

It hardly matters which aspect of the theory is espoused. The
result is the same. The criminal is to be punished simply because he has committed a crime. It makes little difference
whether we do this because we think we owe it to him or because we think he owes it to us. Each theory rests on a figure of
speech. Revenge means that the criminal is paid back; expiation
means that he pays back. The revenge theory treats all crimes

as if they were certain crimes of physical violence: you hurt X; we will hurt you. The expiation theory treats all crimes as if they were financial transactions: you got something from X; you must give equivalent value. Underlying both figures of speech and rendering irrelevant a choice between the figure to be employed is the thought that it is right for punishment to be inflicted on persons who commit crimes. This familiar version of the retributive position, which I shall call the affirmative version, has no useful place in a theory of justification for punishment, because what it expresses is nothing more than dogma, unverifiable and on its face implausible. The usefulness of the retributive position resides, as we shall see later, in what it denies rather than in what it affirms.

UTILITARIAN PREVENTION: DETERRENCE

The utilitarian or preventive position, by contrast, has considerable appeal although, as we shall see, it does not suffice as a justification for punishment. Its premise is that punishment, as an infliction of pain, is unjustifiable unless it can be shown that more good is likely to result from inflicting than from withholding it. The good that is thought to result from punishing criminals is the prevention or reduction of a greater evil, crime. There are many different, and often inconsistent, ways in which punishment may prevent the commission of crimes, but the inconsistencies should not be allowed to obscure the fact that the desired result is the same in every case.

The classic theory of prevention is what is usually described as deterrence: the inhibiting effect that punishment, either actual or threatened, will have on the actions of those who are otherwise disposed to commit crimes. Deterrence, in turn, involves a complex of notions. It is sometimes described as having two aspects: after-the-fact inhibition of the person being punished, special deterrence; and inhibition in advance by threat or example, general deterrence. These two are quite different although they are often confused in discussion of problems of punishment. For example, it is sometimes said that a high rate of repeat offenses, or recidivism as it is technically known, among persons who have already been once subjected to criminal punishment shows that deterrence does not work. The fact of recidivism may throw some doubt on the efficacy of *special* deterrence, but a moment's reflection will show that it says nothing about the effect of *general* deterrence.[2] An even more preposterous argument is sometimes heard to the effect that the very existence of crime or (more moderately but equally fallaciously) the increase in crime rates is evidence that deterrence does not work. Unless we know what the crime rate would be if we did not punish criminals, the conclusion is unfounded. It may well be that some forms of punishment, through their excessive severity, produce a net increase in the amount of crime, but that is a very different issue (although one often confusingly invoked by people skeptical of the deterrent efficacy of punishment). Since these same people are typically proponents of rehabilitation as a goal of punishment (also, be it noted, in the interest of prevention) and since punishment is not the less punishment for being rehabilitative in purpose, it is evident that the argument is beside the point. As so often in debates on this issue, the problem of how severe given forms of punishment should be is confused with the problem of whether punishment is itself justifiable. It cannot be too often emphasized that the severity of punishment is a question entirely separate from that of whether punishment in any form is justifiable.

The idea of deterrence as a mode of crime prevention is often derided on psychological grounds. Criminals do not, so these critics say, pause to reflect upon possible consequences before committing a crime; they act upon obscure impulses that they can neither account for nor control. We may agree that the criticism is probably well-founded, but it is not applicable to very much of what is comprehended by the idea of deterrence. If the term deterrence (like most such high-level abstractions) is to have any functional utility, we must recognize that it does not describe a simple entity. The "one word–one meaning" fallacy is nowhere more pernicious than when words so broadly

---

[2] In the interest of clarity I shall reserve the term "deterrence" for general deterrence and shall use "intimidation" for special deterrence.

connotative as deterrence are used as if they described things rather than clusters of ideas.

The modern psychological criticism of deterrence turns out on inspection to be based on a very simple model, one almost might say a caricature, of what is signified by the term. The model is Jeremy Bentham's, and it is a model of great, although not un-limited, usefulness. It assumes a perfectly hedonistic, perfectly rational actor whose object it is to maximize pleasure and mini-mize pain. To such an actor contemplating the possibility of a criminal act the decision is based on a calculus: How much do I stand to gain by doing it? How much do I stand to lose if I am caught doing it? What are the chances of my getting away with it? What is the balance of gain and loss as discounted by the chance of apprehension? The purpose of criminal punishment, on this model, is to inject into the calculus a sufficient prospect of loss or pain to reduce to zero the attractiveness of the possible gain.

The psychological critics reject the reality of this model.[3] In doing so, they substitute for it a model of man as governed by largely unconscious drives that impel him to act quite without regard to any rational principle of pleasure-seeking. That model, like the Benthamite model that these critics deride, is useful; but like the Benthamite model, it does not come close to ex-hausting the possibilities of human existence. The psychological model, if I may call it that, represents the criminal as murderer —and not as murderer for profit but as perpetrator of the crime of passion. He is the man who kills on impulse because he hates his father, he is sexually inadequate, he lacks control, and so forth. The polemics of the psychological critics are full of case histories that conform to this model. No one would deny their reality, but they do not tell the whole story. The Ben-thamite model may well be a more nearly accurate representa-tion of the acquisitive criminal: the burglar, the embezzler, the con man. Perhaps the purest modern instance is the man

---

[3] E.g., Walter Bromberg, *Crime and the Mind* (New York, 1965); and Gregory Zilboorg, *The Psychology of the Criminal Act and Punishment* (New York, 1954).

who cheats on his income tax. While we should not overlook the significance of irrational drives in even such carefully planned crimes as these often are, it still seems clear that they have a rational hedonistic component. The Benthamite model has considerable relevance to cases of this sort, which—although they do not necessarily dominate the field of criminal activity— cannot safely be ignored.

My point, of course, is not that the Benthamite model of deterrence explains everything, but rather that it explains something about human behavior. The criminal law is a human institution that needs to take account of as many possibilities of human action as seem inherent in the human condition. Bentham gave us a hold on a piece of reality. That hold should not be abandoned simply because it is partial, especially if one concludes that complete views of reality are unattainable.

All that I have been concerned to show so far is that even the caricature of deterrence resulting from a restriction of the idea to the dictates of rational hedonism has some validity as a basis for punishment. But much more needs to be said about the cluster of ideas validly subsumed under the heading of deterrence. The warning given by the threat of punishment as reinforced by the occasional spectacle of its actual infliction has a wider meaning than Bentham's model suggests. One need not see man as an isolated atom, intent only upon making rational choices that will advance his own pleasure, to see deterrence at work. Let us expand our view to take account of what we know of man as a creature whose impulses are subjected from birth to the manifold processes of socialization and whose reactions to situations in which he finds himself are largely automatic. To deny on that view the reality of deterrence is to call into doubt many of our hypotheses about the socializing capacity of human institutions such as the family, the school, the peer group, the community. Or, equally implausibly, it is to single out one social institution—the criminal law—and deny to it the compulsive force that we ascribe to every other institution that conditions human behavior.

Our hypotheses about the operation of general deterrence should be broadened to include also the effect of punishment—

and indeed, of all the institutions of criminal justice—on the totality of conscious and unconscious motivations that govern the behavior of men in society. On the conscious level, moral norms are learned and the learning is reinforced by threats of unpleasant consequences that will follow if those norms are disregarded. The degree to which the norms are accepted depends largely on the vividness with which coercive threats are made. And it is not merely the physical unpleasantness of punishment —loss of life, loss of liberty, loss of property—that makes the impression. Feelings of shame resulting from the social disgrace of being punished as a criminal are feared also. And it is not only Bentham's rational hedonists who are touched by the power of deterrence, but all those who are sufficiently socialized to feel guilty about breaking social rules and whose experience has led them to associate feelings of guilt with forms of punishment. It may be conceded that it is the law-abiding whose moral systems are affected in this way by the force of deterrence. But to say that is not to minimize the force of what is being done, unless we are prepared to say that the threat of punishment, involving as it does both physical and psychic pain, has no role to play in making people law-abiding and in keeping them that way.

At least as much importance attaches to the effect of the threat of punishment on behavior governed by unconscious motivations. On this level, "threat" becomes a much subtler and more complex concept than either the rational hedonists or their critics have been prepared to recognize. The existence of a "threat" helps to create patterns of conforming behavior and thereby to reduce the number of occasions on which the choice of a criminal act presents itself. Every one of us is confronted daily by situations in which criminal behavior is a possible alternative. Sometimes the presentation is sufficiently vivid that we think about it and reject the criminal alternative. More frequently and more significantly, we automatically and without conscious cognition follow a pattern of learned behavior that excludes the criminal alternative without our even thinking about it. Indeed, the arguments for the efficacy of deterrence may become stronger the more one departs from a rational free-will model and the more one accepts an unconsciously impelled, psychological determinism as an accurate description of human conduct. There seems to be a paradox in the rejection by some psychologists of the idea that the threat of punishment (itself reflecting a legal model) can induce people unconsciously to adopt patterns of law-abiding behavior. Guilt and punishment are, after all, what the superego is all about.

The socializing and habit-forming effects of the threat of punishment are not limited to simple, literal observation of threats being made and carried out. There is heavy symbolic significance in the operation of the criminal sanction; for the process of ascribing guilt, responsibility, and punishment goes on day after day against the background of all human history. The vocabulary of punishment (itself heavily influenced by legal concepts and models) with which we become acquainted beginning in early childhood impresses us—some more than others—with the gravity of antisocial conduct. The ritual of the criminal trial becomes for all of us a kind of psychodrama in which we participate vicariously, a morality play in which innocence is protected, injury requited, and the wrongdoer punished. It is not simply the threat of punishment or its actual imposition that contributes to the total deterrent effect but the entire criminal process, standing as a paradigm of good and evil, in which we are reminded by devices far more subtle than literal threats that the wicked do not flourish. These public rituals, it is plausible to suppose, strengthen the identification of the majority with a value-system that places a premium on law-abiding behavior.

When the criminal is seen caught in the toils of this process, any desire people may have that he suffer reinforces the values against which he has offended. In this sense, the retributive and utilitarian justifications for punishment tend to coalesce. The sense of fitness (which, as Holmes wryly remarked, is unqualified only with respect to our neighbors) that we feel at the spectacle of merited suffering becomes a prop for our own sense of identification with law-abidingness. This is, then, an important part of the utility of punishment: not, as the simplistic notion goes, that criminal justice prevents lynching by satisfying community passions for revenge, but rather that blood lust properly tamed reinforces individual rectitude. The symbols change and not all of them are essential; we get along well enough without wigged barristers. But the symbolic richness of the criminal process is a powerful deterrent, something we too often forget especially when desiccating reforms are advanced in the name of the "treatment" of offenders.

When the threat of punishment is removed or reduced, either through legislative repeal or (as ordinarily occurs) through the inaction of enforcement authorities, conduct that has previously been repressed (in two senses of the word) tends to increase. We are so familiar with the phenomenon that there may be no more convincing demonstration than this of the effectiveness and complexity of deterrence. When, for example, laws repressing certain kinds of sexual conduct are no longer enforced with any regularity, the conduct in question is promoted, not merely because people feel that a threat has been removed but also, and probably more significantly, because the subtle process of value reinforcement through the rites of criminal stigmatization comes to a stop.

I have elaborated the elements of deterrence theory because the idea of deterrence has fallen into considerable and undeserved disrepute. I do not want, however, to overestimate the importance of its role in any rational penal system. Deterrence has its limits, and inattention to those limits has doubtless helped to discredit it. To start with the most obvious point, deterrence is not the only mode of prevention available to us, and any ultimate appraisal of its role in a system of crime prevention must wait upon a comprehensive presentation of other possible modes, and an examination of the extent to which they use techniques and work toward goals inconsistent with those peculiar to deterrence. Beyond that, it is clear that the deterrent role of the criminal law is effective mainly with those who are subject to the dominant socializing influences of the day. That it is effective with them is its strength. That it is not effective with others is its countervailing weakness. Deterrence does not threaten those whose lot in life is already miserable beyond the point of hope. It does not improve the morals of those whose value systems are closed to further modification, either psychologically (in the case of the disoriented or the conscienceless) or culturally (as in the case of the outsider or the member of a deviant subculture). And, where the prohibited conduct is the expression of sufficiently compulsive drives, deterrence is made possible, if at all, only by cruelly rigorous enforcement, widespread repression, and a considerable drain on human and economic resources—a price we may well shrink from paying.

Special Deterrence or Intimidation

A second utilitarian justification for punishment is its asserted propensity to reduce or eliminate the commission of future crimes by the person being punished. Again, the concept rests primarily on a rational, hedonistic model of behavior. Once subjected to the pain of punishment, so the theory runs, the individual is conditioned to avoid in the future conduct that he knows is likely to result again in the infliction of pain through punishment.

No aspect of preventive theory has been subjected to such a barrage of criticism in recent years as has the idea of intimidation. The criticism centers on what is thought to be a conclusion emerging from empirical study of recidivism among offenders. Although there is much disagreement over specific figures and even more over their significance, it is universally recognized that persons who have served prison sentences have a high rate of reconviction, perhaps as much as fifty per cent. Superficially, this well-documented fact does appear to raise substantial questions about the efficacy of intimidation. Yet, as we shall see, there are reasons not to reject out of hand its usefulness in crime prevention.

First, there is the obvious but frequently overlooked fact that we do not know how much higher the recidivism rate would be if there had been no criminal punishment in the first place. It is not unreasonable to suppose that the rate would probably be somewhat higher if persons who committed crimes were free to continue committing them without being punished. Second, the argument against intimidation often confuses the severity of punishment with the fact of punishment. By singling out those who have been subjected to the relatively severe sanction of imprisonment, the generalization ignores the effect of such punishment measures as probation and suspended sentences on persons who commit crimes. As we have previously pointed out, the very fact of criminal conviction is itself a form of punishment, particularly to the relatively law-abiding citizen. To be detected in the commission of crime and then subjected to the stigma of a criminal conviction may in itself have a strong impact on the future behavior of the offender. The studies we have on the subject seem to demonstrate that those subjected to the relatively less severe sanctions of probation or of early release from prison on parole have a lower rate of recidivism than do persons subjected to more severe punishment. A related point is that by and large those who are selected for severe punishment are less likely to conform with standards of law-abidingness. They are the more experienced, more hardened criminals who are for one reason or another not amenable to intimidation.

It should also be noted that recidivism rates appear to vary greatly for different types of crime. We need far more specific research than we have yet had on this point, but it does seem clear that "crime" is much too vague an entity to be studied wholesale as the basis for any conclusions about the efficacy of intimidation. There may well be types of offenses (or types of offenders) that are relatively immune to the influence of intimidation. Once such categories are established by empirical evidence rather than, as now, by hunch, the role of intimidation in a system of punishment for such offenses will need to be reevaluated. But we are certainly not in a position now to say that the concept has no utility. Finally, it must be remembered that punishment may serve, and ordinarily will serve, more than one intermediate goal of prevention. Even if intimidation does not seem to be, standing alone, a sufficient justification for punishment, that is no reason to reject the contribution it may make to crime prevention if preventive goals are pursued in the name of such other justifications as deterrence and rehabilitation. To take only one example, there is no hard line separating the effects of rehabilitation and intimidation. The convict who goes straight after his release may do so because he is a "better" man, but he may also do so because he is the same old man under better control. If he refrains from committing further crimes at least in part because he does not want to be punished again, it would take a very lofty view of human nature to assert that he has not been "rehabilitated."

Perhaps the most cogent criticism of intimidation derives from observation of the effect of inhumane punishment on offenders. The combination of the corrupting influence of criminal associations in prison with the feelings of bitterness, hatred, and desire for revenge on society that are engendered by inhumane treatment in a backward prison may well produce a net loss in crime prevention. Whatever feelings of intimidation are produced on the prisoner by the severity of his punishment may be outweighed by the deterioration of his character in prison. His punishment may contribute to the effect of deterrence on others, but in the process he is lost to society.

This antinomy embodies one of the great dilemmas of punishment, reflecting the conflict among intermediate justifications that have the common ultimate goal of crime prevention. Punishment must be severe enough to exert a restraining effect on others, but not so severe as to turn the person being punished into a more antisocial creature than he was before. We will have more to say at a later point about the issue of severity. It is enough now to note that we have not as a society displayed much imagination in this regard. Severity has been by and large equated with brutality; and we have neglected the possibility that not everything that men fear and wish to avoid must necessarily have a brutalizing effect on them if they are exposed to it. Until we have devised measures that avoid this dilemma, we are wise to be cautious in our reliance on intimidation as a guide to penal action.

BEHAVIORAL PREVENTION: INCAPACITATION

The simplest justification for any punishment that involves the use of physical restraint is that for its duration the person on whom it is being inflicted loses entirely or nearly so the capacity to commit further crimes. By contrast with the idea of general deterrence, about whose empirical basis there is continuing disagreement, the empirical basis for incapacitation is clear beyond argument. So long as we keep a man in prison he will have no opportunity at all to commit certain kinds of crimes—burglary, obtaining property by false pretenses, and tax fraud are three of the many types precluded in this way. And his opportunities to commit certain other kinds—such as assault or murder—are greatly diminished by confinement. Of course, such extreme forms of punishment as execution and solitary confinement for life can assure total and near total incapacitation. In a society that was single-mindedly devoted to the repression of crime as a paramount objective of social life, incapacitation would be the most immediately plausible utilitarian justification for the punishment of offenders. On further inspection, however, its plausibility diminishes.

We may start by noting that incapacitation differs radically from general deterrence as a mode of crime prevention and that, in consequence, it must be justified on different bases. Deterrence operates according to the nature of the offense. The personal characteristics of the numerous people who are every day punished for committing crimes cannot be known by the public, to whom the deterrent threat is addressed. The threat of punishment or the spectacle of its imposition creates general awareness that people who do certain kinds of things will be punished if they are caught, no matter what their personal characteristics are. Incapacitation has a much subtler and more attenuated relationship to the nature of the offense. To the extent that there is any connection at all, it rests on a prediction that a person who commits a certain kind of crime is likely to commit either more crimes of the same sort or other crimes of other sorts. This latter prediction does not seem to figure largely in the justification for incapacitation as a mode of prevention. To the extent that we lock up burglars because we fear that they will commit further offenses, our prediction is not that they will if left unchecked violate the antitrust laws, or cheat on their income taxes, or embezzle money from their employers; it is that they will commit further burglaries, or other crimes associated with burglary, such as homicide or bodily injury. The premise is that the person may have a tendency to commit further crimes like the one for which he is now being punished and that punishing him will restrain him from doing so.

Incapacitation, then, is a mode of punishment that uses the fact that a person has committed a crime of a particular sort as the basis for assessing his personality and then predicting that he will commit further crimes of that sort. It is an empirical question in every case whether the prediction is a valid one. To the extent that the prediction is valid, utilitarian ethics can approve the use of punishment for incapacitative purposes, on the view that the pain inflicted on persons who are punished is less than the pain that would be inflicted on their putative victims and on society at large if those same persons were left free to commit further offenses.

It will be seen that this proposition is highly dubious when applied to the issue of whether all of the people who commit a certain kind of offense should be punished for it. How can we say in advance that the quantum of pain likely to be caused by, let us say, murderers as a group if they are left unpunished would exceed the quantum of pain imposed on them by punishment? If we could be sure that they as a group are likely to cause significantly more deaths or bodily injuries than the population at large, we would have the beginnings of a rationale for punishing them as a group in the name of incapacitation. We may have such a basis for offenses that can be shown to be highly repetitive, but we do not have an *a priori* basis for saying it about offenses in general. The incapacitative justification, then, when addressed to the question whether people who commit a certain kind of offense should be punished for it, is no stronger than the empirical evidence available that offenses of that kind are likely to be repeated.

Just as the deterrent and incapacitative modes of punishment differ in their effects, so do they differ as operational criteria for lawmakers. A legislature that is seeking to determine when punishment is justifiable must decide according to the nature of the offenses (which is knowable in advance) rather than according to the personality of the particular offender (which is not).

How reliable is the prediction that people who are once detected in the commission of a certain kind of offense will go on
committing that kind of offense? Some persons commit burglary
under circumstances that indicate they are unlikely to do so
again. Others are known to be making a career of it. We can
hardly say in advance which is which.

There are kinds of conduct that are typically repetitive. Persons who commit theft because they suffer from kleptomania
are apt to go right on doing so. Narcotics offenders, if they
happen to be addicts, are by definition likely to repeat their
offenses. We have learned that there is a typical syndrome involved in the writing of bad checks. It is an activity of such a
compulsive sort that repeat performances are highly probable.
In cases of this sort, the empirical basis for making the kind of
prediction upon which the incapacitative rationale necessarily
rests is quite strong. But note the paradox that this involves.
The case for incapacitation is strongest in precisely those areas
where the offender is least capable of controlling himself, where
his conduct bears the least resemblance to the kind of purposeful, voluntary conduct to which we are likely to attach moral
condemnation. Baldly put, the incapacitative theory is at its
strongest for those who, in retributive terms, are the least
deserving of punishment. That is not, of course, enough to disqualify it as a basis for punishment. It does, however, suggest a
certain tension between the concept of blameworthiness as a
prerequisite of punishment and the dictates of the incapacitative claim. Perhaps the way to dissolve that tension is to abandon blameworthiness as a condition for the imposition of
punishment. That is the thrust of the behavioral theory that
presents one horn of the criminal law's contemporary dilemma.
Incapacitation as a basis for punishment seems particularly
attuned to the demands of the behavioral position.

Another noteworthy feature of the incapacitative theory is its
implication for the question of severity. If it is justifiable to lock
someone up to keep him from committing further crimes, for
how long is it justifiable to do so? One answer may be: until we
are reasonably sure that he will no longer commit crimes of that
sort. But when is that? In the case of crimes that stem from a
personality trait of the offender, we may confidently expect that

he will go on committing the offenses in question until the personality trait changes. If we cannot give the hopeful answer: until he is reformed, then we must say: so long as he remains a danger. But that may well be for the rest of his life, if by "danger" we mean a person with a propensity to commit certain kinds of criminal acts. The logic of the incapacitative position drives us to say that until the offender stops being a danger we will continue to restrain him. What this means, pushed to its logical conclusion, is that offenses that are universally regarded as relatively trivial may be punished by imprisonment for life. It means that, at least, unless we have some basis for asserting that lengthy imprisonment is a greater evil than the prospect of repeated criminality.

The problem is by no means academic. The laws of many states contain so-called habitual offender provisions, the general thrust of which is that upon conviction for two or more offenses at different times the offender may be sentenced to an extended term of imprisonment, sometimes for life. To the extent that there is a coherent rationale for laws of this sort, it rests upon the prediction of continued dangerousness that justifies the incapacitative theory of punishment.

Another difficulty with the incapacitative position is its irrelevance to many forms of criminal conduct. Consider the case of perjury. A witness in a civil trial is persuaded to give false testimony so that his friend, who is seeking damages for injuries suffered in an automobile accident, may win his case. The falsity is detected, and the witness is tried and convicted for having committed perjury. What is to be done with him? Presumably he will be, or at least may be, sent to prison. If incapacitation were the sole justifying basis for punishment, it would seem peculiar to imprison this person. He may have shown a propensity for telling lies under oath (although even that is disputable), but it is hardly likely that he will have the occasion to do so again. It is simply ludicrous to say, "We will send you to prison for three years so that we can be sure that at least for those three years you will not commit any further acts of perjury." Whatever the justification for punishment in this case, it clearly does not rest on the need to restrain the prisoner from committing further crimes. Or consider the use of the criminal sanction to enforce compliance with tax laws. A doctor takes fees in cash that he does not report on his income tax return. This is discovered, and he is tried and convicted for income tax evasion. It strains credulity to suggest that we are sending him to prison for a year so that during that time he will not be able to cheat on his income tax. Even if we lived in a Gilbert and Sullivan sort of universe in which that was the stated reason for punishing tax evaders, we would still face the strong moral objection that alternative, less severe methods of prevention would be just as effective, or nearly so. A rule, for example, that the tax returns of all persons who had been once convicted of income tax evasion would automatically be submitted to detailed audit would probably have the same effect.

Even crimes for which punishments are generally thought to rest at least in part on the incapacitative ground may not, on reflection, reveal much of a basis for invoking that ground. The man who murders his rich aunt so that he will accelerate his inheritance under her will is not imprisoned (or executed) in order to keep him from murdering other people. Indeed, murderers in general have been shown to be among the least recidivistic of offenders. Once released from prison they have a very low rate of reconviction for any criminal offenses, let alone for murder. The justification for punishing such persons must rest on other grounds.

It appears, then, that incapacitation does not present a claim as a sufficient basis for imposing punishment. Of the utilitarian grounds for punishment, only general deterrence has so far been shown to present any such claim. The most that can be said for incapacitation is that it may provide an additional basis for punishment in cases where reasonable evidence concerning the nature of either the particular offender or his kind of offense suggests that he would repeat that offense or commit others if he were not imprisoned.

BEHAVIORAL PREVENTION: REHABILITATION

The most immediately appealing justification for punishment is the claim that it may be used to prevent crime by so changing the personality of the offender that he will conform to the dictates of law; in a word, by reforming him. In that ideal many have seen the means for resolving the moral paradox of the utilitarian position: that punishment is an instrumental use of one man for the benefit of other men. Perhaps "resolving" is too strong a word. After all, the goal sought by the rehabilitative ideal is not reform for its own sake or even for the sake of enabling its object to live a better and a happier life. We hope that he will do so, but the justification is a social one: we want to reform him so that he will cease to offend. He is still being made use of. Whatever moral truth inheres in Kant's famous imperative—"One man ought never to be dealt with merely as a means subservient to the purpose of another. . . . Against such treatment his inborn personality has a right to protect him"—is not made inapplicable by the benevolence of the reformer. Perhaps all we can say is that the ideal of reform mitigates the harshness of the paradox. We are helping society, true. But we are doing so by helping the offender.

It has become fashionable to reject the unpleasant word "punishment" when talking about rehabilitation. For reasons I have given in some detail, this emerging linguistic convention is a misleading one. However benevolent the purpose of reform, however better off we expect its object to be, there is no blinking the fact that what we do to the offender in the name of reform is being done to him by compulsion and for *our* sake, not for his. Rehabilitation may be the most humane goal of punishment, but it is a goal of *punishment* so long as its invocation depends upon finding that an offense has been committed, and so long as its object is to prevent the commission of offenses.

What are the significant characteristics of a system of punishment based on the goal of rehabilitation? Principally, such a system is—like incapacitation—offender-oriented rather than offense-oriented. If rehabilitation is the goal, the nature of the offense is relevant only for what it tells us about what is needed to rehabilitate the offender. To be sure, that relevance is greater than is commonly supposed. In the present state of our knowledge about the human personality and the springs of human action we cannot afford to ignore what a man has done as an index of the kind of man he is and, consequently, of what measures are required to make him better. Still, what he has done is only one measure, and a rough one at that, of what he is. The rehabilitative ideal teaches us that we must treat each offender as an individual whose special needs and problems must be known as fully as possible in order to enable us to deal effectively with him. Punishment, in this view, must be forward-looking. The gravity of the offense, however measured, may give us a clue to the intensity and duration of the measures needed to rehabilitate; but it is only a clue, not a prescription. There is, then, no generally postulated equivalence between the offense and the punishment, as there would be in the case of the retributive or even the deterrent theory of punishment.

It follows from this offender-oriented aspect of the rehabilitative ideal that the intensity and duration of punishment are to be measured by what is thought to be required in order to change the offender's personality. Unlike the related goal of incapacitation, the inquiry is not into how dangerous the offender is but rather into how amenable to treatment he is. If a writer of bad checks can be cured of his underlying disorder only by five years of intensive psychotherapy, then that is what he is to receive. And, of course, no one knows at the outset how much of what kind of therapy will be needed in his or anyone else's case, so it cannot be said in advance what the duration of his punishment will be. It ends whenever those in authority decide that he has been rehabilitated. Of course, if he does not yield to treatment and is thought to present a danger, he will not be released. The two goals always go hand in hand. No rehabilitationist has ever been heard to say that offenders whom we are incapable of reforming should be released when this incapacity becomes manifest. Indeed, some of them eagerly embrace the view that incorrigible offenders must be kept in custody for life, if necessary. They have not been concerned to inquire too closely into the criteria of necessity. In its pure form, the ideology seems to call for cure or continued restraint in every case. Incapacitation, then, is the other side of the rehabilitative coin. It may well seem a dark underside.

There are two major objections to making rehabilitation the primary justification for punishment. The first probably comes very close to settling the matter for present purposes. It is, very simply, that we do not know how to rehabilitate offenders, at least within the limit of the resources that are now or might reasonably be expected to be devoted to the task. The more we learn about the roots of crime, the clearer it is that they are nonspecific, that the social and psychic springs lie deep within the human condition. To create on a large scale the essentials of a society that produced no crime would be to remake society itself. To say this is not to suggest that the goal of so improving society is not worthwhile, or that there is any superior social goal. It is merely to suggest that this is a task to be undertaken in the name of objectives and using techniques that far transcend the prevention of undesirable behavior. One trouble with the rehabilitative ideal is that it makes the criminal law the vehicle for tasks that are far beyond its competence. Surely the point does not require laboring that a general amelioration of the conditions of social living is not a task that can be very well advanced in the context of the institutions and processes that we devote to apprehending, trying, and dealing with persons who commit offenses.

Rehabilitation after the fact, which is all we can realistically propose, suffers simply from a lack of appropriate means. The measures that we can take are so dubiously connected with the goal that it is hard to justify their employment. We can use our prisons to educate the illiterate, to teach men a useful trade, and to accomplish similar benevolent purposes. The plain disheartening fact is that we have very little reason to suppose that there is a general connection between these measures and the prevention of future criminal behavior. What is involved primarily is a leap of faith, by which we suppose that people who have certain social advantages will be less likely to commit certain kinds of crimes. It is hard to make a good argument for restraining a man of his liberty on the assumption that this connection will be operative in his case. It is harder still if he already possesses the advantages that we assume will make people less likely to offend.

We know little about who is likely to commit crimes and less about what makes them apt to do so. So long as our ignorance in these matters persists, punishment in the name of rehabilitation is gratuitous cruelty. In truth, the threat of punishment for future offenses as extrapolated from the experience of suffering punishment for a present offense may be the strongest rehabilitative force that we now possess. To the extent that a man is rendered more prudent about committing offenses in the future by reason of unpleasantness suffered on account of offenses past, he may be said to be rehabilitated in as meaningful a sense of the term as we can generate from present-day experience. For the gross purposes of the criminal law, a man is better when he knows better. As already suggested, intimidation and rehabilitation have more affinities than present fashions in penal thought accord them.

There is, of course, no reason to suppose that our lamentable ignorance about how to reform offenders is a condition that will persist forever. Indeed, there are measures available today that illustrate in a gross kind of way the claims that rehabilitative theory may be able to make tomorrow. One example is the prefrontal lobotomy, a neurosurgical procedure that has the effect among others of reducing the kind of aggressive drives that impel one toward criminal activity. Of course, it is not a very selective procedure; although it reduces drives, it does not discriminate among ways in which the drives find expression, so that the patient who has undergone this procedure is as unlikely to do anything useful as he is to do anything destructive. Nonetheless, if he does have a reduced drive toward criminality it seems fair to say that, insofar as we are interested in reducing the propensity to commit offenses, the patient has been rehabilitated. In terms of the immediate goal sought, it is irrelevant that rehabilitation has been accomplished at the cost of a profound alteration in his personality of a sort that he (and the rest of us as well) has not invited and would probably prefer not to undergo.

Let us suppose, though, that the side effects of some yet-to-be-discovered means of changing the human personality are not such as we would consider objectionable. To put it another way, suppose that the existing empirical objection to the rehabilitative ideal is removed. Should that ideal be permitted to dominate our punishment system? It is with this question that the second major objection to rehabilitation as the primary goal of punishment emerges. If people can be changed for the better without suffering effects that would generally be considered unfortunate, is there any moral case against compelling them to undergo measures designed to produce such change, given the predicate that they have by their past behavior demonstrated a readiness to commit offenses of a sort whose future occurrence will now be reduced? It may be enough to measure our present fumbling efforts against that millennial prospect and assert that until it arrives the question is academic. It may also be that when the day of the good-behavior pill comes, we will be on the one hand so insensitive to such interferences with the personality and on the other hand so eager to enjoy the increased security that its wholesale administration to offenders promises that questions of this order will seem as academic then as they do now. But if we consider the moral dimensions of the question, the answer is by no means clear. Is it quixotic to assert that man has a right to be bad? Perhaps that right will appear to have little substance when the means of change is more readily at hand than it is today. Yet I have serious doubts on this point, and I am impelled to ask whether a theory of punishment that requires acquiescence in compelled personality change can ever be squared with long-cherished ideals of human autonomy.

SUMMARY: THE LIMITS OF PREVENTION

I have so far dealt with rehabilitative theory on the assumption that what is claimed for it is primacy as a goal of punishment, and I have been concerned to point out certain difficulties that stand in the way of accepting this superficially attractive proposition. Before leaving this aspect of the subject, I should like to comment on a claim frequently advanced by proponents of the behavioral view (which we can now see as the advocacy of rehabilitation and incapacitation as complementary goals of punishment). This claim, briefly stated, goes back to the polarity described at the beginning of this discussion: that there are only two views and that one must choose between them. On the one hand, this claim asserts, there is the demand for vengeance, which we call retribution. It is backward-looking to the offense rather than forward-looking to the offender; it is punitive rather than preventive, it is predicated on metaphysical notions about "responsibility" for the offense that bear no relation to the social justifications for punishment. On the other hand, there is the behavioral position, which, as we have seen, can be characterized as an attempt to deal with the prevention of crime by changing the offender or his situation: primarily, through reforming him, secondarily, through incapacitating and intimidating him.

The attitude of proponents of the behavioral position toward deterrence is ambivalent. They do appear to recognize that deterrence, to the extent that it operates, serves preventive goals. But they question whether it does operate, point out that empirical evidence of its operation is lacking, and assert that in the absence of more solid factual demonstration than we now have available, the claims of deterrence should be subordinated to claims for individual treatment of offenders based on the concepts of rehabilitation and incapacitation. Some go further: they assert that deterrence is simply vengeance thinly disguised. To punish a man with the vague hope that doing so will serve to deter others is simply a rationalization, so the argument runs, for a desire to inflict pain on him because he deserves to suffer for his misdeeds. Why not come right out and admit it, these critics say: if punishment is imposed for any purpose other than to make the offender a better man or to protect society against him, it is socialized vengeance and should be rejected by any society that calls itself civilized.

It is doubtless true that there are times when the utilitarian claims of deterrence are used to mask a desire to inflict what is thought to be deserved suffering. The debate over the death penalty is a notable example. Those who support capital punishment on essentially retributive grounds continue to couch their argument in deterrence terms in spite of the lack of evidence to support the claim. But to cite this kind of aberration as evidence that the deterrent position is retributive is to confuse the issue in two ways. First, the argument about the severity of punishment is confused with an argument about the justification for any punishment at all. Second, the assertion is made that because an argument can be misused it has no validity, an obvious non sequitur. A commercial pornographer may favor freedom of speech solely because it enables him to ply his trade unmolested by the law, but this does not in any way prejudice the arguments on the merits for freedom of speech.

The fact that punishment involves suffering is a moral embarrassment. But it is just as much an embarrassment to the behavioral position as it is to the claim that punishment is justified because it deters. The case for incapacitation is every bit as capable of being a mask for vengeance as is the case for deterrence. Life terms for habitual offenders are urged because of an asserted need to protect society from their depredations. Indeterminate commitments for sexual psychopaths and narcotics addicts are urged on the same ground. Our experience with measures of this kind—their genesis in demands for action when the community is shocked by a heinous crime, their operation as wastebaskets for the socially undesirable—suggests that they are just as capable of serving as outlets for feelings of revenge as are undisguised pleas to make the offender pay. Indeed, these claims may be less defensible than a straightforward plea for revenge. To the morally unacceptable urge to punish they add the morally degrading spectacle of widespread hypocrisy and self-deception. And they present a social danger that measures we might reject if they were acknowledged to be based on the urge for revenge will be accepted when put forward in the more plausible guise of scientific utility.

The same danger is latent in the case for rehabilitative measures. Given the lack of any solid empirical basis for supposing that we know how to reform, given the fact that measures of reform may entail just as severe restrictions on personal liberty as measures employed for deterrent or even retributive ends, the danger is equally present that in the name of humanitarian goals we will commit ourselves to measures that are in large part, albeit covertly, inspired by the demands of vengeance. And there is the additional danger that, because such measures are being taken in the name of humanity, we will be less quick to recognize and defend against encroachments on libertarian values.

The proponents of the behavioral position often seem oddly obtuse in the face of modern knowledge, such as it is, about the unconscious springs of human conduct. One would suppose that they of all people would be alert to the ambivalent quality of human motives, especially when they involve large-scale interference with the freedom of others. Helping others rather than punishing them sounds attractive. Substituting amelioration for suffering sounds high-minded. Thinking of crime as evidence of pathology rather than of depravity sounds advanced. But who can be sure that the urge to punish and the urge to cure may not have a common source in some dark recess of the human psyche? At the very least, what is called for is a little trepidation, a little self-doubt, a little awareness of how great a leap is needed to get from the theoretic dictates of the behavioral view to a set of working institutions and processes for dealing with deviant conduct.

I do not make these points in a spirit of disparagement. They are no more telling against the advocates of the behavioral position than is their criticism of the claims of deterrence. But they are no less telling, either. All that I have been concerned to show is that any unitary theory of punishment is inadequate and that all theories—not simply deterrence—that start from the utilitarian premise suffer from the same moral embarrassment. In the words of a distinguished lawyer-philosopher: "[Punishment is] at best, a needed but nonetheless lamentable form of societal control."[4]

I have been concerned to examine in detail the ambiguities in utilitarian theories of punishment precisely because I believe that those theories provide the most satisfactory starting point we possess for an integrated rationale of criminal punishment: one that gives a satisfactory account of the general justification for punishment and that provides a basis for determining both what kinds of conduct and what kinds of people should be subjected to the criminal sanction. Having in mind the ambiguities of the utilitarian position, let us now consider whether a satisfactory integrated theory of punishment can be devised.

[4] Richard Wasserstrom, "Why Punish the Guilty?" *University* (Spring 1964), p. 14.

AND THE PRISONERS WILL BECOME PRIESTS: THE CONVICTS BREAK OUT

Timothy Leary

A Harvard professor and a team of dedicated students came to the prison at Concord, Massachusetts, to experiment with a method of reaching deeply into the beings of the imprisoned men. They hoped to lead these men to new insights and in the course of so doing discover new approaches to rehabilitation. The professor was Timothy Leary, or "Dr. Tim," as the men came to call him. He had a novel approach: psychedelics, consciousness-expansion, that caused the mind to burst forth with visions, thoughts, feelings, and emotions that could be described as hallucinations, fantasies, or just a different reality.

Source: Timothy Leary, *High Priest* (New York: World, 1968), pp. 192–211. Copyright © 1968 by League for Spiritual Discovery Inc. Reprinted by permission of The World Publishing Company. An NAL book.

The "sacrament" was Leary's name for the psychedelics, for even at that point in his career he was developing a religious approach to the drugs. Later, LSD would be embraced by a group that Leary would name the League for Spiritual Discovery. "The sacrament can liberate the imprisoned." Self-help had worked, in Leary's view, with Alcoholics Anonymous and other groups; it could work with prisoners as well. But it would be self-help with insights and group cohesion, and this Leary would provide with the psychedelics.

In the following selection, Leary describes some of the prisoners' reactions to psilocybin—the fear and the awe, the flow of fantasy and the return to reality. And then he goes on to relate what happens to one prisoner who is granted parole. He leaves the prison, to return: but return to what? Seldom, almost never, does a prisoner return to a family, a job, a society extending a hand of welcome; rather, what awaits him is the stigmatized status of being an ex-convict. This makes him as much a pariah as being a convict, but without the latter's security and support. Leary and his group sought to become a family for this particular ex-convict—not with a remarkable success, but with an effort worthy of study.

There is an epilogue to this story of what Leary did with the prisoners, not the sequence of events in Dr. Tim's life, much of which is public information, but rather what happened among the prisoners themselves. They sought, after Leary's departure, to continue as a self-help group, without guidance and without drugs, but with the inspiration he had left with them. Finally, they obtained permission to establish an organization, and for several years they continued to operate, both in prison and out, one of the major efforts of a group of convicts and ex-convicts to rehabilitate themselves through a self-help, voluntary association. But that is another story, and it has been told elsewhere.[1]

---

[1] See William C. Kuehn, "The Concept of Self-Help Groups among Criminals," *Criminologica*, VII (May 1969), 20–25; and Edward Sagarin, *Odd Man In: Societies of Deviants in America* (Chicago: Quadrangle Books, 1969), ch. 7 (this chapter written in collaboration with William C. Kuehn).

◄§

My experience while under psilocybin was so much more than I expected. To begin with I was completely unprepared for what was to happen, what changes were to take place in my beliefs, re-evaluating myself to the point of nothingness.

My whole way of life was so transparent while under psilocybin, that coming out from under the mushroom, I was in a deep state of shock. I use deep shock figuratively. This thirst for knowledge I had . . . is . . . was . . . it seems so meaningless now. More so because I was applying it to some abstract idea, some complicated intrigue of my own.

As to my first awareness of my real self, it was when my conversing

The first psychedelic session at the prison set up powerful repercussions.

First there was the effect on the little group of voyagers. Strong bonds had developed. We had been through the ordeal together. We had gone beyond the games of Harvard psychologist and convict. We had stripped off social facade and faced fear together and we had trusted and laughed.

I felt at home in the prison. It always works this way after a good trip. You die and then you are reborn. The place of your rebirth is home. This is not metaphorical—it is a neurological reality.

During the psychedelic session the nervous system returns to that state of flux and unity-chaos of infancy—and spins beyond familiar time-space where there is no home because all is a two-billion-year process of homing. As the session ends, one is reborn (smoothly or with a jolt). This is the period of reentry—the return from space to the planet. That place to which you return becomes neurologically engraved in your subsequent consciousness. It is a new "home"—a new neurological center. In scientific papers we described this as the process of re-imprinting. A rewiring of the nervous system.

There is a strong biochemical attachment to the people, the objects, the scents and sights, of the place to which you return. This accounts for the LSD cult phenomenon.

In our case the hospital room of the prison had become a center. A home. It was wired into my head.

The morning after the session, driving back to the prison was like going back to some sacred place in my skull.

Meeting the prisoners was like a family reunion.

Our status in the prison was changed. Glances of respect and interest. Prisoners approached us as we walked across the yard to ask if they could sign up for the mushrooms. Guards and parole officers stopped us to ask questions or to request that a favorite prisoner be admitted to the psychedelic group.

We spent the next two weeks discussing the reports that the prisoners wrote and comparing notes on the trip. Then we ran a second session. This time the prisoners were more sophisticated. There was no sitting around on chairs in nervous anticipation. As soon as the energy began to radiate through their bodies they headed for the cot, fell out, and closed their eyes. For the next two or three hours they lay engulfed in the visions, occasionally sitting up to smile or make some Zen comment. The Harvard guides changed the records and sat quietly, watching the cellular clocks in the room whirring, occasionally approaching the voyagers, a hand on the shoulder, a smile, the cosmic nod of affirmation. And the looks of wonder and sharing.

partner, Smithy, was searching for a complicated word in regards to something that needed a very simple word. It was then this idea flashed thru my mind, could it possibly be that what I was looking for is so very simple also. And then to my utter amazement, I realized I wasn't fighting the world, I was fighting myself.

Should I retain this ethical position, or disregard it for the present, to let him understand and see how much more there is to life, than living behind these walls in a state of mental and physical stagnation.

And finally he came to the decision, to show me how much I was missing with just the be feeling, and not being there feeling, let me expound on this for a moment.

Smithy asked me if I missed these different things outside of prison, that he and everyone else was enjoying, and my answer was something to the effect, oh! But I have these same things you have, by just substituting the being there feeling with the be feeling, then he asked me to teach him this feeling, because with this feeling, Smithy believed he would be able to solve the many problems of mankind.

The possibility of saving so much money, pain, mistakes, etc., seemed to him to be so important, and to me so ridiculous, that I explained to him that he was not ready yet, and to this answer he became so sad and unhappy, that I explained to him there wasn't to my knowledge anything to take the place of the being there feeling.

From there we concentrated on communication with the lower levels of intelligence. Smithy's idea was to find a way to plug into their minds for this knowledge we need to attain—this high pin-

Oh Doc! Amazing. This stuff is amazing.

It's all always amazing, Tony. Do you want anything?

Yeah, Doc. I'm thirsty.

I brought the glass of water. In sitting up, Tony spilled a few drops. His eyes riveted on the little wet puddle on the gray blanket.

Water, he said wondering. Life and water. Where does the water come from, Doc? We are water creatures, aren't we? Yeah, my body is the sea.

Sometimes the microscopes of inner vision focused on their lives. Jerry huddled under his blanket sobbing, his head shaking back and forth. Oh Doc, what a selfish fool I've been! My family. Wasted years. Wasted years. Will I get another chance, Doc? Can I go back and try it again?

Nine in the fourth place means:
He climbs up on his wall; HE CAN-
    NOT ATTACK.
Good fortune. (I Ching XIII)

It keeps going, Jerry. Every moment it starts all over again.

We arranged the room in sacred design. Incense. Candles. The convicts would lie watching the flickering flame. Outside the barred windows they could see the prison wall and the guard tower. Candlelight and the flash of sunlight on the guarding rifles.

Why are there prisons, Doc? What are we doing here? Wanted men. It's insane, Doc. We're all insane. Us cons

and the cops and the guards. How did we get into this?

Each session was a cosmic drama. Confusion. Humor, lots of laughter. Olympian multi-level god laughter. Loneliness. Tears. Terrors. Suspicion. Trust.

After the third session the convicts repeated the personality tests to measure changes. We brought the test folders into the hospital room and handed them to the inmates. No secrets. We explained what the tests measured and what the results meant.

They had changed. Showed less depression, hostility, antisocial tendencies, more energy, responsibility, cooperation. The objective indices so dear to the heart of the psychologist had swung dramatically and significantly in the direction of increased mental health.

By explaining their test results to them and letting them handle their own test scores, we were training them the same way we trained Harvard graduate students in psychodiagnostics. To learn what the test meant. How they were changing. The prisoners were becoming psychologists.

They loved it. Fierce debates about personality characteristics. The psychiatric diagnostic game being played by the cons.

After a few weeks of discussion we planned with the inmates the continuation of research. The convicts were to select the new recruits for the group.

nacle of knowledge, and Smithy, believing if we were the superior minds, wasn't it up to us to find a way of communicating with them, and not they with us.

But I disagreed, I believed we should first reach this high level of knowledge, and then if we have any desire to learn what they have, fine, if not it wouldn't make any difference anyway. But as usual Smithy's clear and logical mind took over, he showed me how much fuel could be used from each man's mind along the way. And I agreed to this idea.

So in summation, we found that knowledge alone was meaningless, knowledge must have fuel from these other channels. These everyday pleasures, the loves, the sadness, the small problems. These together with knowledge would balance out, to give man the proper guide in life, without them, man would become hopelessly lost.

The most sobering effect the mushroom had on me, was midway in our conversation. I asked Smithy if he realized that we had not mentioned God once— Smithy's answer verbatim (Have we done anything else). One could not realize the meaning of this answer and what effect it had to my reasoning—unless one understood that up until Monday I believed I was much more than I turned out to be, not a pretty picture for one to witness unprepared.
In conclusion I must state briefly, that I enjoyed the mushroom on one hand, but on the other hand, it frightened me, I say frightened, because I saw

They would learn how to administer the psychological tests. They would give the orientation lectures. They would run the project.

Here the reconciliation that follows quarrel moves nearer. It is true that there are still dividing walls on which we stand confronting one another. But the difficulties are too great. We get into straits, and this brings us to our senses. We cannot fight, and therein lies our good fortune. (I Ching XIII)

At this point we ran into prison politics. The social structure of a prison is like any village. There is a very explicit hierarchy. The inmates themselves run the prison. All the guards and administrators do is keep the peace, but the gut, muscle, moment-to-moment space-time issues are determined by prisoners.

The inmates belong to invisible social clans and the clan leader decides what happens. If the warden and guards violate the dignity and prerogatives of the convict leaders there is trouble. And all administrators want to avoid trouble.

One day when we walked into the hospital there were two new inmate medical attendants. They were men in their forties. Tough, proud, hard customers.

They walked up to me. Doctor Leary, I'm Jim Berrigan. This is Don Sainten. We'd like to talk to you.

Fine, but I'm late for the project meeting. Maybe later.

No. The meeting can wait. Let's talk now. I looked at them closely. They were men of confidence and dignity, power-holders, leaders. Dress them differently and they could be sea captains or chief surgeons or Broadway promoters.

I nodded and they motioned me down the hall. We walked into the hospital kitchen. I'd never been there before. Don walked to the stove and turned on the burner under a coffee pot. Bacon and eggs, Doc? No thanks. Coffee will do.

Jim and Don sat on the high serving counter and grinned. We've been watching this mushroom business, Doc, and it looks pretty good to us and we've decided to join your project. We'll be a lot of help to you. We've arranged transfers to the hospital so we can be right on call.

The words were cool and cocky and seemed to leave no room for question.

I explained that the decisions about who joined the project were made by the convicts in the group. I couldn't interfere but I'd pass their names on to the inmate planning group.

Jim and Don grinned. I don't think that those guys will give us any static, Doc, we usually get what we want around here. Don't we, Don?

Don nodded. There was muscle and hard prick behind the words.

I liked them and had to respect them. And it was more politics. Dealing with the powers that be. I grinned

myself for what I really was, but even tho this picture was seen for what it really was, I look to the future with enthusiasm, and to pursue psilocybin to its end.

What is it like to be under psilocybin, being able to see colors in all its brilliance and absolute splendor, it is by all means an atmosphere I would want to be in all the time—able to understand myself, music, and what it means, the feeling one gets from listening to such superb music as classics.

Actions and thinking that I have done before are being changed to a more magnificent and truer way; thoughts have come to me under psilocybin such as past manners in treating people with a much better attitude and respect.

This has taken me years to do and so after all these years I have found a way, thru the help of psilocybin. It has helped me in spell-

ing and reading. I re-
member when I couldn't
hold ten words in my
head, but now I have
words like antidisestab-
lishmentarianism—long
—yes, but a word with
any accomplishment,
and there are others I
am seeking to accom-
plish in accordance to
psilocybin.

A great deal of the pic-
tures I seen were trans-
parent, clear enough to
see and understand and
to speak about after my
session. It was nice to
experience.

There was nothing vi-
cious about my two ex-
periences, nor was it
extravagant, but it
was extraordinary and
therefore I must praise
and glorify this experi-
ence and all its wonder.
It explored my mind
and opened up a gate
that has been closed for
a long time, and with
this acknowledgment I
can keep it open and let
this memory mellifluous
itself through me be-
cause there is no need

and said, I'm pleased that you're interested. It's a new and good thing we're
doing and it works. It's also fun. I hope
you'll join us.

When I mentioned to our planning
group that Jim and Don had volun-
teered there was an uneasy ripple, and
murmurs about who exactly is in
charge, and I thought the project was
going to be democratic.

By democratic we mean that we
should run it, right?

We had already run into some problems of power and authority in turning
our decisions over to the convicts. The
intoxicating taste of command. Two of
the inmates had thrown themselves
into the doctor-psychologist role with
great energy and had developed pom-
pous professional facades in dealing
with their "clients." They tended to be
fussy and schoolmasterly punitive. The
other cons didn't like it.

And everyone was uneasy about Jim
and Don coming into the project.
They were big men in the prison. They
were boss cons. They'll take over.

Hey, wait a minute. If they come
into the project they'll have to take
the mushrooms.

There was a thoughtful silence and
then everyone began to laugh.

And if they take the drug they'll
flip out of their minds and beyond the
game of being boss convicts. Right?
And they'll be stripped naked like
everyone else. And they'll come back
changed like the rest of us.

If the mushrooms really work, if they produce insight and love, then they'll work for Jim and Don. Yeah, and for the guards too. Let's invite the screws to turn-on.

So it was agreed that Don and Jim could join the group. They were tested and listened to the orientation talks and held out their tough-guy hands one sunny morning to receive the sacrament.

This trip was being guided by Gunther Weil and two inmates from the original group.

After an hour Jimmy Berrigan started to show signs of distress. Jimmy was one of the hardest men in Massachusetts. He belonged to a famous Boston waterfront gang—a rugged, violent tribe. Jimmy was a professional outlaw. Proud. Touchy. Cocky. A man whose culture and whose long life was totally dedicated to strength, bicep control.

And now, as it comes to all men, the ultimate humiliation was coming to tough Jimmy in a sunlit room in the hospital ward in Concord prison.

Jimmy suddenly discovered he had fallen into a trap. He had bulled his way into the project to enhance his power in the prison. The mushrooms were good, and anything good in the prison belonged, by tribal custom, to Berrigan. And now he lay on a cot, rendered weak, his mind spinning away, his control slipping, overwhelmed by a thousand shadowy cel-

to be mendacious, dishonest. It is time to mend that which is broken.

Psilocybin has showed me how wrong I have been in my disinclination, I now care to emulate, strive for the better things in life.

I don't know of any other way for a person to ease tension, but maybe some could try a hobby or listen to music, maybe classical or spiritual. I am sure that somewhere along these lines you will find peace of mind.

On my second session, while I was under psilocybin and laying in bed with the covers over my head, a picture came into view as clear as I have ever seen before, and this was of Christ in the manger with these people standing and kneeling by his side. This picture stayed with me for a few moments, and then thousands of Christmas lights came into view— different. shapes and forms and designs of colors that was of tremendous brilliance and elegance.

I was wondering at one point if I was living, or was this heaven that I had heard so much about. Being able to experience these things have made me do a great deal of thinking in rechanneling my life. One must come a long way before he can find himself and I really hope I have.

I also have now a great conception of classic music whereas one time I would never think of listening to such music.

Psilocybin has a way of opening up the mind and letting you see dif-

lular faces mocking his illusions of strength.

This wasn't what he expected. This was a different high from booze and bennies and happy pills. He had fallen into a diabolic con game perpetrated by Harvard psychologists. After forty-five years of defiance and arrogance Jimmy was fallen. He raged in despair. He should have known better than to trust his natural enemies, these smooth-faced, glib middle-class professionals. What a sucker he was to fall for their line, to forget that power was everything. To let them slip him these immobilizing pills.

Well, he'd go down fighting. He tried to sit up, but his body was a tangle of pulsating wires and warm liquids. It was a nice feeling but he felt strange and weak. He looked around the room which was alive with belted radiance. Where were his tormentors? Ah, there was Gunther, young pip-squeak kid who couldn't hold his own for five seconds in a barroom brawl—now smiling at him in malevolent triumph.

He motioned for Gunther to come over and then fell back on the pillow.

How are you Jimmy?

I'm terrible, I'm dying. Well you got me, you clever bastard, but I'm not finished. You may have me but my brothers and my gang will get you for this. You'll be in a cement-bag in Boston Harbor in one week.

Gunther's face looked blank. Get me for what?

For trapping me this way, you smug Harvard fink.

Gunther felt a flicker of fear. He was turned-on too. Visions of gangland slayings. Cruel, implacable hoodlum revenge. How did he, a well-brought-up middle-class Jewish boy with good school grades get himself involved in this scene of wickedness and violence. Because of the mushrooms. The ecstasy had led him on. He had been warned of this. The grim Judeo-Christian retribution. You pay for your bliss. Now he was paying for his mushroom kicks. He looked down at the face of his murderer, the rugged, waterfront grimacing features of this hood, this devil Berrigan whose dread retribution was to fall on him. Thoughts of escape flashed through his mind. He glanced at the barred windows. He was trapped in the prison, surrounded by thugs who would spring to the command of the master criminal.

Tears came to his eyes. What a tragedy, to be cut down in his promising youth. He cursed the day he had even listened to the mushroom song and all the glib psychedelic teachings, which sounded so good but which just lured you into the void of hell.

The two men stood transfixed in horror and hate. Slim Harvard and grizzled outlaw. Caught together in some cold hopeless whirlpool of cosmic energy. Frightened and frighten-

ferent pictures and gradually you will grasp these significants, and use them as they should be used.

ॐ

Prisoner Trip Report #2:

I feel as an antiquarian does while searching for ancient relics—anticipation before the discovery—once discovered—the journey to make known what is unknown. I find there isn't two paths any longer, but numerous trails to follow.

None are marked in any tangible manner or form—the senses are to be my guide.

I must reject the colorless, barren, unpopulated roads—to travel into the world of beauty, the sun, the flowers, fresh-fragrant air—all the benefits nature has devised for the use of men.

I can do no less since the operation was successful (restoring my eyesight). I have traveled long in the world of darkness, shackled to the segregated misfits. The overwhelming desire to tear the cloth from my flesh, releasing the suffocating sinews to the magical beat of primitive drums.

(The sacred dance dedicated to the beyond.)

I am looking forward to my next session, as a child waits for someone to turn the lights on in the heavens above.

ing each other. Blaming each other. Man hopelessly isolated from man. The other men in the room watched silently.

Jimmy snarled again. My brother will kill you for this.

How can they kill me, Jimmy, I'm dying right now.

Dying. Death. Rebirth. Some long-forgotten wire of memory flickered. Death-rebirth. Trust the process. Gunther closed his eyes and the words came to him. The prayer. He struggled to move his throat and tongue, and then the words came out quavering, shaky, a strange little voice, but the message was there. Jimmy Berrigan looked up in disbelief. His eyes widened. Then he understood. From somewhere in his childhood, his Irish genes, his rugged Celtic past, the same message sparked.

Jimmy began to laugh. Amazing. Unbelievable. God did exist. The old teachings were true. Not in the stilted, phony effeminate accents of the Boston priesthood whose piety he despised, but in the voice which sighed and breathed in his cells.

He reached up and grabbed Gunther's hand, and their eyes met in a smile. And the session reel spun on.

The initiation of Jimmy and Don increased the feeling of centeredness at the prison. Coming to Concord was like returning on pilgrimage to a holy place. A conspiracy was emerging. We started plotting a mass prison break.

It is the nature of fire to flame up to heaven. This gives the idea of fellowship. Here, clarity is within and strength without—the character of a peaceful union of men, which, in order to hold together, needs one yielding nature among many firm persons. (I Ching XIII)

The name of the game was keep-out. We agreed that cops-and-robbers was ridiculous; the prisoner-guard game absurd. The perpetuation of these social dances depended on someone willing to play the part of the criminal. The entire top-heavy administrative structure, policemen, detectives, informers, lawyers, district attorneys, judges, probation and parole officers, guards, wardens, prison psychiatrists —all were dependent on the hero-star-bad-guy to make their good-guy parts have meaning. The criminals were the fall guys, the victims who kept the whole game going.

The solution was obvious. The prisoners had to turn-on, see the game the way it was, and then drop-out. Just stop playing the bad-boy game. See it, laugh at it, and drop-out.

So we made a contract. . . . Everyone in the group would do everything he could to help every member get out and stay out of prison. Not just sessions and discussions in the prison, but practical help in getting out, in finding a job, and dealing with life on the outside.

People I hated for no sound reason, I have come to love. The lies I've told force me to tell the truth and I do not find that it hurts as much as a lie does.

I'm satisfied with myself. I know that this is a new me. I'll always be looking to see if there is a better way to do things and how.

Believe me, I consider my being here the most important factor in my life because this is where I have come to know the meaning of freedom and the joys that come with it. Yes, the road has been a hard one and many tears involved. The going is easy now because I have found the way to the end.

I've been thru a complete change of life, an experience that the average 20-year-old does not go thru but when they do go thru this change, the better things are ahead.

I know myself in such a way that I can account for my thoughts and what they mean and what use they will be put to.

Prison can lead a man down to nothing in a very short time. There were times when I felt myself slipping and filling my mind full of ideas that were no good. The ideas are still there but only as a guide to show me that I cannot afford to make a life of criminal doings.

We were proposing a family, clan-type group. This was very different from professional bureaucratic rehabilitation. The motto of the rehabilitation worker is detachment. Don't get emotionally involved with the client. You will be seduced or conned. A mass-assembly-line rehabilitation sequence, in which the psychologist performs his tests and turns the patient over to the psychiatrist, who treats the patient and sends him cured to the parole board, which decides on the basis of its own criteria whether to allow parole. The parolee is then investigated and supervised by parole officers. Complete depersonalization all the way down the line.

The prisoner is treated this way because he comes from a family which either won't or can't help him. His clan has been fragmented. He is an isolated loner, an anonymous cog in the social machine.

Our strategy was exactly opposite to the detached professional approach. The aim was to build a network of friends who would help each other. To construct a group that could perform some of the functions of the tribe. If a middle-class person gets in trouble he is typically rescued by middle-class know-how which bails him out, gets him a lawyer, talks middle-class jargon to the officials, gets him a job, provides him with a middle-class home to return to.

Our plan was to use the resources of

our group (including middle-class know-how) to weave a web of protection for the convicts.

. . . Said Gandalf . . . Well, let folly be our cloak, a veil before the eyes of the Enemy! For he is very wise, and weighs all things to a nicety. . . . But the only measure that he knows is desire, desire for power; and so he judges all hearts.

. . . Said Elrond . . . the road must be trod but it will be very hard . . . this quest may be attempted by the weak with as much hope as the strong. Yet such is oft the course of deeds that move the wheels of the world: small hands do this because they must, while the eyes of the great are elsewhere. (The Lord of the Rings)

The project moved rapidly into action. One of our members was coming up for a parole hearing. Johnny O'Connell, a genial Irishman. Johnny was caught by the standard dilemma of the lower-class convict. In order to be paroled he needed a job and home. His family was disintegrated, helpless, uncaring and could offer no home. And how could he get a job when he was uneducated, untrained, socially tarnished and, being in prison, unable to canvas prospective employers? Unless something was done he would meet the parole board and be turned back for another year of incarceration for the crime of not having a family, a tribal group to support him.

Since the first mushroom test, my thoughts have always been smooth and more wholesome than ever before.

Nothing seems to drive me to stubbornness as before. I have come a long way into manhood and what I see, I like. What can be better than knowing where you are going and how you are going to get there.

It's pleasant to know that your mind is free and not being guilty of unworthiness.

I want to be at peace
with the world and
have it at peace with
me.

Psilocybin is a wonder-
ful discovery that does
things that nothing else
could do.

Psilocybin brings out
the truth of all around
you, those concerning
you and yourself. The
answers will be yours.
But will you use them?

There are things I seen
but I can't think of all of

So we went to work. First, to get
him a job. Johnny's occupations in the
past had been itinerant and casual.
Dish washer. Handy man. Laborer.
We phoned around Boston to find an
employer who wanted to guarantee
steady employment to a dish-washing
convict who was guilty of a few bad
checks and who drank now and then.
No takers.

For a week I spent most of my time
meeting with restaurant owners and
managers of construction companies.
They were all encouraging but no one
was willing to sign a paper guarantee-
ing Johnny a job.

Then we thought of the home-base
solution. Harvard University was one
of the largest businesses in Cambridge.
Dozens of dining halls. We visited the
Harvard employment office. There the
officials were most sympathetic. Their
interest led them to visit the prison.
They listened attentively to the discussion about sessions and in return gave
brief lectures about hard work, hon-
esty, and responsibility. But for Johnny
there was no help because the month
was May and the Harvard dining halls
closed for the summer.

There was nothing to do but hire
Johnny ourselves. Take him into the
family business. A letter was written
on the stationery of the Harvard Center for Personality Research, guaran-
teeing him a job on our project. We
located a room in Cambridge, paid the
rent, and Johnny had a home.

With these documentary testaments to middle-class support, Johnny was released. Our first reconverted man was on the streets.

When he reported to work for the research project, his first assignment was to find himself a job—and to keep diary notes of his job-hunting.

At five o'clock each afternoon he would return to the center with his report. The only jobs he could get were in large downtown cafeterias where he would be allowed to join that anonymous army of gray-faced, dead-eyed, muscatel-drinking drifters who clear dishes off tables and mop floors today and are gone tomorrow to the drunk-tank. Such a job was guaranteed to push him into alcoholism.

And every day at five-thirty Johnny would leave our office and go to his rented room, anonymous body on an impersonal bed in a strange chamber. The bars had TV and warmth and companionship.

For two weeks he continued to search, made endurable by the support of the graduate students who hung out in the project office (at least there were some people who knew and cared). And then came a job as apprentice baker in a pizza parlor. It was a small shop where he would be known by everyone, where he would be a person.

When Johnny came back from work the first evening, we all listened to his description of the place, what the girl

them because I never seen things like them before. I can't describe them.

There is one time I remember falling upward towards a mass of designs and it was all different colors or lights. It may sound nutty but I was there.

I see other human beings in a different light. I seem to place everyone on an equal level. Regardless of race, creed, or color and education.

I have never found it difficult to talk with most people. However, after the mushroom experience I find it much easier.

What can it do for others? I don't know. I will say this however, if the mushroom leaves the same impression on others as it has on me, then I suggest that everyone should be confronted with its virtues.

The main thing I received from my first experience with mushrooms, was to look at myself and the entire human race from a different angle. One of

cashier looked like, what the boss said to him, what his duties were.

We passed the story on to the cons at the prison, and they listened carefully to all the details.

There was still the bad business of Johnny living by himself and having no friends. The only thing that he could do after work was hang out in the bar. This was expensive. It was also dangerous—leading to hangovers and oversleeping.

But Johnny didn't know any other way of spending time or money. Free dollars and free hours automatically went to the saloon. The ideas of saving money, of purchasing anything except immediate essentials, of taking a vacation, of planning a career were as foreign to Johnny as to an Australian bushman. Middle-class behavior was as far removed from his experience as life on Mars.

So let's emigrate Johnny to Mars. Let's expose him to the day-to-day routine of middle-class American life where he could learn by observation. Johnny moved into my house, into the third-floor attic that Bill Burroughs had just vacated.

Johnny was a congenial householder. Jolly with kids. Easy with adults. He'd come home from work every night about midnight and have a beer and tell us about the pizza parlor.

When the parole officer would drop around to make his surprise visits, the fibers of the house braced in empathetic protection. We were all members of a benign conspiracy to keep Johnny out of jail. For the first time in his life he had a home and a protective family.

But the price was expensive. It took commitment, caring, concern, sharing. An emotional thing that can't be taught in the professional schools or obtained by voting large appropriations for criminal rehabilitation.

Back in prison the program went on. Psychedelic trips, two or three a week. Moments of confrontation. Moments of terror. Moments of joy.

We were using the prison as a training center. The convicts were learning how to guide psychedelic drug sessions. Harvard graduate students were coming to go through the program themselves. There was less distinction between psychologists and inmates. The new Harvards were assigned to veteran inmates for orientation and guidance.

In session after session the inmates guided the Harvards, and the Harvards guided the convicts.

The energy generated by the sessions continued to spill out beyond the prison walls. The psilocybin session room became a show place. Whenever visitors came to Cambridge inquiring about psychedelic drugs, we took them out to the prison. The convicts sat around the table giving lectures on their mystic experiences to Gerald Heard and Alan Watts and Aldous

friendliness and sincerity. Not what I can do everyone out of—but what I can do for them and with them. I hope to find deeper and clearer meanings to these other things the next time I take the mushroom. . . .

By nature, I am a very restless person. Always wanting to move. Yes, I would even go as far as to say wanderlust. I couldn't sit still if someone was talking to me and most of the time it would bore me to listen to them talk. Since the mushroom, I don't feel that way. I seem to be more relaxed. Less impatient. I want to listen and I don't want to be moving around. To get away from the things around me, now, seems to have vanished.

Then I was scared. I thought someone had pulled a trick on me and the little man disappeared. I thought to myself, someone has dubbed the record with their voice, someone who I don't know, someone very clever in his trickery. Someone wanted to hypnotize me, make me the living, speaking dead. Then I realized that I had seen this little green man before in my last trip.

The last Indian record came on and I closed my eyes, nothing, no color, nothing at all. I opened my eyes and felt very dizzy, so I closed my eyes again. All of a sudden a vision came unto me. Waver of sound, strings waving with sound, the music its very strings danced before me. The strings were gold, bright and brilliant.

Huxley and the ex-King of Sarawak and coveys of visiting psychiatrists.

The instinctive strategy was to do everything possible to enhance self-esteem, pride, and sense of accomplishment. Every power we could turn over to the convicts was a fiber in the body of growth we were constructing.

As in any tribe there were sectors of friction, resentment, and disappointments.

Johnny O'Connell lost his job when the pizza parlor went out of business. For a few days he looked for a new job and then he took to sitting around the house watching television and drinking beer all day. We tried LSD. Heavier and heavier doses, with no results. Johnny always treated psychedelics with the bravado of the Olympic booze champion. I can outdrink any man in the house. His pride was to prove he could take more and more sacrament without passing out.

So one afternoon we gave him five times the normal dose of LSD. Johnny flipped out of his mind and spun up to heaven. He raved about the beauty. He laughed with joy. He saw it all.

How do you like heaven, Johnny?

The answer was straight one-hundred-proof Irish. Tell God he's flubbed his job, Doc, there's no beer joint in heaven.

So we bundled up in overcoats to take Johnny to a bar. We thought he might see through the booze scene. He walked into the bar with bravado, but it was too much for him. The bottles leered and mocked. Gotta get the hell out of here.

Later that night he went back to the bar, ordered a beer, and turned to the man next to him. Mister, you'll never believe where I went today and what I saw. The man next to him didn't believe him. Neither did Johnny. The next day he was back to TV and beer. My irritation grew but Johnny couldn't be moved. I gave him a week to find a job and then I gave him fifty dollars and told him he was on his own.

In two weeks he was back in prison —not for crime, because Johnny wasn't a criminal, but for idleness and beering.

By the fall of 1962 we had over thirty-five convicts and fifteen Harvards in the group. And the men started being paroled out to the streets two and three a month.

True fellowship among men must be based on a concern that is universal. It is not the private interests of the individual that create lasting fellowship among men, but rather the goals of humanity. That is why it is said that fellowship with men in the open succeeds. (I Ching XIII)

We started project CONTACT. The ex-cons and the Harvards were signed up in buddy-system teams to visit the ex-cons in their homes. We'd drive around the slum areas of Brockton, Fall River, Worcester, looking for our man. Then we'd go out and have a

A voice came from the strings mystical and Godlike in its tone, precise in its pronunciation, faraway and abstract in its meaning to me. Then I saw the little green man again, emerald green, robe about him, long legs and arms wrapped about himself, bald head shining with light, long thin ears, bright green eyes, sly wide grinning mouth. He had gold earrings in his ear, long, thin eyebrows and darker and a little beard growing from his chin. He spoke of the music, of the very strings he sat upon.

I could only see part of his face, a small pointed beard covered his cheeks and chin, his eyes glowed with a yellow light and his nose was long and thin. He seemed to be speaking but I could not hear him. Maybe he was praying. I spoke to him, "Hey man, what are you doing here. I know you. I saw you before on a mountain." No answer. I could not help talking jive talk, abstract words. Then the vision disappeared and did not return.

A criminal, at least myself and most all I've ever met, were either unloved children or lost individuals. Lost between right and wrong. What they wanted and the means to it. They knew their ends, power, wealth, money could not buy friends, loved ones, happiness, beauty, intelligence. I saw how foolish the game I played was. Just saw thru it, saw the ends I would find, instead of the ends I'd imagined. It sickened me.

beer and find out how he was doing. There was a twenty-four-hour telephone to rush help in case of emergencies.

Maxwell found himself broke, his wife leaving him, and ready to knock over a store in rage and frustration. He'd phone our number and someone would drive over to meet him and spend an hour talking to him in an all-night cafeteria and lend him ten dollars. We bailed them out of jail, sobered them up, hid them from the parole officer, cooled out angry bosses. We did in short what the family does for its confused members. And we kept them out of jail.

By this time operation Keep-Out had become a three-ring circus. There was the prison. There was the outside CONTACT project and there was the less visible but equally important task of keeping the state administrators and officials happy. We kept a steady flow of memoranda and progress reports to the myriad departments which focus a jealous eye on the work of rehabilitating criminals.

It was clear to us that if a week went by without contacting the bureaucrats, clewing them in, making them a part of the game, the whistle would be blown on our game.

What we were doing was highly implausible from the administrative point of view. Week after week for two years we ran ecstasy sessions in a state prison—turning-on with the prisoners, turning-on visiting psychiatrists. We had converted the hospital ward into a spiritual center complete with incense candles and music.

We did this with the approval of the most skeptical, wary group of politician-pros on the American scene—cops, jailers, and parole officials. Our key was direct human contact. I spent one-third of my time in face-to-face interaction with the state officials. We invited them to the prison. We spent long hours over the lunch table, long hours driving to the state house and to the probation headquarters. A lunch at the Harvard Faculty Club for the Commissioner of Correction and his top lieutenants. Sharing of space-time. Caring for them, caring for their opinions and for their approval.

We even ran sessions for parole officers and correction officials. Some of them had unhappy trips. People committed to external power are frightened by the release of ecstasy because the key is surrender of external power. One chief parole officer flipped-out paranoid at my house and accused us of a Communist conspiracy and stormed around while Madison Presnell curled up on the couch watching, amused at the white folks frantically learning how to get high. He grinned at me. So you call it the love drug?

But the next day the parole officer looked back at where he had been and his voice shook in reverence.

The administrators let the project

What was life, a life of this kind, just misery for myself and those who loved me.

I again asked what I wanted from life and at once I got an answer—love, peace, plenty, intelligence, not power, but friends.

I reached the top. There was the same rock, the softness of it is still here. On this rock was a man. A man both young and old. He had about his slim body a liquid robe of the bluest blue. He had his hands folded in his lap.

His fingers seemed to glow. They were long and bony and his hands seemed slim and fine. He was looking into the sky and did not hear me. He had long, womanlike hair, smooth and shiny and black, coal black.

It has a way that moves me and relaxes me and through this relaxation I find myself in a much better atmosphere, and also put myself into better environment, which in the future will prove how great psilocybin really is.

Under psilocybin I have taken on a different attitude toward people and friends. I was always

go on for the same reason that administrators do anything—fear of criticism. Our work was succeeding and the prisoners knew it. Not just the inmates at Concord but all over the state. The politicians had to go along with it.

Harvard was backing the project and Harvard couldn't be flouted. But there was an underlying skepticism. A basic distrust about any enthusiastic new approach to prisoner rehabilitation. Let them try their newfangled experiment, but the old hands knew that cons are cons and nothing can change them.

In politics and administration the great sin is idealism, bright-eyed vigor —and the highest virtue is cynicism. Faith, hope, and charity are dirty words. Nothing really changes except who has the power, who has the money.

Everyone in the Massachusetts correctional system believed in his heart that our project would fail. That we would not lower the recidivism rate, that we could not convert hardened criminals. We just couldn't do it because we were running against the cultural momentum of American society which is more laws, more cops, more lawyers, more judges, more prison psychiatrists, more control, and we were saying: give power away.

If we were right, then the sphincter clasp of society would have to be released. Deep religious commitments were involved in the use of our little pill.

I came into the warden's office one morning to report the most recent statistics. We had kept twice as many convicts out on the street as the expected number. We had halved the crime rate. He listened politely but he kept glancing toward the corner of the room. When I finished he got up and clapped me on the back and led me to the corner. Look at that, he said proudly.

It was an architect's color drawing of a super prison. Look. Two football fields. This wing is for admitting and orientation. Two more cell blocks. Mess halls double in size. We'll have capacity for twice as many inmates and we can double the staff all the way down the line.

His eyes were glowing like anyone showing you his dream plan. Success. His fantasy was coming true. A prison and an organizational table twice as big! The bureaucrats' goal.

But warden, you're not going to need a larger prison. His face registered surprise. Why not? Because we're cutting your recidivism rate in half, remember. You won't need to have all the cells you have now. You won't need to have half the guards you now have, if you let us turn-on your prison.

The warden laughed. He liked me and felt protective toward our hopes. Well, we're getting some of your men back. Kelly returned today in handcuffs. He was one of your men, wasn't he?

Yes, Kelly had come back to the

different in manner and just the opposite of what this drug brought out.

Impulse has been the main factor in my doing things and through these impulses I have been incarcerated, but I am looking for a way to turn away from impulse.

As I was laying in the bed with the blanket over my head, I kept getting these wonderful feelings, all through my body. I can't explain how they felt, but they felt so good that I was hoping that they would last all day, but they didn't.

For a little while after that, I went through a great deal of suffering. It seems that I was strapped down to a table or something, and I was cut open from my chest to my stomach, and it seems that I could taste blood in my mouth.

As I was laying there bleeding, there were some people standing over me, saying too bad, but they weren't trying to help me.

It was then that I seemed to be fighting something, when Dr. Presnell came over to me and took the blankets off my head. I had felt then that he had just saved my life.

prison and so were some others returning. They had not committed new crimes. They were returning cheerfully, peacefully, quietly, not making it on the outside. Dropping-out.

Kelly was a good example. He had been paroled and went back to the slum housing project where his wife and four children awaited him. He walked in on a financial crisis. The state support money for families of prisoners stopped the day he got out. He had no job. Five reproachful mouths to feed. His relations with his wife, never good, had been further strained by his imprisonment. His occupational assets, never good, were weakened by his prison record.

Kelly was plunged, ill-prepared, into a tense, frustrating, almost hopeless situation. The pride and enthusiasm and insight of his psychedelic sessions were eroding fast. Our outside contact team met with him and tried to get him a job. Kelly was hard to sell to an employer.

Now, if you put yourself into Kelly's head, you get this perspective. The outside society of Boston is cold, demanding, degrading, inhospitable, heavy with responsibility, empty of reward. Kelly looks back at the prison, free food and lodging and a job. There, he is a wanted man. He has a place. A role. But more than that, in the prison is the warmth of the group, the pride of belonging to the mushroom-elite, the rare unexpected ecstasy and adventurc of the psychedelic drug trip, the companionship. The session room was home. Like a hummingbird, Kelly starting circling back to Concord. It was so easy. Just be drinking beer when the parole officer comes to inspect, and sound unenthusiastic about getting a job.

Sorry, Kelly, but we have to pull your parole. You're going back. Kelly was going home, back to his cellmates.

The problem was that the close tribal fabric of the prison group was pulled apart in the city. Everything in the Boston culture was geared to push Kelly back to crime.

We needed a tribal center, a half-way house. A place in Boston where the ex-cons could reinstate the closeness of the prison group. The tribal tie has to be strong to protect its people in the brutal anonymity of the city.

We started looking around for a house to rent. We ran into the usual problems. Landlords turned off when they learned that we were planning a center for ex-convicts. We didn't have the money or the energy to set up a house. It was obvious that we would have to live in the house ourselves with the ex-cons. Sit around the homefire with them, become inmates with them, and we weren't ready to make that big step of love and commitment.

We sat in our offices at Harvard and made great plans and sent men out to look for real estate. And then at five o'clock we returned to our comfortable

I got up to go to the bathroom, and I got a little dizzy. Everything that I saw, and the color of them seemed to be more intense. After I came out of the bathroom, I went over to one of the windows and looked out. I was feeling very happy.

Dr. Leary came over to me and asked me how I felt. I told him I felt free. As soon as I said that, the happiness left me. I started to think what I was free from. I looked around the room, and for the first time, I noticed the bars on the windows.

The walls that were keeping me from freedom. I said to myself, is this all that I have to look forward to for the rest of my life? I started to walk up and down the floor; I looked out of the window, and the walls seemed to be closing in on me. They kept getting closer and closer. I got scared. I looked around the room for some place to hide. I didn't hide. I decided to face it. I looked at the walls and said, "You are not going to get the best of me," and the walls moved back to their regular position.

ॐ

homes in the Boston suburbs and the ex-cons went back to the slums.

Sixth in the second place means: Fellowship with men in the clan. Humiliation. There is danger here of formation of a separate faction on the basis of personal and egoistic interests. Such factions, which are exclusive and, instead of welcoming all men, must condemn one group in order to unite the others, originate from low motives and therefore lead in the course of time to humiliation. (I Ching)

In the sessions we were all gods, all men at one. We were all two-billion-year-old seed centers pulsing together. Then as time slowly froze we were reborn in the old costumes and picked up the tired games.

We weren't yet ready to act on our revelation. The spark we had lit within each one of us was there and we guarded it, but the sun-flame had not yet burst forth.

THE JUDGMENT
FELLOWSHIP WITH MEN *in the open.*
Success
It furthers one to cross the great water.
The perseverance of the superior
  man furthers.

(I Ching)

VENGEANCE IS MINE, SAITH THE LORD

Karl Menninger

Karl Menninger is not only one of America's most eminent psychiatrists but also a truly eclectic behavioral scientist. He brings to the study of punishment the informed insights of anthropology, social psychology, and sociology, as well as decades of observation of the administration of criminal justice. Wholly alien to Dr. Menninger's experience and viewpoint is the pseudoscientific attempt to impose on students of human behavior the rigors, concepts, methods, and principles of the mathematical and physical sciences. Nowhere in Dr. Menninger does one find the process of dehumanization implicit in the strictures of the sterile objective-quantitative social scientists. These men would deny to the scholar in the behavioral and social disciplines not only his strong sympathy for the abused, brutalized, deprived, disadvantaged, and discriminated against among mankind, but also his rights as an informed citizen-scientist to polemicize for reform and progress.

Source: Karl Menninger, *The Crime of Punishment* (New York: Viking Press, 1968), pp. 190–218. Copyright © 1966, 1968 by Karl Menninger, M.D. Reprinted by permission of The Viking Press, Inc.

In our view, Karl Menninger's lifelong dedication to the cause of abolishing the death penalty and reforming our penal system enhances rather than diminishes his stature among his criminological colleagues.

The Crime of Punishment, from which this excerpt is taken, is polemical and reform-oriented; it describes a penal system that creates criminals rather than rehabilitates them. Few students of penology will question Dr. Menninger's premise "that all the crimes committed by all the jailed criminals do not equal in total social damage that of the crimes committed against them." The latter are crimes committed not because judges, juries, prosecutors, police, or even that totality which we call society may be cruel, stupid, and stultifying, but because all of us are emotionally bound to traditional practices that defeat their own purpose. Instead of being socially protective, these practices are self-destructive and neither deter nor repress criminality; rather they aggravate it.

Vengeance, writes Dr. Menninger, "no matter how glorified or how piously disguised . . . must be personally repudiated by each and every one of us. . . . Unless this message is heard, unless we the people . . . can give up our delicious satisfactions in opportunities for vengeful retaliation on scapegoats, we cannot expect to preserve our peace, our public safety, or our mental health."

The great secret, the deeply buried mystery of the apparent public apathy to crime and to proposals for better controlling crime, lies in the persistent, intrusive wish for vengeance.

We are ashamed of it; we deny to ourselves and to others that we are influenced by it. Our morals, our religious teachings, even our laws repudiate it. But behind what we do to the offender is the desire for revenge on someone—and the unknown villain proved guilty of wrongdoing is a good scapegoat. We call it a wish to see justice done, i.e., to have him "punished." But in the last analysis this turns out to be a thin cloak for vengeful feelings directed against a legitimized object.

It is natural to resent a hurt, and all of us have many unfulfilled wishes to hurt back. But in our civilization that just is not done—openly. Personal revenge we have renounced, but official legalized revenge we can still enjoy. Once someone has been labeled an offender and proved guilty of an offense he is fair game, and our feelings come out in the form of a conviction that a hurt to society should be "repaid."

This sentiment of retaliation is, of course, exactly what impels most offenders to do what they do. Except for racketeers, robbers, and professional criminals, the men who are arrested, convicted, and sentenced are usually out to avenge a wrong, assuage a sense of injury, or correct an injustice as they see it. Their victims are individuals whom they believe to be assailants, false friends, rivals, unfaithful spouses, cruel parents—or symbolic figures representing these individuals.

In the old days no one apologized for feelings of vengeance. Poets, playwrights, and other artists have been preoccupied with it for centuries. One goes to the opera and listens to beautiful music that was inspired by such sordid vengeance-dominated plots as those of *Tosca, Il Trovatore, La Forza del Destino,* and a hundred others. Or one thinks of the fascination that *The Count of Monte Cristo, Hamlet, Othello,* and many other revenge stories have had for millions of people for hundreds of years. What has changed in our modern thinking or feeling that this noble urge to repay, at all costs, the wrong done to me and mine is no longer so highly esteemed? Has Christianity actually had some effect? Or is it merely a surface repudiation of our pre-civilization character in the interests of a decent social facade?

"Vengeance is mine," God is quoted as declaring. But vengeance by the individual worked its way back in, somehow. Various scriptural citations imply that God expects some human assistance in dealing out vengeance. His spokesmen and His agents have always laid about them with zealous vigor and great self-assurance to do what the Lord wanted done, and to whom. "Thou shalt not suffer a sorceress to live." [Ex.22:18] "Ye shall tread down the wicked; for they shall be ashes under the soles of your feet." [Mal.4:3] "Happy shall he be, that taketh and dasheth thy little ones against the rock." [Ps.137:9] (Or see King David's last words to his son.)

Angry at the poor rebellious peasants in 1525, Martin Luther wrote:

> For a prince and lord must remember in this case that he is God's minister and the servant of His wrath (Romans XIII), to whom the sword is committed for use upon such fellows. . . . If he can punish and does not—even though the punishment consists in the taking of life and the shedding of blood—then he is guilty of all the murder and all the evil which these fellows commit, because by willful neglect of the divine command, he permits them to practice their wickedness, though he can prevent it and is in duty bound to do so. Here then, there is no time for sleeping; no place for patience or mercy. It is the time of the sword, not the day of grace. . . . Stab, smite, slay, whoever can. If you die in doing it, well for you.[1]

The initiation of official retaliation for crime is sometimes inaccurately ascribed to the Anglo-Saxons, to Calvin, to the Romans, and to the children of Israel. Clear demands for legal tit-for-tat appear in much more ancient documents. Typical citations from the Babylonian code of Hammurabi, four thousand years ago, are these:

196. If a man destroy the eye of another man, they shall destroy his eye.
200. If a man knock out a tooth of a man of his own rank, they shall knock out his tooth.
195. If a son strike his father, they shall cut off his fingers.

The Hammurabi Code (1750 B.C.) and the Lipit-Ishtar Code (1900 B.C.) were harsh, but they were meant to limit the revenge. *No more than this penalty may ye take!*—that was the essence of it. Hammurabi apparently instituted the law to control practices of family and tribal revenge that went further than the offenses being repaid and which were perpetuated in feuds. Revenge has a tendency to do this.

But three hundred and fifty years before Hammurabi, a more civilized people than the Babylonians had a criminal code imbued with a far more humane philosophy. King Ur-Nammu of Sumeria was a most enlightened monarch who instituted many social and moral reforms. He ruled against the "chiselers and

[1] Martin Luther, *Works of Martin Luther*, Vol. IV. Philadelphia: A. J. Holman Co., with the Castle Press, 1931.

grafters" of the kingdom, described in the code as "the grabbers of the citizens' oxen and sheep and donkeys." He established a method for "honest and unchangeable weights and measures." He saw to it "that the orphan did not fall prey to the wealthy" and that the "widow did not fall prey to the man of one mina (sixty shekels)." The crowning, dramatic feature of Ur-Nammu's law code was the elimination of vengeance from criminal procedures. Restitution and monetary fines rather than the infliction of pain were the official consequence of wrongdoing.[2]

This was over forty centuries ago. Jesus of Nazareth came about midway between then and now and recommended that we turn the other cheek. The early Christians did so and were martyred; the German Jews did so and were cremated. Isn't it natural to defend oneself and one's home and one's honor?

Eighteen hundred and twenty-six years after the advent of Jesus, a great and really very humane statesman, Edward Livingston, proposed in his "System of Penal Law for the State of Louisiana" that the following be inscribed on every murderer's cell:

In this cell is confined, to pass his life in solitude and sorrow, A.B., convicted of the murder of C.D.; his food is bread of the coarsest kind, his drink is water, mingled with his tears; he is dead to the world; this cell is his grave; his existence is prolonged, that he may remember his crime and repent it, and that the continuance of his punishment may deter others from the indulgence of hatred, avarice, sensuality, and the passions which led to the crime he has committed. When the Almighty in his due time shall exercise toward him that dispensation which he himself arrogantly and wickedly usurped toward another, his body is to be dissected, and his soul will abide that judgment which Divine Justice shall decree.[3]

What is behind such vindictiveness? Certainly not Christianity, not Judaism, nor indeed any religion! And yet certainly not specific hatred! And surely not an expectation of eliminating crime!

[2] Samuel Noah Kramer, *History Begins at Sumer*. New York: Doubleday, 1959.
[3] Edward Livingston, *Complete Works on Criminal Jurisprudence*, 2 Vols. New York: National Prison Association of the United States of America, 1873.

Today criminals rather than witches and peasants have become the official wrongdoers, eligible for punitive repayment. Prosecuting attorneys have become *our* agents, if not God's, and often seem to embody the very spirit of revenge and punition. They are expected to be tough, and to strike hard.

Pierre Berton, traveling through the town of Goderich in southern Ontario in 1959, was horrified to learn that a fourteen-year-old boy had been sentenced to hang for murder. He wrote this poem:

Requiem for a Fourteen-Year-Old

In Goderich town
The sun abates
December is coming
And everyone waits:
In a small, stark room
On a small, hard bed
Lies a small, pale boy
Who is not quite dead.
The cell is lonely
The cell is cold
October is young
But the boy is old;
Too old to cringe
And too old to cry
Though young—
But never too young to die.
It's true enough
That we cannot brag
Of a national anthem
Or a national flag
And though our vision
Is still in doubt
At last we've something
To boast about;
We've a national law
In the name of the Queen
To hang a child
Who is just fourteen.

The law is clear
It says we must
And in this country
The law is just.
Sing heigh! Sing ho!
For justice blind
Makes no distinction
Of any kind;
Makes no allowance for sex or years,
A judge's feelings, a mother's tears;
Just eye for eye and tooth for tooth—
Tooth for tooth and eye for eye:
If a child does murder
The child must die.
Don't fret—don't worry . . .
No need to cry
We'll only pretend he's going to die;
We're going to reprieve him
By and by.

We're going to reprieve him
(We always do),
But it wouldn't be fair
If we told him too.
So we'll keep the secret
As long as we can
And hope that he'll take it
Like a man.[4]

[4] *The Atlantian*, Fall 1965, pp. 24, 26.

No less an authority than Chief Justice William Howard Taft wrote in 1928 that the "chief purpose of the prosecution of crime is to punish the criminal and to deter others tempted to do the same thing from doing it because of the penal consequences. . . . It is a mistake of huge proportion to lead criminals by pampering them, and by relaxing discipline of them and the harshness of prison life, to think that they are wards of the state for their comfort, entertainment, and support."[5]

One attorney says: "Despite attempts to curb the vengeful urges of district attorneys, however—and despite Constitutional restrictions upon 'cruel and unusual punishments' and other methods of venting sadistic feelings—modern American law goes to considerable lengths to help *express* vengeful strivings."[6]

"I think," said the distinguished jurist Sir James Stephen as late as 1883, "it is highly desirable that criminals should be hated, that the punishments inflicted upon them should be so contrived as to give expression to that hatred, and to justify it so far as the public provision of means for expressing and gratifying a healthy natural sentiment can justify and encourage it."[7]

The prison sentence, determined by law, intended to prevent both the abuses of tyrants and the bloody orgies of mob vengeance. We no longer inflame the public with such scenes as these:

The sheriffs, attended by two marshals and an immense number of constables, accompanied the procession of the prisoners from Newgate, where they set out in the transport caravan, and proceeded through Fleet Street, and the Strand; and the prisoners were hooted and pelted the whole way by the populace. At one o'clock, four of the culprits were fixed in the pillory. . . . Immediately a new torrent of popular vengeance poured upon them from all sides— blood, garbage, and ordure from the slaughter house, diversified with dead cats, turnips, potatoes, addled eggs and other missiles, to the last moment. . . . The vengeance of the crowd pursued them

[5] William Howard Taft, "Toward a Reform of the Criminal Law." In *The Drift of Civilization.* New York: Simon & Schuster, 1929.

[6] C. G. Shoenfeld, "In Defense of Retribution in the Law." *Psychoanal. Quart.,* 35:108–121, 1966.

[7] Sir James Stephen, A *History of the Criminal Law of England,* Vol. II. London: Macmillan, 1883, p. 81.

back to Newgate, and the caravan was filled with mud and ordure.
No interference from sheriffs and police officers could restrain the
popular rage. . . .

Then—it was June, 1594—the three men, bound to hurdles,
were dragged up Holborn, past the doctor's house, to Tyburn. A
vast crowd was assembled to enjoy the spectacle. The doctor, standing on the scaffold, attempted in vain to make a dying speech; the
mob was too angry and too delighted to be quiet; it howled with
laughter . . . and the old man was hurried to the gallows. He was
strung up and—such was the routine of the law—cut down while
life was still in him. Then the rest of the time-honored punishment
—castration, disembowelling, and quartering—was carried out.
Ferriera was the next to suffer. After that, it was the turn of Tinoco.
He had seen what was to be his fate, twice repeated, and close
enough. His ears were filled with the shrieks and moans of his
companions, and his eyes with every detail of the contortions and
the blood. . . . Tinoco, cut down too soon, recovered his feet after
the hanging. He was lusty and desperate; and he fell upon his execu-
tioners. The crowd, wild with excitement, and cheering on the
plucky foreigner, broke through the guards, and made a ring to
watch the fight. But, before long, the instincts of law and order
reasserted themselves. Two stalwart fellows seeing that the executioner was giving ground, rushed forward to his rescue. Tinoco was
felled by a blow on the head; he was held firmly down on the scaffold; and like the others, castrated, disembowelled, and quartered.[8]

What was "socially acceptable" behavior toward criminals in
1594 is not so today. The avid curiosity and brutality of the
public toward the miscreant who is caught must find less revolt-
ing expression. But the savagery is still there.

"Distrust," said Nietzsche, "all in whom the impulse to punish is
strong." No one is more ferocious in demanding that the murderer
or the rapist "pay" for his crime than the man who has felt strong
impulses in the same direction. No one is more bitter in condemning the "loose" woman than the "good" women who have on
occasion guiltily enjoyed some purple dreams themselves. It is never
he who is without sin who casts the first stone.

Along with the stone, we cast our own sins onto the criminal. In
this way we relieve our own sense of guilt without actually having
to suffer the punishment—a convenient and even pleasant device

[8] Sol Rubin, *The Law of Criminal Correction*. St. Paul, Minn.: West
Publishing Co., 1963.

for it not only relieves us of sin, but makes us feel actually virtuous. A criminal trial, like a prizefight, is a public performance in which the spectators work off in a socially acceptable way aggressive impulses of much the same kind that the man on trial worked off in a socially unacceptable way.[9]

The man who wrote these eloquent lines was a former winner of the Isaac Ray Award, Professor Henry Weihofen. In his book, *The Urge to Punish*, he shows how clearly and piously this phenomenon replaces an unavowed wish for vengeance. We all have it, but some people deceive themselves more than they deceive others.

The man on the street knows so little about the total situation that it is not surprising that he explodes in rage at the news of some horrendous crime. He is merely saying loudly that he is against evil. He wants to believe that "things are being taken care of," that the brave, tough "cops," the "good guys," deal "adequately" with the tough "bad guys," and so all is well—or as well as things can be in our rough-and-tumble world. So he is not too much disturbed to hear it alleged that (some) police have usurped the power to punish and believe that the use of "legitimate violence" is their occupational prerogative and monopoly. If the police thereby obtain "results," the community is satisfied. And since "those who suffer are most often the poor, the ignorant and the friendless, no one complains (except to the American Civil Liberties Union or to some minority organization) and the police can congratulate themselves on the improvement of their public relations."[10] Most policemen would deny any feelings of vengeance toward offenders—just necessary and legitimate counterviolence.[11]

[9] Henry Weihofen, *The Urge to Punish*. New York: Farrar, Straus & Giroux, 1956, p. 138.

[10] David J. Dodd, "Police Mentality and Behavior." *Issues in Criminology*, 3:54, 1967.

[11] I work constantly with police officers and have a strong identification with them and a concern about their public image. I belong, as an associate member, to the National Fraternal Order of Police. Yet I myself have been roughly dealt with by policemen for no more serious offense than asking a question about a gathering crowd in New York's Central Park. Such gratuitous rudeness and bullying is, of course, to be balanced against the courtesy, dignity, and genuine helpfulness of many other policemen; but with more belligerent, embittered subjects, an experience such as mine is enough to start trouble for which all of us have to pay—including the police.

But there are a few political leaders, writers, and even psychiatrists and other scientists who are heard from now and then in terms that leave no doubt about their vengefulness. And here, to top the list, is what a man of God, committed to teaching the gentleness of Jesus and the forgiveness of Christian love, recently published in a syndicated column:[12]

Modern literature . . . has now gone to the . . . extreme where pity is for the rapist and not for the raped, for the criminal and not the victim. This false compassion started with novelists like William Saroyan and John Steinbeck who presented the "lovable bums," the shiftless, the drunks, as "beautiful little people." The next stage was to excite pity for the genial rapist, the jolly slasher, the dope pusher, the adulteress playing musical beds, the rich kid who sells "goofballs," knifers, sluggers, muggers, and the homosexuals.

But today, thanks to a few social workers, a few incompetent judges, and woolly-minded thinkers, and many "sob sisters," compassion is extended not to the one who was mugged, but to the mugger, not to the policeman, but to the dope pusher, not to the girl killed by a dope fiend, but to the rich boy from an interesting family. [Could this be an appeal to class distinction?] No blame may be laid at the door of the criminal or the degraded. The new saviors of a perverted society say: "Neither do I condemn thee. Go, and sin some more."

With what *result?* [Italics mine.] Crime increases about nineteen per cent a year in the United States. [!!]

Contrast this with the following letter by Professor Anatol Hold,[13] father of a three-and-one-half-year-old girl slain by an honor student, which was written early in the morning a few hours after the confession had been obtained:

Dear People of Philadelphia:
I write to you this morning, at the rise of dawn, still in the midst of a tormented wake, the most terrible grief which has ever seared my soul.

Yesterday afternoon, on June 4, I lost the most precious thing that life ever gave to me—a three-and-a-half-year-old girl child of surpassing purity and joy; a being profoundly close to the secret

12 *Kansas City Star*, June 4, 1966.
13 Copyright 1959, *Philadelphia Evening Bulletin*.

wellsprings of life itself—a closeness from which she derived great unconscious strength which made her irresistibly attractive to human beings with whom she came in contact.

She was murdered at three in the afternoon, in the basement of a house only a few doors away from ours, by a fifteen-year-old boy. . . .

The boy himself has also always given an excellent formal account of himself—honor student, gentle in manner, handsome and all the rest. . . .

I am sure that his parents have been God-fearing, upright citizens, too uneducated in matters of the human soul to have recognized the plight of their child during the years of his growth.

They undoubtedly took naïve pride in his constant good behavior, neat appearance, and good performance at church and school, never suspecting that this very goodness was a serious cause of worry in the light of what must have been left unaccounted for.

It is, of course, worrisome, from the social point of view, that there are parents with such lack of understanding. It is, I submit, much more profoundly worrisome that it should have been possible for this boy to go through his whole fifteen years without anyone who was responsible for his upbringing—such as his school and his church—having taken note (out of uncaring or lack of understanding) of the danger signals before the tragedy.

Beware, citizens. The human animal cannot be cheated forever. It will have love, or kill.

You will understand that I am not lecturing to you for the pure joy of sounding wise. I am hurt to the depths of my being, and I cry out to you to take better care of your children.

My final word has to do with the operation of the machinery of justice. Had I caught the boy in the act, I would have wished to kill him. Now that there is no undoing of what is done, I only wish to help him.

Let no feelings of cave-man vengeance influence us. Let us rather help him who did so human a thing.

[Signed] A Sick Father

The final sentence of this letter deserves immortality.[14]

---

[14] Still another instance of the repudiation of vengeance is this historical vignette: Perhaps nothing in President McKinley's life was equal in greatness to his last moments. Standing in a reception line at the Buffalo Exposition, he patted a little girl on the head and, as she passed on, he turned and smilingly extended his hand to the next in line. This was his assassin.

In sharp contrast is the following case, which has also been in my files a long time:

Last week a man was tried in New York State for the shooting of his son-in-law, who had seduced his daughter. He was acquitted of murder or manslaughter on some unintelligible point of unwritten law. The trial was brief but exceedingly painful. At great cost to herself, the widow of the murdered man came to give evidence. Resisting her father's embraces in the courtroom, she still testified in order to save him, though she made it clear to everyone that she loved the man who had been killed. Her father confessed he was drunk when he killed the youth, but he said the youth was of evil life, and this allegation, tending to give horror to the seduction, probably weighed greatly with the jury. At any rate, they acquitted him, amid the cheers of a friendly crowd.

So long as one could assume ordinary human comprehensions on the part of the acquitted man, this verdict need not seem dead loss. In some ways it approximates the ideal of many people, leaving the culprit to his own conscience. But even if this is pure romanticism, the acquittal could be condoned if the trial had made some effect. Hear, however, some reflections of the exonerated citizen, imparted to a reporter of the *World*:

"This is without doubt the merriest and happiest Christmas of my life. True, my daughter is not herself, but I guess she will be all right in a few days. . . . Do I think she saved my life? Why, no! I am sure that even without her help I would have been acquitted. You see, I did not know what I was doing; so how could I have been guilty? Anna knew she had disgraced us and so she wished to do all that lay in her power to atone.

"While I certainly would undo my act if it lay in my power, I feel sure Anna will be happier with us than if she were the wife of Eugene Newman. Marriages of that kind always end in misery, whereas now she will just take up the threads of her former life and be happy. She intends to resume her music. She is a splendid pianist. When she recovers her health all will be as before.

Knocking aside the proffered hand of the President, the assassin lunged forward and shot McKinley through the abdomen. A security officer leaped forward and knocked the assassin to the floor. As McKinley slumped back into a chair, his eyes followed his killer and McKinley was heard to say, "Don't let them hurt him." And then, in a whisper, "My wife! Be careful how you tell her. Oh, be careful." (Courtney, John F.: "Doctors and the McKinley Assassination." *The Resident Physician*, 14:72–80, March 1968.)

"I never said I was going to sign a pledge never to drink again. I always have drunk like a gentleman.

"Has my daughter forgiven me? What do you mean? What has she to forgive? Our relations are most loving. She was always a most obedient child—quiet, unexpressive, but with a sweet disposition. I could not understand her disobeying us the way she did by going with this boy and marrying him in view of our expressed objections. But now that is all over, and she is again our sweet loving daughter."

The daughter, according to the reporter, is completely crushed. She loved her husband, but she guesses her parents knew best, for "see what her disobedience has done."[15]

Angry as it makes us to see a father so indifferent to his great guiltiness—guilt for a heartless murder, guilt for brutal sadism to his crushed daughter—what would *we* like to do with him? What would appease our aroused sense of injustice? We want him to be sorry, but he is not, and we cannot make him feel sorry for what he has done. Even if we could, it will not comfort his daughter or return her husband to her, and it may even deprive her of a meal ticket. We might tie him to the public whipping post, as they have long done in Delaware, and *hurt* him. He would suffer, and be very sorry about *that*, and also very angry. He then, as well as we, would feel the sense of injustice. But we would carry an additional burden of having done a cruel thing pointlessly, trying to make ourselves feel better and not succeeding. In kind, if not in degree, we then line up with the Marquis de Sade, who believed in pleasure, especially pleasure derived from making someone else feel displeasure.

We cannot expect the public to be objective, either in judging the criminal or in judging us psychiatrists. Especially we cannot expect them to understand our repudiation of punishment, if not as an actual "treatment" device, then at least as a matter of (Kantian) principle. It is a part of the common folkways, a standard value judgment. Robert Waelder[16] has written

---

[15] *The New Republic*, December 26, 1914, pp. 9–10.

[16] Robert Waelder and Clarence Morris, "The Concept of Justice and the Quest for a Perfectly Just Society—A Dialogue." *U. Pa. Law Rev.*, Vol. 115, No. 1, November 1966.

of this, urging us to "go easy" in denouncing punishment and pushing the principle to its extreme form. For the public believes in punishment deeply, although it is willing to make many exceptions to the rule if these are properly stipulated. Gradually the public will come to realize that not *some* cases, but *all* cases are exceptions. But in the meantime, we should perhaps give lip service to the possible merits of punishment in some instances.

PRICE, PENALTY, AND PUNISHMENT

It is time for me to speak unequivocally about the inference of the title of this book. Is it true, I am asked, that you oppose *all* punishment for *everyone?* Think of some of the fiendish crimes that we all hear about from time to time. Do you think such persons should go unpunished? You seem to favor penalties; how do they differ from punishments?

Certainly the abolition of punishment does not mean the omission or curtailment of penalties; quite the contrary. Penalties should be greater and surer and quicker in coming. I favor stricter penalties for many offenses, and more swift and certain assessment of them.

But these are not *punishments* in the sense of long-continued torture—pain inflicted over years for the sake of inflicting pain. If I drive through a red light, I will be and should be penalized. If a bridge player overbids, he is promptly and surely penalized, and his opponents can even double the penalty. If he cheats, he may be excluded from the game, but no one beats him or locks him up.

If a man strikes a rock in anger, his suffering from a bleeding hand is a penalty, not a punishment. If another man oversmokes and develops lung cancer, the affliction is a penalty, not a punishment. If we disregard traffic signals we are penalized, not punished. If our offense was a calculated "necessity" in an emergency, then the fine is the "price" of the exception.

Price is an agreed-upon, predetermined value, voluntarily tendered in exchange for a desired goal or gain. Penalty is a predetermined price levied automatically, invariably, and categorically in direct relation to a violation or infraction of a pre-set rule or "law." In a sense it, too, is voluntary; the payer of the penalty knew from the outset what it would be if he incurred it.

All legal sanctions involve penalties for infraction. But the element of punishment is an adventitious and indefensible *additional* penalty; it corrupts the legal principle of *quid pro quo* with a "moral" surcharge. Punishment is in part an attitude, a philosophy. It is the deliberate infliction of pain in addition to or in lieu of penalty. It is the prolonged and excessive infliction of penalty, or penalty out of all proportion to the offense. Detention in prison was supposed to be a mollification of pain infliction, but it is often more cruel and destructive than beating. What is gained for anybody when a man who has forged a check for sixty dollars is sentenced to the penitentiary for *thirty years* (at public expense, of course)? I saw such a case in 1967. The judge's rationalization was that the man had offended in this way *twice before* (!) and had served shorter sentences without reforming!

This is not penalization. This is not correction. This is not public protection. (Is any check forger so dangerous as to require such expensive precautions?) This is not reformation. It is sadistic persecution of the helpless at public expense, justified by the "punishment" principle.[17]

When a seventy-seven-year-old woman driving her car in heavy traffic struck and killed an eight-year-old child, everyone concerned, including the parents of the child, the judge, and the woman herself, agreed that she should renounce automobile driving forever; this was her penalty. No "punishment" was imposed.[18]

[17] A particularly eloquent statement on the justification of punishment is quoted from Sir Edward Fry by Mercier: "Punishment, in short, is an effort of man to find a more exact relation between sin and suffering than the world affords us. . . . It seems to me that men have a sense of the fitness of suffering to sin, of a fitness both in the gross and in proportion; that so far as the world is arranged we realize this fitness in thought, it is right; and that so far as it fails of such arrangement, it is wrong . . . and consequently that a duty is layed upon us to make this relationship of sin to suffering as real and actual and as exact in proportion as it is possible to be made. This is the moral root of the whole doctrine of punishment." (Mercier, Charles: *Criminal Responsibility.* New York: Physicians and Surgeons Book Co., 1926, pp. 37–38.)

[18] "Woman Vows Not to Drive." *Topeka Daily Capital*, June 7, 1956.

If a burglar takes my property, I would like to have it returned or paid for by him if possible, and the state ought to be reimbursed for its costs, too. This could be forcibly required to come from the burglar. This would be equitable; it would be just, and it would not be "punitive." Just *what* the penalties should be in the case of many offenses is a big question, I realize, but it could be answered if all the public vengeance and lust for seeing people hurt by punishment could be ignored.

I do not think this means that we psychiatrists are too sentimental. Being against punishment is not a sentimental conviction. It is a logical conclusion drawn from scientific experience. It is also a professional principle; we doctors try to relieve pain, not cause it. It is the unthinking public who is sentimental—sentimental in the sense of reacting emotionally to the first impact of unpleasant, grievous "news," i.e., a few of the bare facts of a case. A wave of emotion sweeps over them; they are shocked, horrified, alarmed. Instinctively, they want quick, eliminative action which they think of as punitive. Let some time elapse, and a little more of the facts become known, and the swift resolution about dispatching the offender becomes altered. It may even swing to the opposite pole so that the public is moved to pity or even shame by the revealed circumstances. Then it wants instant restitution and release.

So far as prisoners are concerned, there is an uncomfortable hypocrisy about our professed repudiation of vengeance. The conviction, the punishment, is in some way or other implicit in the concept of justice. We have to keep things even, or equal. I do not think anyone really believes this, but they feel it. They express it. What they feel is a wish for vengeance.

Most of the great philosophers, beginning with the Greeks and repeated later by Hobbes, Locke, Spinoza, and others, had this idea. For example, Protagoras said, "No one punishes the evildoer for the reason that he has done wrong—only the unreasonable fury of a beast acts in that manner. But he who desires to inflict rational punishment does not retaliate for a past wrong which cannot be undone. He has regard for the future, and is desirous that the man who is punished, and he who sees him punished, may be deterred from doing wrong again. He punishes for the sake of prevention, thus clearly implying that virtue is capable of being taught."

And Plato said that no man is to be punished "because he did wrong, for that which is done can never be undone, but in order that, in the future times, he, and those who see him corrected, may utterly hate injustices, or at any rate abate much of their evil-doing." Yet he also goes on to say that the law "should aim at the right measure of punishment." This qualification seems, in turn, to be balanced by his remarks on the death penalty, which he thinks should be imposed only on the incurable who cannot profit from punishment and whose execution "would be an example to other men not to offend."[19]

Immanuel Kant declared that the offender *must* be made to suffer, not to deter him—Kant knew this was nonsense—but to balance his evildoing. He insisted that the purpose of punishment is *not* the deterrence of others from doing the forbidden deed, not the reformation of the criminal, not the welfare of society, not even that tricky business about official violence holding down the urge for public violence (mob law). Kant did not even concede the need for vengeance as a proper factor. "Juridical punishment," he said, "can never be administered merely as a means for promoting another good, either with regard to the Criminal himself, or to Civil Society, but must in all cases be imposed only because the individual on whom it is inflicted *has committed a Crime*. [Italics mine.] . . . The Penal Law is a Categorical Imperative; and woe to him who creeps through the serpent-windings of Utilitarianism to discover some advantage that may discharge him from the Justice of Punishment, or even from the due measure of it."[20] Kant gave the illustration of an "abandoned island." Suppose, he said, that a

[19] Encyclopaedia Britannica, *The Great Ideas: A Synopticon of Great Books of the Western World*, Vol. II. Chicago: Encyclopaedia Britannica, 1952, pp. 488–495.

Plato also said, "The right of retaliation . . . properly understood . . . is the only principle which . . . can definitely guide a public tribunal as to both the quality and quantity of a just punishment." (As quoted in *Eighteenth Century Penal Theory* by James Heath. New York: Oxford University Press, 1963, p. 272.)

[20] Encyclopaedia Britannica, *op. cit.*

society living on an island plans to leave that island because it is going to disintegrate. Before doing so, those condemned to death must be executed. This punishment is not done for the benefit of the inhabitants, inasmuch as they will soon be leaving; the executions must be accomplished simply because there exists a superior moral law that requires punishment.

But to renounce vengeance as a motive for punishing offenders leaves us with the equivocal justification of deterrence. This is a weak and vulnerable argument indeed, for the effects of punishment in this direction cannot be demonstrated by sound evidence or research. Furthermore, to make an example of an offender so as to discourage others from criminal acts is to make him suffer not for what he has done alone but because of *other* people's tendencies. Nevertheless the deterrence theory is used widely as a cloak for vengeance. As Bittner and Platt comment, in discussing this point:

> The idea that punishment simply executes some norms implied in the ideal of justice did not disappear from penological polemics, but it carried relatively little weight. . . . Punishment has grown progressively milder and milder. It is important to emphasize that the decline in the severity of punishment is not a development accompanying the growth of civilization in general, rather, it belongs peculiarly to the 19th and 20th century.[21]

I, myself, find it difficult to restrain my own feelings of vengeance in connection with the parents of what have come to be called "battered children." There is no question now that many parents are fiendishly, but covertly cruel in their home treatment of children—breaking their bones, lacerating their flesh, and often killing them. Some of these parents are brought for psychiatric examination, and it is hard to be objective in performing one's professional duty.

Nevertheless, I once examined the father of a child whose terrible beating was observed by the horrified neighbors who had him arrested. I had read about it in the newspaper and felt almost obliged to disqualify myself as an examiner. When I in-

21 Egon Bittner and A. M. Platt, "The Meaning of Punishment." *Issues in Criminology*, 2:79–99, 1966.

terviewed him, and learned all the details of the case, I felt very
penitent for having been so righteously indignant, so just plain
vengeful in my thoughts. The essence of the case was that this
man really loved his child; he was perhaps the only person who
did. He was usually most kind and gentle with his son who,
however, had bitterly disappointed him on this occasion. But
there were many other factors that brought his rage to the
boiling point at the particular moment when the beating occurred. It was not excusable, but it was really understandable.
No one was more penitent than this father, and I am glad to
be able to report that he was immensely helpful subsequently in
obtaining for the child much-needed opportunities of growth
and development.

I must confess, too, that sometimes after reading about some
particularly shocking crime, like everyone else I let myself
wonder if it would not be simpler and cheaper and more "satisfactory" all around if such an individual could just be quietly
exterminated. He has done irreparable and horrible damage; he
can never recover; he can never be any good to the world; he
will always remind us of terrible sorrow; his continued existence
is a burden to himself and a burden for us.[22] But then I reflect
that I myself am becoming unobjectively and inconsistently
sentimental. The principle of *no* punishment cannot allow of
any exception; it must apply in every case, even the worst case,
the most horrible case, the most dreadful case—not merely in
the accidental, sympathy-arousing case.

Let us return for a moment to the question as to whether the
spectacle, the threat, or the experience of punishment actually
does deter repetition of the offense by the offender. Scientific
research regarding the effectiveness of punishment as a controller of individual behavior shows that it varies with a wide
variety of "parameters," as psychologists call them. Dr. Richard
L. Solomon of the University of Pennsylvania, editor of *The*

[22] Eichmann is a case in point. He might have been kept alive but in
confinement, to brood over his evil past. He might have been minutely
studied as a specimen of human depravity, or he might have been spared
the torture of his conscience by being quietly executed. Perhaps the last
was the most merciful of the three. But was that the intention of the
judges?

Psychological Review, summarized some of the factors affecting punishment as a controller of instrumental behavior in a recent study:

[The] (a) intensity of the punishment stimulus, (b) whether the response being punished is an instrumental one or a consummatory one, (c) whether the response is instinctive or reflexive, (d) whether it was established originally by reward or by punishment, (e) whether or not the punishment is closely associated in time with the punished response, (f) the temporal arrangements of reward and punishment, (g) the strength of the response to be punished, (h) the familiarity of the subject with the punishment being used, (i) whether or not a reward alternative is offered during the behavior-suppression period induced by punishment, (j) whether a distinctive, incompatible avoidance response is strengthened by omission of punishment, (k) the age of the subject, and (l) the strain and species of the subject.[23]

What all this says in plain English is that common sense is correct in thinking that the swift, on-the-spot infliction of sufficiently painful stimulation to sufficiently influence animals—dogs or human beings—will tend to dissuade them from certain types of behavior of which we do not approve and which we wish to teach them not to do. But it does not deter *others* not so treated.

It is facile and fallacious to assume from this fact that human beings in general can be conditioned by threats of punishment or by the delayed infliction of penalties of attenuated painfulness from yielding to the temptation of impulsive crimes. If society were able to catch most offenders, and then if it were willing to punish them promptly without any discrimination, inflicting the penalties fairly but ruthlessly, as it were, most crime would be prevented. But society is neither able nor willing to do this. Almost no crime is punished promptly. Many crimes are punished unfairly. And some crimes are punished so severely that the whole world reacts against the action.

It is a curious thing, first called to my attention by my colleague, Dr. Sydney Smith, that in juvenile cases where the ques-

[23] Richard L. Solomon, "Punishment." *Amer. Psychologist*, 19:239–253, 1964.

tion of punishment comes up there seems to be a tacit assumption that the child who has gotten into trouble has somehow miraculously escaped previous experiences of punishment. One hears some vengeful judges declaiming against the wickedness of youth and the waywardness of adolescents and the need for stern punishment as if the child had never had any. Dr. Smith has said eloquently:

Granted there are instances in which children have been reared in an atmosphere of inconsistency where value training of any kind was entirely missing; but even in these cases it is the lack of loving guidance and structure rather than the lack of punitive retribution that has triggered the behavioral manifestations of delinquency. *In a high percentage of court cases, there is evidence that the child has met with punishment that has not only been frequent but in many cases excessive.* [Italics mine.] In fact, one of the sources of the child's own inadequate development is the model of open violence provided by the parent who has resorted repeatedly to corporal punishment, usually because of his own limited imagination. This indoctrination into a world where only might makes right and where all strength is invested in the authority of the mother or of the father not only makes it easy for the child to develop aggressive patterns of behavior but makes him emotionally distant and distrustful.[24]

Drunken driving is almost nonexistent in Scandinavia, where the sureness, swiftness, and severity of the penalty is well known. But the legislators of many states in this nation have repeatedly rejected proposed bills entailing severe punishment for drunken drivers. Do we need to ask why?

Legislators are much less frequently inclined to rob banks or commit burglaries than to drive while intoxicated. Hence it is much easier to legislate severe penalties for these much less dangerous offenses, and the rest of us approve. We approve severe penalties for those offenses which most of us feel little temptation to commit.

Occasionally something goes wrong with the system and the usual exemptions do not work. An example of this is the sen-

[24] Sydney Smith, "Delinquency and the Panacea of Punishment." *Fed. Prob.*, 29:18–23, 1965.

tencing of seven executives from leading manufacturing companies in 1961. Although found guilty of sizeable crimes, these men were sentenced for very short terms. Twenty of them drew suspended sentences.

All were prominent citizens; many were officers in their churches; one was president of his local chamber of commerce; one was a bank director. Each one was described by his lawyer as an "honorable man." The crimes were described by the Attorney General as being "so willful and flagrant that . . . more severe sentences would have been appropriate." One of the attorneys declared that the company in question "abhors, sought to prevent, and punished this conduct." The judge disagreed with this statement, declaring that the company's rule "was honored in its breach rather than its observance."

"No further punishment is needed to keep these men from doing what they have done, again," one of the attorneys said. "These men are not grasping, greedy, cut-throat competitors. They devote much of their time and substance to their communities." Another attorney made a general attack on the government's demand for jail terms. He said government lawyers were "cold-blooded" and did not understand what it would do to a man like Mr. —— to "put him behind bars" with "common criminals who have been convicted of embezzlement and other serious [*sic*] crimes."[25]

It is true that even a short jail sentence was a terrible thing for these men. It is a terrible thing for *any* man. The real meaning of such protests is that we have a gentleman's agreement that people with money and good names and highly placed friends, when caught in derelictions, are not supposed to be dealt with like poor people who are not well known and who do not have highly placed friends.

One value of this sad episode may be to bring home to the public the fact that there is a difference between a penalty (which I advocate) and punishment which the law prescribes. It would have been far more equitable in this case to have allowed the company to assess the penalty on the men involved—

[25] Anthony Lewis, "7 Electrical Officials Get Jail Terms in Trust Case." *The New York Times*, February 7, 1961.

which their attorneys say it did—and then let the court assess a penalty on the company, which it also did. The penalty on the company ought to be something other than the mere expense item of a fine. No fine is going to be of any value unless it is large enough to wipe out the profits made by illegal activity. But *who* deserves the "punishment"?

Violence to Children Repaid

For many years the essence of vengeance against the offender has been implicit in the upbringing of the child. Perhaps it is too farfetched an illustration, but is there possibly some connection between the thesis of the popular German nursery rhyme by Hoffman, *Der Struwelpeter*, and the ethics and the social philosophy of Nazi Germany in the 1930s and 40s? Take this verse from the version of the nursery rhyme by Maxine Kumin:

> Now look at Konrad the little thumb-sucker.
> *Ach!* but his poor mama cries when she warns him
> The tailor will come for his thumbs if he sucks them.
> Quick he can cut them off, easy as paper.
> Out goes the mother and *wupp!* goes the thumbkin in.
> Then the door opens. Enter the tailor.
> See in the picture the terrible tongue in
> His grinning red mouth! In his hands the great shears.
> Just as she told him, the tailor goes *klipp und klapp*.
> Eight-fingered Konrad has learned a sad lesson.
>> Therefore, says Fräulein, shaking her chignon,
>> Suck you must not or the tailor will chop![26]

This quaint nursery (!) rhyme seems funny to some. It has been considered *good* for children by millions of intelligent, civilized people. But its sadistic, vengeful essence is obvious. And surely we are all aware of the unjustified, unexcused, unadvertised cruelty to children that abounds in some levels of society.

The late Dr. Adelaide Johnson and some of her colleagues in the Mayo Clinic were especially impressed with the way in

[26] *The New Yorker*, January 14, 1961.

which the violent destructiveness of the criminal is so often a reflection of the cruel and violent way in which he was treated as a child. I cite two of her many cases to show again that the fruit of violence is violence, vengeance for vengeance, hate for hate. It is a vicious circle.

CASE 1. In a jealous rage, a thirty-year-old man found an ax and, in the presence of neighbors, killed his former sweetheart. Originally, he had seduced her away from his brother when the latter went to Europe on military duty.

This man, the second of six children, had been the target for the most violent uncontrolled brutality on the part of the father, who, although he had a good job as a shop foreman, was a philandering alcoholic and a physical and mental sadist in his relationships with the prisoner's mother. The father's wild beatings of the boy were so frightening that neighbor men often interceded. The mother said she continued to live with the father only "to be sure he did not kill one of the boys," while at the same time her husband doted on the older daughter, of whom the prisoner was violently jealous. The father often beat and choked the mother in the children's presence. He shouted that she was a whore and that he would kill her some day. From the time the boy was three years old, the mother said, he recurrently ran away from home because he was so terrified of the father. From the time the boy was fourteen years old, his father accused him of vicious sexual practices with girls, a charge which was not true at the time. The mother said that the father constantly "spoke evilly about other people's sex lives" in the presence of the children. At no time did the father ever accept any responsibility for his brutal acts, and he never expressed any remorse. The boy never dared to bring a young friend into the home.

The mother offered no protection to the child against the father's attacks, but she did console him afterward. She never called the police to protect the boy. She and the prisoner leaned on each other emotionally, and apparently he was always tender with her. At no time did the mother express any guilt or responsibility for having kept the boy in such a savage environment, and at the time we saw her the next oldest son was experiencing a similar life with the father. The prisoner said that without her warmth and comfort he would have killed himself long ago. He cried and moaned about his love for her for fifteen minutes when she was first mentioned in the interview. He could not recall any conscious hostility toward his mother.

CASE 2. The prisoner was twenty-seven years old when he strangled his sweetheart. When we saw him he was unable to account
for his killing her. "Those twelve months with her—I wouldn't
trade them even to being in this prison for life." He murdered her
when she refused to marry him.

He said he wondered if he had not "misidentified" his victim
with her interfering mother, of whom he said in all seriousness he
would "gladly wring her neck." He also remarked, "If it hadn't been
Rosie I killed, it would have been someone else—it was inevitable."

He was exceedingly bitter toward his own mother. "Mom hated
me since the day I was conceived. I was an unfortunate burden on
her. It wasn't my fault I was born. She has punished me ever since,
though, for it. I can remember all the unmerciful beatings she gave
me. She is happy now that she has completely destroyed my life."

He said she was vicious; she would choke him and beat him so
hard with a barrel stave that he became bruised and bleeding. She
used to say to him: "What did I ever do that God thinks I
deserved to have you wished on me!"

The mother told us of how her father "ran out" on the family
when she was five years old, and she said he never supported them.
. . . It is clear how this hostility toward her father had carried over
toward the son. . . .

"His whole childhood was filled with anger," said the mother.
She said she always thought he would get into trouble. "He grew up
thinking the same way. He felt everyone was against him." At the
time we saw her, she said she was glad the son was in prison and
she hoped the authorities would never release him.[27]

More recently, Nevitt Sanford has described this principle
clearly. We all know that in most cases of vicious acts there is
a harsh, brutal father or mother in the childhood background.
Sanford says that this is frequently an immigrant father who
struggled against odds to adapt himself to a strange environment and saw his authority undermined and flouted. He quotes
from the autobiography of the son of a Greek immigrant serving
a sentence for armed robbery:

My first memory has to do with Dad beating Mother. It seems
that Mother and Aunt Catherine, who in the meantime had arrived

---

[27] Glen M. Duncan, Shervert H. Frazier, Edward M. Litin, Adelaide
M. Johnson, and Alfred J. Barron, "Etiological Factors in First-Degree
Murder." *JAMA*, 168:1755–1758, 1958.

from Greece, were having an argument. I do not recall its exact nature. However, Dad entered the room cursing Mother. He called her a son of a bitch and an old whore, and kicked her in the stomach. I began to cry and felt extremely sorry for Mother, who with her hands pressed to her abdomen had fallen into one of the dining room chairs. . . .

Dad came home angry one night. Business had fallen off; he was discouraged and was thinking of closing the store. Mother said that it was too bad. If she said anything else, I cannot remember it. Dad swore at her. She ran from the table. Dad kicked back his chair and started for her. She ran out in the hall toward the piazza. Dad ran and kicked her. She cried, "Don't." He stood there and cursed. . . . I ran and put my hand on his leg and between sobs asked him not to hit Mother. He told me to get away from him and struck at me. I ran up the hall. Poor Mother, heavy with child, stayed on the piazza until he had become quiet and then with a red nose and a drawn, haggard face crept into bed, afraid to speak, afraid to open her mouth for fear that her husband would kick her. Years later, when he would begin to curse, this scene would unfold itself, and I would rise and for every vile epithet he used, call him one in return, while four young children sat and listened.[28]

In our book, *Love Against Hate*,[29] my wife and I tried to suggest how this vicious circle of vengeance evokes vengeance, and evoked vengeance tends to be perpetuated not only in and out of the courtroom and jails but within the family. Clinical experience has indicated that where a child has been exposed early in his life to episodes of physical violence, whether he himself is the victim or, as in the case just described, the witness, he will often later demonstrate similar outbursts of uncontrollable rage and violence of his own. Aggression becomes an easy outlet through which the child's frustrations and tensions flow, not just because of a simple matter of learning that can be just as simply unlearned, not just because he is imitating a bad behavior model and can be taught to imitate something more constructive, but

[28] Nevitt Sanford, *Self and Society*. New York: Atherton Press, 1966, p. 123.

[29] Karl Menninger, *Love Against Hate*. New York: Harcourt, Brace and Co., 1942.

because these traumatic experiences have overwhelmed him. His own emotional development is too immature to withstand the crippling inner effects of outer violence. Something happens to the child's character, to his sense of reality, to the development of his controls against impulses that may not later be changed easily but which may lead to reactions that in turn provoke more reactions—one or more of which may be "criminal." Then society reacts against him for what he did, but more for what all of us have done—unpleasantly—to one another. Upon him is laid the iniquity of us all, *unless* he can be shown to have been touched (punished) by God—absolved from guilt by a *previous* affliction. This is the philosophy of the irresponsibility doctrine.

The whole question of reading the nature of the malignant (or otherwise) intent in the offender's mind is one which the public is loath to refer to psychiatrists. Psychiatrists applaud this, because they have even greater doubts about the ability of *anyone* to determine accurately anyone's *intent*. If the criminal lacks a special self-evident excuse, a King's X of some kind, the vengeance of the people will often rise like a windstorm and sweep away all humanity, intelligence, Christianity, and common sense.

The scientists, and penologists and sociologists I know, take it for granted that rehabilitation—not punishment, not vengeance in disguise—is the modern principle of control. But in practice it is not. In the law it is not. Somebody is being "kidded."

SELF-CONTROL IS MENTAL HEALTH

For a long time it was popular in psychiatry to declare the mental healthiness of getting rid of one's aggressions. Inhibition and remorse seemed to be our most dreadful enemies and we encouraged patients to turn their hairshirts wrong side out and feel better. We never meant to say, as we have been interpreted as having said, that everyone should be as belligerent and aggressive as the spirit moved him to be. We never advocated that society return to the primitive days when "every man did that which was right in his own eyes" (Judges 21:25).

At any rate, the new psychiatry, faced with scenes of mounting and persistent rage of desperate and embittered people, must reemphasize the equal necessity for plain self-control. We must scotch the impression that it is always mentally healthy to get rid of one's anger promptly and directly. The present danger is upon us, and we are all suddenly realizing that vengeance is a two-edged sword, and that we cannot cure ourselves by stabbing one another. Nor can we justify our stabbings by calling our offenders dangerous or communistic or members of a gang. "Shoot to kill," cries an excited mayor to his policemen, thereby urging them to commit crime to stop crime, and start a new chain of revenge.

For an effective program of making the offender suffer by beating him to his knees, there must be unassailable power ranged against him, otherwise he will rise up in *his* vengeance and pay us back. *He* will do a little punishing according to *his* lights. "They that live by the sword shall die by the sword" is what we were taught. But we never have believed it.

Portugal has beaten two colonies into submission. It takes no great political prescience to predict that Portugal is on the way out, following the same route that far more powerful nations have taken. But whether this fight into historical prophecy has any basis, it is no secret that in all the great cities of the world today we are experiencing the phenomenon of revenge for dissatisfactions being turned against those nearest at hand and least prepared for the onslaught. We have always said that there were many people less than sane, but we have never really expected to see this "insanity" rise in great masses and turn in bitterness against *our* "sanity."

When a young lawyer, Governor William H. Seward, later Abraham Lincoln's Secretary of State, learned of a man in the Auburn State Prison who had apparently been driven mad by the flogging and other tortures that had been given him there, Seward went to see the man. Later he defended him in court—unsuccessfully. But this experience so aroused his interest in such problems that at the risk of professional, political, and personal ruin, he undertook the defense of an obviously demented old Negro accused of murder. In Seward's own words:

I sat here two weeks during the preliminary trial. I stood here between the prisoner and the jury nine hours, and pleaded for the wretch that he was insane and did not even know he was on trial: and when all was done, the jury thought, at least eleven of them thought, that I had been deceiving them, or was self-deceived. They read signs of intelligence in his idiotic smile, and of cunning and malice in his stolid insensibility. They rendered a verdict that he was sane enough to be tried—a contemptible compromise verdict in a capital case; and then they looked on, with what emotions God and they only know, upon his arraignment. . . . Gentlemen, you may think of this evidence what you please, bring in what verdict you can, but I asseverate before Heaven and you, that, to the best of my knowledge and belief, the prisoner at the bar does not at this moment know why it is that my shadow falls on you instead of his own! . . .

I speak with all sincerity and earnestness; not because I expect my opinion to have weight, but I would disarm the injurious impression that I am speaking merely as a lawyer for his client. I am not the prisoner's lawyer. I am indeed a volunteer in his behalf; but Society and Mankind have the deepest interest at stake. I am the lawyer for Society, for Mankind; shocked, beyond the power of expression, at the scene I have witnessed here of trying a maniac as a malefactor![30]

Seward lost his case, of course (until the appeal). He was politically persecuted, reviled in the press, and denounced from the pulpit. Why? Because he suggested that punishment of an offender be suspended. And mark well that he suggested this *not* because he opposed punishment for criminals, but because the man they were bent on punishing was sick! (And, of course, sick men cannot appreciate punishment.)

Cases like this dramatize how much the attitude of society has changed in a hundred years. But the punitive attitude persists. And just so long as the spirit of vengeance has the slightest vestige of respectability, so long as it pervades the public mind and infuses its evil upon the statute books of the law, we will make no headway toward the control of crime. We cannot assess the most appropriate and effective penalties so long as we seek to inflict retaliatory pain.

[30] Earl Conrad, *Mr. Seward for the Defense*. New York: Rinehart & Co., 1956, pp. 258–259.

THE JUSTIFICATION OF PUNISHMENT

Edmund L. Pincoffs

At one time, philosophers and theologians held a monopoly over the dialogue justifying, rationalizing, or, less frequently, condemning punishment. More recently, men in a variety of professions have entered the discussions—legal scholars, criminologists, police and correction officers, behavioral scientists, and "armchair" experts. All of these have contributed to the continuing controversy between the two camps: those whose moralistic-judgmental orientation compels them to hold a vindictive, retributive, *lex talionis* stance, and those who condemn our major reliance on a system of punitive deterrents. The latter group, perhaps, is of a more permissive, sympathetic, and understanding nature, or their hard-nosed pragmatic-utilitarian analyses have convinced them of the futility of punitive deterrents.

Now comes philosopher Edmund Pincoffs to summarize and balance, to clarify and refine the major approaches, although ad-

Source: Edmund L. Pincoffs, *The Rationale of Legal Punishment* (New York: Humanities Press, 1966), pp. 115–138. Reprinted by permission of Humanities Press, Inc.

mitting that attempts to reconcile the polar camps have thus far proved futile.

Pincoffs is more utilitarian than retributive. He argues a moral justification for punishment and questions, most intelligently and by inference sympathetically, a wholly therapeutic approach to those unable or unwilling to abide by society's laws. But he opposes the death penalty and calls for radical curtailment in the use of imprisonment.

"Why, and by what right," asks Leo Tolstoy in *Resurrection*, "do some people lock up, torment, exile, flog, and kill others, while they are themselves just like those they torment, flog, and kill?" More than two thousand years of dialogue has provided us with no totally satisfactory rationale, no completely acceptable answer to this question. But in addressing himself directly to it, Professor Pincoffs guides us skillfully and in the main objectively through the developmental history and logic of the conflicting approaches to the eternal problem raised by the great Russian writer.

By what right do some people punish others?
TOLSTOY

No one can know how many reasons there are or might be for wishing to modify or reject punishment. And as we offer the case for the institution of legal punishment, we wish to reveal as candidly as possible the vulnerable underpinnings on which the argument rests. For it is not a justification for all space and time, but one which applies only under certain conditions. These conditions are not local or peculiar, but it is easy to conceive of a world in which they did not obtain.

I

What, in principle, would constitute an adequate defense of the institution of legal punishment? Before attempting an answer we must raise a prior question: What kind of undertaking *is* a "defense" or "justification" of an institution or practice?[1] Not, how do we go about it? But, what is it we are going about?

We are offering reasons for the conclusion that punishment should be retained, not abolished. In doing so, we are thinking of the practice of punishment not as a rib of the universe, but as a device which serves certain purposes well or ill. It is not a device in the sense that it is a "dodge" or "gadget" which can be used today and abandoned tomorrow. But it is something which has been devised—not all at once, or consciously, perhaps; but it is an invention of man. It is an arrangement which we (the writer and most of the readers of this book) find already present in the culture of which we become bearers; but our culture could have been otherwise. There are cultures in which there is no legal punishment. To justify legal punishment is, then, to show that there are better reasons for retaining than for abolishing it.

Strictly speaking, if we subscribe to the principle that the burden of proof is on him who would institute a change, all that is necessary in the defense of a going practice is to show that no adequate grounds for changing it have been brought forward. But it is not merely because it is there, and change always makes difficulties, that punishment should be retained. A positive case can be made out for it which would warrant instituting legal punishment if it were not already the practice.

How, then, should we go about offering a justification of legal punishment? What, in principle, would constitute an adequate general defense or justification of punishment or of any social practice?[2] To justify a practice is to show two things: that under the circumstances, *a* practice is necessary, called for, or would be useful; and that of the alternatives available and acceptable, the practice in question would likely be the most effective. We will refer to the reason why some practice must be instituted as the "guiding principle" of justification; and to the

[1] We will settle here on the wider term, "practice," since we wish to compare punishment with possible alternatives which would qualify as practices but not as institutions.

[2] "Justification," in general, is discussed in Chapter VI [of the book from which this selection is taken].

considerations by reference to which the practice is rejected as nonacceptable even though it seems the best of the available alternatives, in the light of the guiding principle, as the "limiting principles" or justification. It is with respect to the guiding principle that a proposed practice can be more or less effective; but it may be rejected, even though effective, by a limiting principle.

These are general formal conditions of the justification of a practice. It is a necessary condition of an adequate justification of a practice that of the available alternatives it most efficiently serves the purpose for which a practice is needed; it is a necessary condition that the practice not be ruled out by a limiting principle; and it is a necessary and sufficient condition that the practice serve the purpose as well as possible within the bounds set by the limiting principles.[3] This schema is at least useful in approaching the problem of the justification of a specific practice. It forces us to distinguish between the questions whether *a* practice is necessary; whether the practice in question best fills the need; and if, even so, it must be rejected.

But Tolstoy's question, with which we wish to come to grips

[3] The general view of the justification of punishment presented here is perhaps closer to Ross' than to any other traditional view. The distinctions made here, however, give us certain advantages over Ross' account. Ross speaks of the balance between the *prima facie* duty of "injuring wrongdoers only to the extent that they have injured others," and the *prima facie* duty of "promoting the general interest." (*The Right and The Good*, Oxford, 1930, Ch. II, Appendix II, "Punishment"). In the first place, our account avoids the implication that we simply balance these considerations one against the other like weights on a scale (*op. cit.*, pp. 63 and 41). It is not a question of choosing either justice or utility or a balance between, but of finding the most useful social device consistent with the demands of justice. Secondly (though Ross might well not agree that this is an advantage) the emphasis is more on standing on, or holding a principle, than on knowing that something is true. Third, our account is not open, as Ross' is, to the kind of objection raised by J. S. Mill (in *Hamilton*) to the effect that we cannot very well balance the maxims of justice against those of utility, since what one maxim of justice demands may be incompatible with what another maxim of justice demands. On the present account, such conflicts, which I believe are real, need not concern us; since if the practice in question conflicts with any maxim which we adhere to, then it is ruled out; and we must look about for one which is acceptable. But, like Ross, we are able to avoid the charge that, by setting in motion an utilitarian engine of justification uncurbed, we are likely to justify too much.

in this chapter, concerns the right to punish. It requests a specifically moral justification. Like an economic or aesthetic justification of a practice, a moral justification will have guiding and limiting principles. But whatever principles we accept must be shown to be *morally* defensible. This may seem to present insuperable difficulties, for there are apparently irreconcilable differences over the ultimate principles of morality. Hence, what is morally defensible to one school will not be so to another. Utilitarians, self-realizationalists, intuitionists might fail to agree on the moral defensibility of the guiding and limiting principles by which punishment must be morally assessed as a practice. It may come out this way. But it may not. What is morally defensible from one point of view need not be indefensible from another. And it may be that the schema we use will point up the complementarity rather than the incompatibility of the leading moral views. For who wishes to deny that a practice must be shown to serve some purpose? The retributivist can, as we have seen, argue with real plausibility, that particular decisions concerning punishments should not be made on the ground that some supposedly good purpose would be served by punishing. And the retributivist can argue (less plausibly I believe) that all penal laws should be passed solely on the ground that justice demands them.

But is it really plausible to argue that justice demands *a* practice? Is it not more plausible to argue that when a practice can be shown to be necessary on utilitarian grounds, it should meet the demands of justice? Does justice demand the institution or practice of law, or marriage, or private property, or coined money? Or, at least, that there should be *an* institution which serves the purposes served by these? To say Yes, is to say that there are burdens and privileges existing prior to an institution or practice, which the practice should be invented and adopted to protect. But then the question is how we can know what these burdens and privileges are, prior to any practice within which they operate. To say that the institution should be invented and adopted to protect these burdens and privileges is like saying that basketball should be invented so that fouls and points for goals can be recognized and penalized or rewarded.

But, outside of basketball there are no fouls and points for goals. What would it mean to say that there are burdens and privileges which persons have, to protect which it is essential that we adopt the practice of marriage?

This might seem more plausible with respect to punishment. Is punishment as an institution justified because justice demands that there should be an institution which accords punishment to ill desert? The ill desert must then be supposed to exist independently of any practice in terms of which it can be defined. The crucial point here is that it is impossible to account for the *existence* of desert in the absence of a practice in terms of which desert can be assigned. What may lead us to think that desert can exist independently of a given punishment-practice is that desert is a concept in not one but several practices: legal punishment being merely the most clearly articulated of them. But if we stop to think of it we would realize that we could not speak, for example, of what Johnny deserves for pouring ink on the oriental rug were it not for *some* prior understanding of a practice. According to this practice, those persons playing the role of parent are given the authority to assign penalties not only for certain kinds of acts in advance, but also for acts adjudged "bad" or "naughty" after the fact: like pouring ink on rugs or putting glue in the seats. Punishment of such acts is justified, even though there is no rule promulgated in advance against them. But whence do parents derive the moral authority to identify and punish such acts? Surely not from some table beyond the tables of rules. Then we would simply have to ask for the credentials of that table, and of any table from which it was derived, and so on. It is not that the ill desert exists prior to the role of parent, but that parents are persons who are given discretion, according to a practice, to make decisions concerning ill desert.

It might seem that, nevertheless, there is ill desert independent of the practices of punishment, because the decisions of parents or judges are not merely arbitrary: decisions concerning desert are not right simply by virtue of being made by the proper authorities, but by virtue of being made in accordance with standards which the authorities should observe. We can criticize the authority's decisions on rational grounds. But the analogous point holds for fouls in basketball, or balls and strikes in baseball. Here too we can criticize the decision of the umpire by reference to the criteria by which he should be governed. But it does not follow that there could be balls and strikes were there no game of baseball. The assertion that a person deserves severe punishment is significant if and only if there is some practice according to which some authority could, by discoverable criteria, rightly award severe punishment. To say that justice is a limiting principle of possible practices of punishment is not to say that practices should somehow meet the requirement that some abstract, extra-practice "desert" should be given its due. It is but to say that the practice must, in virtue of its arrangements, give everyone concerned a fair shake. This point will be expanded below.

II

Let us now turn to the question what the circumstances are which give rise to the need for some practice, be it legal punishment, or an alternative. Here we will list certain very general assumptions of fact which, taken together, give rise to the problem. To the extent that these assumptions of fact are shaky, the justification of punishment totters; for the problem punishment and its competing practices are designed to meet alters or disappears. The assumptions of fact in question fall naturally into three different categories: assumptions concerning human nature, human society, and nature or "supernature."

Concerning human nature, we assume that humans are non-ant-like in that they do not order their affairs by instinct: *i.e.*, without rules. We assume also that whatever rules or regulations men set for themselves, there will be tension between the rules and the private interests, desires, or passions of persons falling under these rules: that there will not be automatic submission.

Concerning human society we assume that it is necessary to set some rules if men wish to survive, simply because human beings, being without enough instinctual equipment, are incapable of carrying on common activities necessary for their survival unless they are shown, told, taught, how to conduct themselves, what to do, and what to refrain from doing. And we assume that it is *desirable* to set *other* rules if the common life is to enhance the well-being (however that is defined) and reduce the misery and unhappiness (easier to agree upon) of all.

Concerning nature or "supernature," we assume that no natural or supernatural forces either compel action in accordance with the rules, or counter each violation with retribution. Lightning does not, as a matter of course, strike down either the man whose hand is raised with murderous intention or the murderer whose intention has been fulfilled. If lightning, pestilence, or tornado operated in either of these ways, social arrangements to ensure compliance with rules would be redundant.

To these factual assumptions we must now add a moral one. We assume that survival in conditions not merely miserable, and with some hope of happiness, is a value worthy of protection. We shall assume, indeed, that to interfere with these modest prospects and possibilities is morally wrong; and that each community has a collective moral right to prevent such interference.

Granting, then, that men wish to survive, and to decrease their misery and enhance their well-being there must be rules; and some social arrangement must be found which will counter the tendency to violate rules. Two points should be noted here. The arrangement in question is not required to be one which equally discourages the violation of all rules; some rules are more important for survival and well-being than others; and the effectiveness needed in the prevention of some rule-violations is not demanded for the prevention of all rule-violations. And, whatever practice may be instituted, its application in the prevention of rule-violations will be justified only to the extent that the rule and/or rule-set is justified. This latter point must be expanded.

Legislators[4] may be in a position to enact any rules they choose. In enacting rules, they may or may not have sufficiently in mind the survival or well-being of the citizens. Their laws

[4] The term is used here in the broad sense explained in Chapter V [of the book from which this selection is taken].

may be designed to enhance their own well-being. The state may be administered like the legislators' private plantation, the citizens regarded as serfs—and it may be badly administered even on these terms. Can any practice designed to encourage compliance with the rules of such a legislature be justified? The alternative practices in question are not designed to encourage compliance with any particular set of rules, but are devices to encourage compliance with *rules*. To show that there may be bad rules is not to show that the practices are bad practices. The practices are *needed* to counter the tendency to violate rules which for our survival and well-being we must have; but this, unfortunately, does not prevent their *being used* to enforce rules which may even go against the ends of survival and well-being. To reject them on this account is like rejecting hammers because they may be used by murderers, or representative government because we disapprove of the Senator from Mississippi.

There is a limit beyond which this argument should not be pressed. For telling counter-examples can be given. Should we not reject the practice of carrying hand-guns, *e.g.*, even though it arose for a defensible set of purposes: to provide a light gun, capable of being carried on long trips, which can be used for small game and, in wild country, for self-defense? Should we not have rejected duelling, even though it may originally have been a desirable substitute for simple unorganized mayhem? But the analogous argument in the present discussion would have to show that the conditions which gave rise to the demand for a practice designed to encourage compliance with rules are now so changed that practices originally meeting that need are now needed and are used for unjustifiable ends. While this does not now seem a plausible pair of contentions, it should be conceded that they could be, under circumstances now hard to foresee. If the great majority of human beings were in some way transformed so that the tension between rules and personal interests, passions, and desires disappeared; then the circumstances which gave rise to the need for a practice would have disappeared. And it could be that, under those circumstances, the practices originally designed to encourage compliance with rules, and now no longer necessary, were being used instead merely as instruments of oppression.

III

Suppose it be granted that, conditions being what they are, some practice to encourage compliance with rules is needed. Should punishment be preferred to other possible practices? Before attempting to assess the relative merits and demerits of punishment and its competitors, we must discuss the grounds of comparison. These, as we have noted, concern effectiveness and acceptability.

Punishment is *not* the most effective possible method for discouraging crime. Probably the most effective way to discourage —better, abolish—crime is to annihilate the human race. Or if this seems a little extreme, no doubt we could go a long way toward the elimination of crime by the use of drugs: the tranquilization of the human race. These possibilities are mentioned to point up the absurdity of arguing solely on grounds of effectiveness in the reduction of crime. Even though the procedures mentioned would work to eliminate crime, they would not be acceptable. What are the boundaries of acceptability? To what limiting principles may we appeal in rejecting an effective practice?[5]

Above, we mentioned not only justice but also humanity. By denominating humanity a limiting principle, we mean that one possible ground for refusal to accept an effective practice is that it is inhumane. It is apparently usually assumed in theoretical writing that any practice which is inhumane is by the same token unjust, since humanity as a separate limiting principle is not discussed. Yet it is not absurd to suppose that a given practice could be just but inhumane: that it might violate none of

---

[5] How many limiting principles are there? This is like asking how many ways there are for an effective practice to go awry. Limiting principles reject the proposed practice because it can be seen in advance that once this device is set in motion there are ways in which it would operate which we could never accept. But because the demand for *a* practice is sometimes very great, the grounds on which a candidate may be ruled out as non-acceptable are naturally very much curtailed. Justice and humanity, in that order, seem to be the limiting principles which bind with the greatest stringency; but for less important practice-choices, many more limiting principles can enter in. Compare the choice of a practice for assigning responsibility for the rearing of the young, to the choice of a practice by which recipients of the "keys of the city" are to be designated.

the maxims of justice and still demand treatment of individuals which we would agree is cruel or degrading. The "solution" of the problem of crime by annihilation or drugging could be not only effective, but just—in that it did not violate any of the maxims of justice by discriminating between persons: drugging or annihilating everyone impartially. This possibility gives rise to the maxim that justice should be "tempered with mercy"— and to a certain confusion attending this maxim. For justice is not inherently opposed to mercy: what is just may be humane enough; but it need not be humane at all.

How is it to be decided whether a proposed practice is inhumane? It will not do to speak briskly of setting up cardinal or ordinal scales on which there is a zero mark between minus-inhumane degrees and positive-humane ones. The question would then be how we know where to place any practice on the scale. Is it possible to find a purely formal criterion of inhumanity in a practice? It may be, but if so it would have to be developed in conjunction with a criterion of the justice of a practice, to which problem we now turn.

What is it for a practice to be just?[6] We shall take it that a practice is just if, knowing that it is necessary that there should be *a* practice and that this one would be effective, each of us would be willing to accept the practice not knowing in advance what role we would play. To expand: the assessment of the justice of a practice involves the conception of a particular view

[6] The definition of and test for justice in a practice are topics which lead way beyond the scope of the present discussion. What is offered here is merely an approach which seems to me promising. One might agree that justice is a limiting principle even though one disagreed that it could be defined as it is defined here. Much of what I have to say here has been suggested by John Rawls' article, "Justice as Fairness" (*Philosophical Review*, 1958, pp. 164–194). For a more complete discussion, the reader is referred to the whole of this article. I do not adopt Rawls' device of positing that the uncommitted individual we must picture is completely self-interested. He is but a construct, and we can do with him what we please, but to require that he be merely self-interested is to risk misleading comparison with Hobbes, and to make him more artificial than is necessary for my purpose. His recognition that *a* practice is needed may be based in part on altruism: a regard for the well-being of (even remote) others. But he would not likely join that society which would not give him, or anyone, a fair shake.

of the practice. It is the view taken of it by a person who realizes that a practice is necessary, and that this one will fulfill the need; who also realizes that in any practice there are going to be burdens and privileges;[7] and who must decide whether these privileges and burdens are fairly apportioned in view of what the practice is designed to accomplish. The test of fairness of apportionment of burdens and privileges is whether the person contemplating the practice would be willing to commit himself to it not knowing which role he might have to play; not from benevolence or self-sacrifice, but because he, along with everyone else, needs the practice.

Our hypothetical uncommitted person might be unwilling to commit himself to a proposed practice for fear of discrimination, not only within, but in assignment to the roles of the practice; and these two types of discrimination are worth distinguishing here. I might be able to predict now that I would (because of the color of my skin, say) be more likely than other persons to be assigned to a given burdened role in a proposed practice (criminal, defendant). Or the role itself (slave) might be such that whoever has to play it is the victim of discrimination, no matter how effective the practice may seem for no matter what good purposes. Slavery, then, may doubly discriminate: in its choice of persons to play the burdened role, and in its allocation of burdens and privileges between roles. It is with discrimination in the second sense that the justice of practices is, strictly speaking, concerned. But by thinking whether a person situated as described could agree to the practice, we will not lose sight of the first form of discrimination either.

We may now return to the question of the criterion of humanity. More accurately, what is wanted is a criterion or criteria by reference to which it can be determined whether a practice is inhumane. Duelling may be a useful example. It is one of the several alternative practices by which quarrels can be settled.[8] A

[7] Compare "burdened" and "privileged" vessels in the International Rules of the Road.

[8] This, of course, is over-simple. The quarrels in question often arose out of supposed insults which, according to the code of honor, could only be expunged by duelling; so that it was the code of honor as a whole which had to give way, not duelling alone.

practice was needed. Whether it was a just practice may be questioned. That it was inhumane to cause a man to lose his life as the price of losing an argument, seems clear—to us, here, now. Why, on what ground, would we call it inhumane? It was not inhumane in that it resulted in the loss of life. Lives were lost in the transportation of freight from harbor to harbor; and the practice of exchanging goods was not on that account inhumane. Duelling was inhumane because it resulted in *unnecessary* mutilation, suffering, degradation, and loss of life: unnecessary because there were available equally efficient and just ways of settling quarrels.

There is another way in which a practice can impose unnecessary, and thus inhumane, degradation, suffering, or death: it can be, unlike duelling, a practice which serves no necessary purpose at all. It is hard to think of examples, partly because when a practice becomes a part of the way of life of a people it begins to play roles not originally envisaged for it, even if it ceases to be needed for the original purposes. But unless we are willing to subscribe to the thesis, so far as practices are concerned, that whatever is is right, there will be ritual and other practices which because of the degradation and suffering they cause individuals falling under them are inhumane and hence no longer acceptable. Examples might be the *suttee*, and the taking of heads as trophies.

If the criterion of inhumanity in a practice is to be that suffering, misery, death or degradation are imposed unnecessarily, then what is a test by which we can know that a given practice is inhumane? Analogously to the test for injustice of a practice, we can ask whether a person, acknowledging the need for a practice, acknowledging that this practice would be efficient in fulfilling that need, acknowledging that the practice in question fairly distributes the burdens and privileges it creates, would nevertheless not want to commit himself to the practice on the ground that there are other equally efficient and fair practices which do not (as this one does) impose suffering, misery, degradation or death.[9]

[9] The discussion here is, admittedly, barely opened. How, by what test, do we decide that degradation, misery, or death are *unnecessary?* And,

IV

We may now return to the justification of legal punishment. We have tried to show that *a* practice is needed, and we have tried to specify criteria of comparison between punishment and alternative practices. What alternative practices are available, and how do they compare to punishment in the light of these criteria?[10]

We will not here attempt to cover all the kinds of practice which would be used to encourage compliance with rules, but will limit ourselves to those which presuppose a system of law. We are thus taking it for granted that it is not only advantageous to have rules but to have legal rules. Our only excuse for such a leap is that to do more than sketch, as we have done, the general justification of rules, is to embark on a question, the justification of law, which cannot be handled within the scope of this book. A full answer to Owen and Tolstoy, who attack the system of law as well as punishment, would require a very much larger book than this one.

---

even more difficult, what is to *count as* misery, suffering, and (most difficult) degradation? But even though the theoretical explication of our test for humanity of a practice may be difficult, still the test can be used prior to explication; for, by and large and never-mind-how, we do agree on what is unnecessary, and on whether suffering, misery, and degradation (to say nothing of death) are imposed. Or, if we do not agree, we know how to go about discussing the point. Explication could only start from the considerations we take as relevant in such discussion.

[10] Justice may be thought of as a virtue of practices, or actions, or of men. If we start from justice as a virtue of practices we will tend to think of acts and men as just insofar as they conform to the practices; and if we start from justice as a virtue of acts we will tend to think of practices as just insofar as they require the kinds of acts which we already, prior to the practice, consider just. But there is something odd in the notion that there can be justice of actions prior to justice of practices (though there is nothing odd about the notion of justice of actions prior to justice of institutions), and that the justice of practices consists in making these, prior, just actions possible. Does punishment, as a practice, exist to make possible that balance of punishment and desert which is known, independently of the practice, to be what justice demands? This is not at all plausible if we think in wide, generic, terms of the "practice of punishment." It becomes more plausible as we confine ourselves to particular practices or those formal practices we call institutions.

There is in principle no limit to the devices which human imagination could create for encouraging compliance with legal rules. Some of these we have noted (and rejected) in passing, such as telishment, the practices which would make of judges or legislators mere social engineers or mere balancers of the scales of justice, and "treatment." There are at least four remaining general sorts of practice which should be mentioned: (1) Practices which punish failure to comply with the law by informal means rather than the formal procedure of legal punishment involving legislators, judges, and jailers. Varieties of social suasion other than punishment have been described for us by cultural anthropologists; and while (is this analytic?) there will be no statutes in preliterate tribes, it is conceivable that social suasion could be relied upon to enforce statutes. For example, it might be the practice that if a man commits incest, he is shamed in public by anyone knowing of the deed; or if he fails to support his in-laws his wife will leave him. (2) Practices according to which compliance with the law is rewarded. (3) Practices according to which men are persuaded to abide by the law. (4) Practices according to which men are conditioned (drugs, neo-Pavlovian techniques) to obey the law. Of these, all are really consistent with legal punishment. And "adequate" is to be understood in terms of the criteria already mentioned.

Social suasion is perhaps the strongest candidate of the four. What is envisaged is the possibility that criminal statutes should be enacted with no penalty attached; that courts should decide guilt but not sentence; that, instead, suitable publicity should be given the crime, and the criminal returned to home and community. The assumption is that the public opinion of the home and immediate community would prove a stronger deterrent and reformative agent than the formal and more impersonal workings of a penal system.

This is a topic as large as the varieties of social suasion and the experience of the human race in their application. It is eminently worthy of research by social scientists, and, so far, little developed. The practice of leaving the punishment to the community has in its favor the point that for any individual the most meaningful punishment is that which is inflicted by those closest to him. It is the opinion of his peers that he values far more than the opinion of some vast and faceless "general public" represented by the sentencing judge. It is a point in its favor, also, that it makes for no discontinuity between the legal and moral community in the way that legal punishment does, in setting off some offences as subject to the sway of jails and jailers while other offences, morally as heinous, are not so subject.

There are, on the other hand, serious disadvantages in social suasion as compared to legal punishment. These turn largely around in the concept of "community." In the first place, there can be not only deviant persons, but deviant communities; and where this is so we cannot rely upon the opinion of peers to enforce laws which are for the public good. The deviant community may not regard laws necessary for the well-being of the larger community as incumbent upon it. Perhaps, the term "deviant" should not be overstressed. It has inevitable connotations of criminality; and while we wish to include gangs and mobs in these remarks, we wish also to include any community insofar as it pursues its own (supposed) interests to the exclusion of the interests of the larger community, in survival, avoidance of suffering, and enhancement of well-being. If we leave the sanctions of laws designed to further these ends of the larger community up to any smaller community, the system may not be viable, since with respect to the purposes of the laws in question, the smaller community may be deviant. And to rely on the social pressure of the larger community is to weaken the claim of social suasion to operate with the force of the judgment of peers—since the most effective peer-judgment comes from the most immediate communities.

Secondly, were the sanctions left up to the community, the same crime would be punished in many different ways rather than in the one way set by the legal penalty; but this would be unjust. It might be answered that the crime would still be punished in accordance with its seriousness, since in communities where it is a heinous offense it would be punished severely, but where it is only a venal offense it would be punished lightly. But this answer only begs the question, raised in the previous paragraph, whether the smaller community may not be deviant in regarding as venal, *e.g.*, what would be inimical to the well-being of the larger group.

Bearing in mind these reasons for rejecting social suasion as a substitute for punishment, we may without contradiction acknowledge its importance for legal punishment. The force of the threat contained in the penal clause of a criminal law is great not merely because the person contemplating crime fears the pain or suffering the penalty would impose if inflicted. Perhaps it is not even mainly this; for he also greatly fears the judgment of his peers symbolized by this official pronouncement of guilt and sentence. In fact, distinctions are made in everyday life and in legal debate between those penalties (*e.g.*, fines) which do not necessarily carry this public disapprobation with them, and those (imprisonment, execution) which do. Justice Brandeis is quoted by Hall[11] as saying, "It is . . . imprisonment in a penitentiary which now renders a crime infamous." But it is a necessary condition of this disapprobation, or infamy, that the criminal has been sentenced to a penitentiary; so the disapprobation is not here to be considered a substitute for punishment.[12]

Let us turn to the practice of rewarding rather than punishing crime. It is not clear how such a practice would operate. Would there be a reward for each person who goes through a year without breaking a law? A reward for each person who, though severely tempted in given circumstances, refrains from violating the law? Such practices are indeed conceivable, but would be subject to grave objections. Those laws which it is most important to enforce are often those there is the greatest temptation to violate. How could we prevent by means of rewards those crimes which in their nature are extremely profit-

[11] Jerome Hall, *General Principles of Criminal Law*, Indianapolis, Ind., 1960, p. 327.

[12] The question, presently much discussed, whether or not a given piece of legislation is punitive in intent, is likely to turn on the question not merely what suffering it imposes but also on the way in which the suffering is imposed will be generally regarded. A suggested test for legislation punitive in intent is to determine "whether the legislative concern underlying the statute was to regulate 'the activity or status from which the individual is barred' or whether the statute is evidently 'aimed at the person or class or persons disqualified.' " [*Fleming* v. *Nestor*, 363 U.S. 603 (1960)].

able, such as embezzlement, or forgery? And would the prospect of reward deter a man about to commit a crime of violence? More importantly, would it be morally defensible to reward a person abiding by (presumably necessary and just) laws?

There *is* a sense of the word "reward" in which it is used synonymously with "positive reinforcement." In this sense, reward provides indispensable support for legal punishment. For here reward is indistinguishable from social suasion, the reinforcement in question consisting in the repeated approval of one's abiding by the law under temptation to violate it.

Concerning the possibility of substituting of persuasion for punishment, we would follow Aristotle in his assessment of human nature when he says ". . . most people obey necessity rather than argument, and punishments rather than the sense of what is noble."[13] This should be immediately qualified (as Aristotle qualified it) by our assertion that we would much prefer to use persuasion rather than punishment, since punishment is a practice forced on us by the "human condition" rather than chosen as something positively desirable on its own account. It should also be said that persuasion may have a kind of pyramiding effect with respect to building respect for rules. That is, to the extent that we risk persuasion rather than punishment, we help develop people amenable to persuasion and not needing fear of punishment as a motive for abiding by the rules. Unlike some other alternatives, then, the side-effects of persuasion as a practice are good: better than the side-effects of punishment.

The cause of persuasion is one open to the advocate of punishment, Aristotle's assessment of human nature being granted as a generalization, but not taken to imply that any given person may not change in his amenability to persuasion. Persuasion as a means of encouraging compliance with the laws should clearly be promoted. This means that the rationale of laws should be the subject of public discussion, that only demonstrably necessary or desirable legal rules be enacted, and that some attempt be made to render the body of law intelligible. If persuasion must be rejected, it is not as an adjunct but as a substitute for

[13] *Ethica Nichomachea*, 118a, 3–13.

punishment. And it is not by virtue of its running afoul of the limiting principles that we must reject it as a substitute for punishment, but as failing to measure up to the demands of the guiding principle.

The achievement of a law-abiding community by the use of drugs or Pavlovian conditioning seems in principle perfectly possible, but the side-effects of such procedures we would not, on grounds of humanity, be willing to accept. We would not accept them because they are unnecessarily degrading: unnecessarily, because law-abidingness can be attained at lower cost in human degradation. Thus, as opposed to persuasion, we would accept conditioning so far as the guiding principle is concerned, but reject it for violating the limiting principles.

The case for punishment so far is that, granting certain very general assumptions of fact, the disvalue of misery, and the consequent need for rules, a practice is needed to encourage compliance with rules. And of the alternative practices some (*i.e.*, rewarding, persuading) fail to measure up to the guiding principle as well as punishment, and others (*i.e.*, conditioning, social suasion) are ruled out on the ground that they conflict with justice or humanity. This argument is deficient in two respects. It is not conclusive; since there may be alternatives not taken into account which would compete more successfully with punishment. If this is the case, then it is open to the opponents of punishments to propose these alternatives and compare them to punishment by the criteria of efficiency and acceptability. It is also deficient in that it offers no positive justification of punishment. It says only, so far, that punishment is the least undesirable of the alternatives.

V

There is much to be said for the thesis that punishment is just that: not anything we would want to have in the best of all possible worlds, but something we must accept for lack of something better in the world in which we live. Yet it may be well to note how it measures up to the criteria of efficiency in encouraging compliance with rules, of justice, and of humanity.

But before turning to these, we should note that there are some very general assumptions of fact, beyond those which give rise to the need for *a* practice, upon which any justification of the practice of punishment must rest.

The first of these assumptions is that men are capable of calculating their own interest; and that in general they will. Obviously the efficacy of the threat contained in a criminal law rests on this assumption. If a man is unable or unwilling to look ahead to the probable consequences for him of bank robbery then of course the possibility of a prison sentence is no deterrent.

Zilboorg tells us that "The indifference of the criminal to the penalty that is ahead of him, even if this penalty is death, is more the rule than the exception."[14] Bentham, on the other hand, argues:

When matters of such importance as pain and pleasure are at stake, and these in the highest degree (the only matters in short that can be of importance) who is there that does not calculate? Men calculate, some with less exactness, indeed, some with more: but all men calculate. I would not say, that even a mad man does not calculate.[15]

The case seems to me to be overstated on both sides. Bentham does not need to claim that everybody calculates. Even if the percentage of people who calculate is relatively small, punishment would so far be worthwhile; for by the threat of punishment crime could be reduced. And more moderate psychiatrists do not accept such conclusions as Zilboorg's. Robert Waelder, for example, tells us that the claim of "a very small but articulate number of psychiatrists" that punishment does not deter is "a radical contention in view of everybody's daily experience in office and shop."[16]

The second assumption is that, in general, men are able to

[14] Gregory Zilboorg, *The Psychology of the Criminal Act and Punishment*, New York, 1954, p. 32.

[15] *Principles of Morals and Legislation*, XIV, 28.

[16] "Psychiatry and the Problem of Criminal Responsibility," *University of Pennsylvania Law Review*, 1952, p. 383.

govern present impulses by the thought of future consequences. If they were not, the threat of punishment would be useless. This, so far as it applies to criminals, is also challenged by some of the more extreme psychiatrists.[17] Third, it is assumed that it is possible to find "evils" which are more or less universally dreaded. If there were no general desire to avoid fines or jail, then these "evils" would not be eligible as punishment. But unless the legislator can find some "evil" which qualifies, the institution of punishment fails; or is modified to allow judges complete discretion in the choice of punishment. Whether this would still be punishment and this "judge" a judge are open questions. Certainly a door would be left ajar for radical abuse of power. There are advocates of the "individualization of punishment" who would be willing to take this risk for the supposed gain in reformatory effectiveness. But what is gained here may well be lost on the side of deterrence of would-be offenders, who could never know what the penalty is, for the crime they contemplate.

To turn to assumptions concerning human society, we assume, first, that there is a virtual monopoly of coercive power in the state. Suppose that each man has an H-bomb which he threatens to explode if molested. Then force could be used on a man only by his consent, and legal punishment would break down. Secondly, we assume that the culture is such that it is possible for people to grasp what it is to be an official in a legal system. If not, sentencing and the execution of sentences will be understood as moves made by particular persons against particular persons; and deterrence will give way to cycles of retaliation. This may help explain why for Tolstoy, who refused on principle to allow the distinction between what is permissible for an official of a system and for an individual falling under the system, punishment was a moral nightmare.

To the extent that any of these assumptions, or the assumptions on which the need for *a* practice is predicated, are false,

---

[17] Cf., *e.g.*, Karpman's definition of criminal behavior, p. 102 [of the book from which this selection is taken. Karpman's definition reads: "Criminal behavior is an unconsciously conditional psychic reaction over which (the criminals) have no conscious control."—Eds.].

the case for legal punishment breaks down. We shall not argue for them, but simply assume their truth. Assuming them true, it seems *a priori* likely that punishment would be effective in encouraging compliance with legal rules. More than this: the experience of centuries of civilization constitutes evidence that it is effective. But not very conclusive evidence. We do not know to what extent social suasion and intellectual conviction have been responsible for the tendency of the masses to abide by the law. We do not have controlled social experiments in which punishment is compared in point of efficacy to treatment, or social suasion, or persuasion. In those chaotic revolutionary situations in which the recent history of the human race abounds, we would hardly have dared rely on less than the strong medicine of legal punishment. Yet perhaps in more orderly times, less drastic practices can be encouraged.

Under the heading of the effectiveness of punishment as a practice we should note (what has sometimes been recognized) that punishment is at least more ingenious than its alternatives in that it works like a pricing system in reverse. Whereas the storekeeper tries to price his wares in such a way that there will be as many purchasers as possible, the legislator tries (or should try) to "price" crimes in such a way that there will be as few takers-of-the-risk of criminal behavior as possible. And—as we realize from our survey of Bentham—it is more subtle than this. It is not merely that we want few takers, but that we want less takers of the worst crimes. So on these we put the highest price and our "pricing" can—on the practice of punishment—be carefully adjusted to the disvalue of the crimes: just as (inversely) the storekeeper can progressively encourage the taking of his wares by lowering the price.

What must be borne in mind is that if the evidence for the effectiveness of punishment in encouraging compliance with legal rules is less than satisfactory, the evidence for the comparatively untried alternatives is even less satisfactory. But the burden of proof is on him who would make a change, on the principle that we should change only where there is a likely advantage in doing so. And this principle seems worth defending, since changes, in deep-rooted practices especially, inevitably involve difficult readjustments, and sometimes involve consequences not foreseen.

What is also required in justification is that punishment should be shown as acceptable, *i.e.*, as not violating the limiting principles of justice and humanity. Is the practice of punishment, as such, unjust or inhumane? To say that it is, is to say that a person so far uncommitted to a society, recognizing the need in any society for an effective practice to encourage compliance with rules, recognizing that these must be burdens and privileges under whatever practice is chosen, would be willing to enter that society and fall under that practice, even though he does not know in advance and from this uncommitted standpoint what role he might have to play and what burdens or privileges would fall to his lot. To say that he would not commit himself to the society on the ground that he might through no fault of his own fall into a role which is at a disadvantage in the distribution of burdens and privileges, receiving, compared to other roles, most of the burdens and none of the privileges, is to say that the practice is unjust. To say that he would not commit himself to the society on the ground that the burdens which must be carried by the players of some roles (even though they may be fairly distributed) are at the same time very heavy and not necessary for the attainment of the purposes of the practice, is to say that the practice is inhumane.

Is the practice of punishment unjust? There is a heavily burdened role, criminal, into which any of us might fall; but not, we may assume, without fault. The proper answer to the person who refuses to commit himself to the society containing this practice, on the ground that he might fall into the unfavored role of criminal, is that once he commits himself to society and practice, whether he then plays or avoids the role of criminal is still open. He *can* have the advantages of the practice, and at the same time avoid the burdens of the unfavored role. And should he fall into the role of criminal, there is nothing inherent in the practice which would make the burden borne by one category of criminal out of proportion to that borne by others, granted the need to distinguish between more and less dangerous crimes.

Is it inhumane? Since, as practice, it does not specify the burdens to be borne, but only that they shall be adequate to the purpose of discouraging crime, the practice does not *as such* demand that there should be burdens not warranted by its purpose. It does not follow from the fact that there may be "cruel and unusual" punishments that the practice of punishment is therefore inhumane. Contrast the practice whereby the rulers administer drugs to the population at large which ensure that whatever laws are enacted will not be violated. This could work only if the critical faculties were so deadened that the individual could no longer distinguish between good and bad laws, and between occasions on which even good laws should and should not be violated. But, since there are alternative ways of encouraging compliance with the laws, which do not involve these consequences, they are unnecessary, and the practice is inhumane.

Morally speaking, if our very general assumptions of fact be granted, and our judgment that widespread misery is a disvalue, then rules are necessary, and some way must be found to make them effective. But if the best and most acceptable way is the practice of legal punishment, then those persons who find themselves playing the roles of judge and jailer have the moral right to sentence and carry out sentences. They have this right as officials of a practice which is, by hypothesis, for the good of everyone alike.

VI

So much, then, for the justification of the practice of legal punishment. It may be well to point out some things this justification does *not* pretend to do. (1) It does not pretend to offer a conclusive argument for punishment, whatever that would be. It presents the case for punishment: a case which must be compared with the case which can be made out for available alternative practices. (2) It does not, as we have noted, claim to warrant punishment as preferable to other practices regardless of context. It could well be that, for example, in a simple, stable, closely interdependent society, where there is more emphasis on character than on rules, punishment would be out of place.

(3) It does not justify any particular mode of punishment, such as capital punishment or imprisonment.

The objection that capital punishment or imprisonment are inhumane does not, even if accepted, necessarily weigh against the practice of legal punishment; since there are other modes of punishment which can be used. However, there is a finite number of modes, and if we were unable to find effective and acceptable modes, this would undercut the case for legal punishment.

The argument over capital punishment tends to turn in the wrong gimbals. Even if it should be shown that capital punishment is more effective than some other mode of punishment in discouraging certain sorts of crime, this would not be sufficient to justify its use; for it might be ruled out as acceptable by justice or humanity as limiting principles. So far as justice is concerned, capital punishment can be as impartially administered as any other mode of punishment. It is argued, with great force, that it is not in fact impartially administered, and that those executed tend to be the poor and the ignorant. This would not make any great difference, unfortunately, between capital punishment and imprisonment, were it not for the important point that there is no way of rectifying a judicial error arising from inadequate legal representation, once a man has been executed. Since there is the possibility of an irreversible error stemming from inadequate representation, it seems clear that our uncommitted individual, contemplating societies with varying modes of punishment, and not knowing whether he would play the role of rich or poor man, should he join the society, would prefer a society which did not have capital punishment to one which did. On this test, capital punishment is unjust.

But the capital punishment society may fail the test of humanity as well. For if our uncommitted onlooker can see no clear case for the thesis that capital punishment is necessary for the encouragement of compliance with the law, and is aware of alternative less cruel modes of punishment which singly or together are as effective, then he will naturally avoid the capital punishment society, even though he may think sentences to capital punishment are nondiscriminatory. And this much is clear: that no clear-cut case showing the necessity of capital punishment as a means of discouraging crime has been brought forward.

It might be argued that it is an unfair burden of proof to place upon the advocate of capital punishment to require him to show that his mode of punishment is necessary for the discouragement of crime, whereas the same burden is not placed upon the advocates of imprisonment and fines. But the difference is that capital punishment is admittedly more cruel than imprisonment[18] and fines and therefore should, upon the principle of humanity, be ruled out if it can be dispensed with. And, we may add, there is ample evidence that capital punishment can be abolished without an advance in the rate of crimes it purportedly discourages.

There are some persons who argue that life imprisonment is more cruel than capital punishment, and there is much to be said for this thesis, but there seems to be no way of deciding *in general* which is more cruel. Our test would have to be the same; namely to ask ourselves whether an uncommitted outsider would choose a capital punishment society in preference to a life-imprisonment society. And (granting for the moment that "life-imprisonment" really means imprisonment for life) we cannot be certain how he would answer, since we do not know whether he would be young or old, well or ill, disdainful or not of the prudent preservation of mere existence. However, the choice fortunately does not have to be made, since the sentence of life imprisonment today rarely means that in fact the criminal will remain in prison for the rest of his life.[19]

What, then, of imprisonment as a punishment? The live question here is not whether imprisonment, which unlike capital punishment admits of degrees, is justifiable, but what kind and how much imprisonment is justifiable. What has not been sufficiently recognized by the general public, in spite of

[18] See qualifications below.
[19] "Life imprisonment means, on the average, only about ten years." (H. E. Barnes and N. K. Teeters, *New Horizons in Criminology*, 3rd ed., Englewood Cliffs, N.J., 1959, p. 59).

the writings of G. B. Shaw,[20] Galsworthy,[21] John Barlow Martin[22] and others is that imprisonment can be a kind of torture worse than mutilation or the rack. Whether it is will depend upon the conditions and duration of imprisonment, and, inevitably, upon the character and personality of the offender. It is clear that from the standpoint of justice and humanity, to say nothing of efficiency, imprisonment as a mode of punishment should receive careful scrutiny. It is by and large only by the latter criterion that it tends to be measured. Here the argument sometimes slides from the inefficiency of a given penitentiary system to the undesirability of imprisonment as a mode of punishment (or even to the undesirability of punishment as a practice.) Yet it does not follow that because a given mode of imprisonment is inefficient that imprisonment as a mode of punishment is inefficient; and, since efficiency is a comparative criterion, it must be shown that there are more efficient modes of punishment which can replace imprisonment. And of course even if imprisonment were the most efficient mode of punishment available, it would not follow that, by the same token, it should be accepted.

The careful scrutiny of imprisonment as a mode of punishment not only from the standpoint of efficiency (here excellent work has already been done) but also of humanity and justice would result, I believe, in a radical reappraisal of the conditions and duration of imprisonment: in bold experiments, at least, in the shortening of legal penalties. For without such probing experiments the burden of proof, which humanity requires, that the penalties presently in force are necessary for the discouragement of crime, will not have been shouldered.

What we say here implies, correctly, that we believe that the schema of guiding and limiting principles can be applied not only to the justification of the practice of punishment but also to the justification of penal legislation. This we will not under-

[20] *Imprisonment*, New York, 1924.
[21] John Galsworthy, *The Silver Box*, New York & London, 1909; and *Justice*, New York, 1913.
[22] "Prison: The Enemy of Society," *Harpers*, April, 1954, pp. 29–38; and many other articles and books.

take here, but the main lines of the venture should be clear. Here the questions would be, first, whether a law is necessary, and, second, whether the proposed law would be the most efficient of the acceptable alternatives. But justice and humanity as limiting principles of legislation cannot be defined or applied in the same way as they are above. The uncommitted bystander must have committed himself to the practice of punishment, and must now consider alternative laws under that practice. Should we then attempt to apply our schema to the justification of sentences? If so, our uncommitted bystander must have accepted not only the practice but the law violated, along with its attached range of penalties.

Whether the distinction between guiding and limiting principles can be maintained in the justification of sentences is a difficult question not to be undertaken here. It is enough, for our purposes, if the conclusion . . . that the judge cannot be reduced either to a social engineer, or to a balancer of the scales, [be allowed to stand].

The short answer to Tolstoy's question, "By what right do some people punish others?" is that, needing a practice, we do not know any better one than legal punishment. The long answer would begin with this chapter and move back to the justification of legislation, penalties, and sentences. This book may provide an outline and some material for that venture.

THE STRUGGLE
FOR PENAL
REFORM IN
AMERICA

W. David Lewis

American criminologists have long been interested in the history of penology, particularly its domestic history. Some of the outstanding among them have turned their attention and talents to tracing the history of various facets of penology from colonial days to the present. They have written about the penitentiary system, the fight for penal reform, and the opposing outlooks on corporal and capital punishment. The names of some of these men and their work that come to mind are Harry Elmer Barnes, *The Evolution of Penology in Pennsylvania* (1928); Negley K. Teeters, *The Cradle of the Penitentiary* (1955); and Thorsten Sellin, *Pioneering in Penology: The Amsterdam House of Correction* (1944).

Source: W. David Lewis, *From Newgate to Dannemora: The Rise of the Penitentiary in New York, 1796–1848.* (Ithaca, N.Y.: Cornell University Press, 1965), pp. 230–255. Copyright © 1965 by Cornell University. Reprinted by permission of the publisher.

Historians, however, have rarely been interested in criminology and penology, as such, so that much of the best historical work came from men better equipped to understand the nature of crime and punishment than to deal with problems of historiography and the reconstruction of times past. An exception, and a notable one, is W. David Lewis.

Criminology and penology have probably never before been enriched by a history so meticulously constructed and so beautifully researched from obscure primary sources. In a manner that is uniquely the metier of the historian, Lewis has captured the spirit, the detail, and the personnel of the movement for penal reform in America as well as the reaction against that movement.

The people who appear in these pages are obscure and for the most part today unknown. Few have heard of Eliza W. Farnham and John Bigelow, but the movements they represented and at times led are more familiar. As described in this selection, they will provide the reader with a rich insight into the manner in which penology was involved in the struggle over free will and determinism, over deterrence and retribution, and over punishments so cruel as to shock even the most calloused reader. Here one will find the intertwining of reform and pseudoscience, the exploitation of prison labor by unscrupulous employers, the diminution of prison reform as a social movement as American liberalism focused its major attention on antislavery. For the pleasure of reading about an important moment in history, for the admiration that one must feel for the author who so vividly captures the buried past, for the light that he sheds on the nature of cruelty and punishment, and for the analogies that suggest themselves to social movements and social actionists today, this selection will prove exceptionally rewarding.

Although the reform administrators who came into power in the prisons of New York during the 1840's agreed upon certain fundamental premises, they were by no means in complete accord on all matters of penal policy. They shared a common disinclination to use violent punishments, a belief that criminals could and should be rehabilitated, and a disposition to use kindness whenever this did not impair discipline. On the other hand, there remained considerable room for disagreement on the causes of crime, the nature of guilt, and the precise means that should be taken to produce amendment of the offender. Some officials were more eager than others to break away from traditional ideas involving the felon and his treatment. As a result the period between 1844 and 1848, during which the movement for a more humanitarian administration of New York's penitentiaries reached its peak, was marked by acrimony and debate. Disputes over certain ideas and techniques became so acute that a split occurred between reformers who shared a common aversion to older methods. This played into the hands of critics who had never wanted a change in the first place, and reaction set in before the decade came to an end.

Foremost among the tendencies to which penological conservatives objected during the 1840's was the way in which popular sympathy and pity were replacing the aversion and animosity with which criminals had only recently been regarded. Paradoxically, some of this sympathy and pity had unquestionably been stimulated by the excesses which had occurred under the stringent rule of such men as Lynds and Wiltse, so that the repressive school was being haunted by its own zeal. The roots of the new attitude, however, could be found in the same optimism which was reflected in the increased emphasis upon rehabilitation in the prisons. In a period of lessened concern about the safety of democratic institutions, and of faith in the inevitability of progress, hatred of the offender could not feed upon widespread fears of social upheaval and citizens could afford to be indulgent. The spread of sentimentalism, which exalted pity as a virtue, also contributed to the new image of the lawbreaker, and was especially influential in the progress of the antigallows movement.[1] In addition, the romantic emphasis upon the organic unity of mankind reinforced latent Christian attitudes about human brotherhood

---

[1] See Herbert R. Brown, *The Sentimental Novel in America, 1789–1860* (reprinted ed.; New York: Pageant Books, 1959), p. 142; David B. Davis, "The Movement to Abolish Capital Punishment in America, 1787–1861," *American Historical Review*, LXIII (October, 1957), 29–30.

and the implication of the group in the sins of the individual.[2] The result, in the eyes of some critics, was a further threat to property and morality in an age of misguided reformism. "Nobody has any *rights* except scoundrels, and slaves and debtors," exclaimed James Watson Webb's New York *Courier and Enquirer* in 1847 in an attack upon current penal practices. "Laws must consult their convenience and advantage solely."[3]

One manifestation of a sympathetic outlook toward the criminal in the 1840's was the willingness of many citizens to absolve him from guilt, either wholly or in part, by shifting blame to various environmental deficiencies. The influential *Democratic Review* asked its readers in 1846 to consider the extenuating circumstances which existed with regard to certain illegal acts, and "to inquire how far even the most virtuously disposed might have fallen before them."[4] Even more outspoken was a statement by Lydia Maria Child to the effect that "Society is answerable for crime, because it is so negligent of duty," printed in the New York *Tribune* in 1844.[5] Popular novelists who had been influenced by such European works as Edward Bulwer-Lytton's deterministic *Paul Clifford* portrayed felons as victims of circumstance. In *The B'hoys of New York* and *The G'hals of New York*, for example, Ned Buntline (Edward Z. C. Judson) cast young delinquents in the role of frustrated and injured persons who had been corrupted and wronged by relatives and acquaintances.[6] The influence of environmentalism was apparent at the first meeting of the New York Prison Association in 1844 when William Henry Channing, one of the charter members of the organization, spoke of

[2] See especially Merle Curti, *The Growth of American Thought* (2nd ed.; New York: Harper & Brothers, 1951), pp. 372, 381.

[3] New York *Courier and Enquirer*, May 5, 1847, as quoted by New York *Tribune*, May 7, 1847. Italics are as given.

[4] Anonymous, "Prison Discipline," *United States Magazine and Democratic Review*, XIX (August, 1846), 129.

[5] Lydia Maria Child, "Kindness to Criminals—The Prison Association," copied from Boston *Courier* by New York *Tribune*, Dec. 20, 1844.

[6] David B. Davis, *Homicide in American Fiction, 1798–1860: A Study in Social Values* (Ithaca, N.Y.: Cornell University Press, 1957), pp. 217–221.

"the conviction, fast becoming general, that the community is itself, by its neglects and bad usages, *in part responsible* for the sins of its children; and that it owes to the criminal, therefore, aid to reform."[7]

Such arguments obviously ran counter to the beliefs of those who regarded the felon as a strictly accountable being. So did the contentions of reformers who asserted that criminality indicated disease or faulty cerebral endowment rather than willful depravity. Although Anglo-American jurisprudence had accepted the M'Naghten Rules of 1843, based upon John Locke's theory that a man should be adjudged legally sane if he understands the nature and quality of his actions and can distinguish right from wrong, this principle had already come under vigorous attack by such eminent alienists as Isaac Ray, whose arguments greatly concerned citizens fearing that the worst types of crimes might now be excused on the grounds of insanity. Such terms as "homicidal mania," "moral insanity," and "irresistible impulse" were cropping up in popular discussion and seemed slippery indeed to those who insisted that some hard and fast line of demarcation, such as Locke provided, was needed to separate the guilty from the innocent. Ray's theories received a particularly spectacular airing in New York in 1846 when William H. Seward based his famous defense of William Freeman in part upon them.[8]

The idea that criminal acts were attributable in many cases to defective endowments received considerable support from the pseudoscience of phrenology, which was particularly distasteful to defenders of traditional moral theories. Phrenology postulated that the human mind was composed of various faculties, generally grouped into "propensities" and "sentiments." Under the heading of "propensities" were subsumed such characteristics as amativeness (the desire for sexual love), combativeness, de-

---

[7] New York Prison Association, *First Report* (1844), p. 31. Italics are as given.

[8] Davis, *op. cit.*, Chap. 3, *passim.* Freeman, part Indian and part Negro, had murdered four members of the wealthy Van Nest household near Auburn and wounded others. Seward failed to secure an acquittal, but the prisoner died in his cell before execution. See Frederic Bancroft, *The Life of William Seward* (New York: Harper & Brothers, 1900), Vol. I, pp. 174–80.

structiveness, secretiveness, and acquisitiveness. The "sentiments" included benevolence, veneration, self-esteem, conscientiousness, and love of approbation. Each of these faculties was controlled by a given area of the brain. The "propensities" had their proper uses; they gave people courage to face difficulty, determination to resist aggression, and the desire to provide against want. Nevertheless, they could become so overdeveloped as to induce men to commit savage crimes. The "sentiments" were also potentially liable to abuse. Firmness, which could be manifested in such desirable characteristics as perseverance, could also produce intransigence and "tenacity in evil." If the various faculties were improperly developed or out of harmony with one another, criminal behavior might occur. This would be especially likely if the propensities were stronger than the sentiments that should normally have held them within bounds.[9]

To the phrenologist, therefore, wrongdoing did not stem from depravity, it had a physical basis. Because the strength of each faculty was governed by the extent of a given brain area's development, one could sometimes identify a criminal merely by looking at him. He was likely to have a "ruffian head," characterized by a low forehead, a flat or depressed skull, and large amounts of brain area behind his ears. By spotting which propensities were especially well developed, one might even be able to tell the precise crimes such a man was most likely to commit. If he had pronounced areas of covetiveness and combativeness, for example, he was probably an armed robber; if he possessed marked covetiveness with cautiousness, however, he might well be a sneak-thief or a pickpocket.[10]

[9] See the list in George Combe, *The Constitution of Man Considered in Relation to External Objects* (Boston: W. D. Ticknor, 1836), pp. 50–53, and the diagram in John D. Davies, *Phrenology, Fad and Science: A Nineteenth-Century American Crusade* (New Haven, Conn.: Yale University Press, 1955), p. 6.

[10] Charles Caldwell, *New Views of Penitentiary Discipline, and Moral Education and Reform* (Philadelphia: W. Brown, 1829), pp. 18, 25. See also the analysis in Amos Dean, *Lectures on Phrenology: Delivered before the Young Men's Association for Mutual Improvement of the City of Albany* (Albany, N.Y.: Oliver Steele, and Hoffman & White, 1834), pp. 103–104. For a brief general treatment of the relation of phrenology to penology, see Davies, *op. cit.*, pp. 98–105.

If these theories were true, it was wrong to hold a criminal strictly responsible for his offenses. The cerebral organization of certain people, stated a New York phrenologist in 1835, was such as to produce strong impulses to steal. To require the same behavior from such individuals as was expected of citizens with good phrenological developments was just as senseless "as it would be to require of man, constituted as he is, that he should visit the depths of the ocean with the fish, or penetrate the mid-heavens with the eagle." A person could be held responsible only for the proper exercise of faculties which he actually possessed.[11] This did not mean, however, that the criminal's mental processes were unchangeable. "The condition of the brain, like that of the muscles and organs of sense," affirmed a prominent phrenologist, "can be altered, and greatly improved by exercise." If one wished to weaken a dangerous propensity, he should place the person who possessed it in an environment which would give such a faculty little chance for activity. At the same time, he should surround the afflicted individual with uplifting influences. These would gradually strengthen the areas of the mind that controlled the higher sentiments. The criminal could thus be changed into a better man.[12]

Rehabilitative treatment was therefore the only phrenologically intelligent policy; subjecting a culprit to violent punishment merely strengthened the very faculties that needed to be inactivated. Flogging was a great mistake, for it excited resentment and hatred, and stimulated a desire for revenge. Traditional methods of dealing with offenders were also unsound in other respects. The fact that a man committed repeated crimes, for example, served only to show that he had an especially bad cranial development and was in critical need of therapy. Because of public ignorance, however, multiple offenders were usually treated with ever greater severity. The concept of "making the punishment fit the crime" was another fallacy. Instead, the treatment should fit the cerebral development of the individual offender.[13]

---

11 Dean, *op. cit.*, pp. 102–103n.
12 Caldwell, *op. cit.*, pp. 3, 14–15, 22–23.
13 *Ibid.*, pp. 3–4, 41; Marmaduke B. Sampson, *Rationale of Crime, and*

Phrenology had not been unknown to early New York prison reformers. During his trip to Europe in 1818, John Griscom had attended a lecture by Franz Joseph Gall, the father of studies in this field, but had come away from it filled with skepticism.[14] In the 1820's however, phrenology gained several notable exponents in the United States. One of these was Charles Caldwell, a professor at Transylvania University; another was John Bell, an outstanding Philadelphia physician who edited the *Eclectic Journal of Medicine*. In 1832, the visit to the United States of Gall's leading disciple, Johann Gaspar Spurzheim, also stimulated great interest in phrenology, as did the American tour of the Scots writer and lecturer George Combe later in the decade. After Combe spoke in New York City in December, 1838, a distinguished group of jurists, physicians, university professors, and philanthropists tendered him a resolution asserting that phrenology opened up "a new era in mental and physiological science, in which we believe human inquiry will be greatly facilitated, and the amount of human happiness essentially increased." The list of believers in the theories of Gall and Spurzheim included such eminent men as Nicholas Biddle, Henry Ward Beecher, Horace Mann, Samuel Gridley Howe, and Henry Schoolcraft. Amariah Brigham, who became supervisor of the New York State Lunatic Asylum at Utica and founder of the *American Journal of Insanity*, was also a disciple.[15]

The moral relativism associated with phrenology, however, appalled various citizens in New York. David Meredith Reese, a critic of many popular "isms," contemptuously attacked the

---

Its Appropriate Treatment: Being a Treatise on Criminal Jurisprudence Considered in Relation to Cerebral Organization, ed. Eliza W. Farnham (New York: D. Appleton Co., 1846), p. 11n.

[14] John Griscom, *A Year in Europe* (New York: Collins & Co., 1823), Vol. I, p. 259; Vol. II, pp. 56, 259, 351–53.

[15] Davies, *op. cit.*, pp. 13–14, 16–20; Arthur E. Fink, *Causes of Crime: Biological Theories in the United States, 1800–1915* (Philadelphia: University of Pennsylvania Press, 1938), pp. 4, 9–10, 12; Robert E. Riegel, "The Introduction of Phrenology to the United States," *American Historical Review*, XXXIX (October, 1933), pp. 75–76, 78; Roswell W. Haskins, *History and Progress of Phrenology* (Buffalo, N.Y.: Steele & Peck, 1839), pp. 199–200.

ideas of Gall and his followers as devices for "easing a loaded conscience."[16] Another detractor feared that "the midnight assassin may go with phrenology in one hand and the dagger in the other, and execute his dark design without compunction and without responsibility."[17] When phrenology began to be applied in the New York prison system, therefore, it was not surprising that it encountered strident opposition from those who believed that man was a free moral agent who should be held strictly accountable for his transgressions. Typical was the reaction of the New York *Courier and Enquirer,* which complained bitterly in 1847 about new ways of dealing with convicts according to cranial bumps and propensities. "The quacks that now vex the public ear with their clamor, and threaten utterly to destroy the body politic with their nostrums," it confidently predicted, "will have their day, and then go to their own place and be heard of no more. Heaven speed the day!"[18]

The principal target of this criticism was Eliza W. Farnham, who was chiefly responsible for introducing phrenology into the state penal system after becoming matron of the woman's prison at Sing Sing in 1844. Reading about the work of Elizabeth Fry among criminals had stimulated in Eliza, as a young orphan growing up in western New York, "an intense curiosity to penetrate the innermost centre of the stained soul, and observe the mysterious working of that machinery by which so fatal a result was produced."[19] Years later, as the articulate and reform-conscious wife of a young lawyer, explorer, and author named Thomas Jefferson Farnham, she received her chance when John W. Edmonds, looking for someone who might be able to establish order among the female convicts, interviewed her and gave her the job.[20] A woman of independent mind who not long

[16] David Meredith Reese, *Humbugs of New York: Being a Remonstrance Against Popular Delusion* (New York: J. S. Taylor, 1838), pp. 75–76.

[17] Quoted in Plattsburgh *Republican,* Jan. 13, 1844.

[18] Quoted in New York *Tribune,* May 7, 1847.

[19] Eliza W. Farnham, *Eliza Woodson, or, The Early Days of One of the World's Workers: A Story of American Life* (2nd ed.; New York: A. J. Davis Co., 1864), pp. 248, 350–51.

[20] Georgiana B. Kirby, *Years of Experience: An Autobiographical Narrative* (New York: G. P. Putnam's Sons, 1887), p. 190.

before had returned with her husband to New York after a few years of pioneering on the Illinois prairies, Mrs. Farnham was not hesitant about introducing new techniques at Sing Sing, and was prepared to defend her ideas in print with considerable writing ability. Firmly convinced of the rightness of her views, and tending to make harsh judgments with regard to those who opposed them, she had all the makings of a controversial figure and quickly became one.[21]

So far as the new matron was concerned, her charges could not be held fully responsible for the crimes which they had committed. "We knew that they were the products of their circumstances," stated an assistant matron and intimate friend who shared Mrs. Farnham's philosophy: "of their inherited tendencies and the conditions into which they were born. Given ignorance and weakness in the blood, and back alleys populated by the degraded and friendless, who can wonder at the outcome?"[22] The proper way to treat a felon, the matron believed, was to follow phrenological doctrines and remove those elements from his environment that stimulated his animal propensities. The substitution of proper influences would in time strengthen his better faculties while the vicious ones withered away. "Those sentiments which have lain dormant or been crushed by outrage and defiance," Mrs. Farnham declared somewhat rhapsodically, "must be gently summoned into being, and tenderly and patiently nursed by continual influences, which fall pleasantly upon and around them like dew upon the sickly seedling."[23] Such a process could never be consummated through the use of harsh and violent punishments; nor could it be furthered by harping upon an inmate's degraded past. Instead, the emphasis had to be upon positive and hopeful incen-

[21] The matron's former experiences in Illinois are recounted in Eliza W. Farnham, *Life in Prairie Land* (New York: Harper & Brothers, 1846), *passim*. Her occasional censoriousness was clearly revealed in her correspondence with John Bigelow, a member of the Sing Sing board of inspectors. See especially Eliza W. Farnham to John Bigelow, Dec. 28, 1845; July 20, Aug. 6, and Oct. 1, 1846; Feb. 20 and 22, 1847; and June 29, 1848, Bigelow Papers, New York Public Library.

[22] Kirby, *op. cit.*, p. 200.

[23] See Mrs. Farnham's editorial comments in Sampson, *op. cit.*, pp. 66, 73.

tives. "We never spoke to them of their past as vicious," recalled a co-worker in later years; "it . . . pleased us to love these low-down children of circumstances less fortunate than our own. We gloried in being able to lift a few of them out of the slough into which they had fallen, or in which they had been born, and to sustain them while they were trying to take a little step upward in the direction of the light."[24]

One of the most efficacious of the "continual influences" which could be brought to bear, the matron believed, was education, previously hampered by the practice of instructing the inmates only singly in their cells. Soon she broke precedent by assembling all of her charges in the chapel every morning for schooling. On some occasions she lectured to them on American history, astronomy, geography, physiology, and personal hygiene; on others she read to them out of "some instructive or entertaining book." Women who knew how to read and maintained a good behavior record were given books to take to their cells, especially George Combe's phrenological treatise, *The Constitution of Man*. Illiterates were allowed to have picture books. Starting with a library which was limited to seventy-five copies of Richard Baxter's *Call to the Unconverted*, Mrs. Farnham was able to prevail upon friends for such works as "Sergeant's Temperance Tales, Hannah More's Domestic Tales, Miss Edgeworth's Popular Tales, Miss Sherwood's Works, and some little books of history, geography, and travels." Some volumes were obtained through the efforts of Margaret Fuller, who visited the prison in December, 1844, and delivered a lecture to the women.[25]

Books and lectures, however, were not enough. To the matron, the very environment of a penitentiary, with its despon-

[24] Kirby, *op. cit.*, pp. 225–226.
[25] *Documents of the Senate of the State of New York* (1846), Vol. I, No. 16, p. 94; *Documents of the Assembly of the State of New York*, 70th Session (1847), Vol. VIII, No. 255, Part 2, p. 49; Sampson, *op. cit.*, p. 66n; Anonymous, "The Rationale of Crime," *United States Magazine and Democratic Review*, XX (January, 1847), p. 53; Kirby, *op. cit.*, pp. 192–194; New York *Tribune*, Dec. 26, 1844. The *Documents of the Senate* and of the *Assembly of the State of New York* are hereinafter referred to as DS and DA, respectively.

dency and gloom, was calculated to have a bad influence upon minds aspiring to better things. She therefore set out to brighten the tone of inmate life. Flowerpots were placed in the windows, maps were hung from the walls, and large lamps with reflectors were installed in the ceilings. Holidays were observed, and on one Fourth of July Mrs. Farnham and her staff chipped in to buy candy and other delicacies for the convicts. Music became a part of institutional life when Georgiana Bruce, a former participant in the Brook Farm experiment, became an assistant matron and brought her piano to the prison. The temper of one unruly inmate was calmed when she was allowed to have a rag doll and cradle, much to the indignation of a conservative critic who happened to visit the penitentiary. In addition, the women were encouraged to engage in handicrafts, and a glass case was set up where the items they produced could be displayed for purchase by outsiders who toured the institution. The proceeds went toward the acquisition of more books for the library.[26]

Mrs. Farnham believed that positive incentives should replace coercive measures whenever this was practicable, and inaugurated a system of classification soon after her administration began.[27] On July 4, 1844, she arranged to have Edmonds visit her department and award large bouquets to the inmates who were chosen by their peers as the kindest and "most amiable." Each of the other convicts received a smaller bunch of flowers on the same occasion.[28] Although the matron was encouraged by the results of such experiments, she found that strong disciplinary measures could not be eliminated completely. "There is a class of criminals who are susceptible to nothing but fear of punishment," she concluded sadly in 1847. "They are incapable of appreciating the motives which would prompt other treatment, and are quite certain to misconstrue them, and so meet it with contempt or ridicule rather than respect."[29] She was there-

[26] Kirby, op. cit., pp. 190–226 passim; New York Sun, Aug. 19, 1846; DA, 70th Session (1847), Vol. VIII, No. 255, Part 2, p. 49.

[27] DS, 68th Session (1845), Vol. I, No. 9, p. 7.

[28] New York Tribune, July 27, 1844.

[29] DA, 71st Session (1848), Vol. I, No. 10, p. 78.

fore constrained on occasion to use chains, mouth gags, strait-jackets, and other devices, however reluctantly.[30]

In general, she believed, moral growth presupposed a certain degree of liberty, and could not be achieved by overburdening the prisoners with rules and regulations. "The nearer the condition of the convict, while in prison, approximates the natural and true condition in which he should live," she declared, "the more perfect will be its reformatory influence over his character." She therefore considered "the smallest number of rules with which our prison can be soundly governed, the most favorable for the improvement and elevation of its inmates." With such precepts in mind, she threw out the rule of silence in January, 1846, and allowed conversation "at all convenient times when it would not interrupt or retard labor." This privilege was at first allowed only to certain inmates, but by the end of the year it had been extended to every woman.[31]

In pursuing her reform program, Mrs. Farnham enjoyed the support of valuable allies both within and without the institution in which she worked. One consistent defender was Horace Greeley, who had known her before her appointment and praised her efforts despite the fact that she was a Democrat who owed her position to a Jacksonian board of inspectors.[32] As chairman of that body, Edmonds gave her solid backing until he resigned early in 1845 to accept a judgeship in New York City. His successor, James Powers, was an elderly jurist from Catskill who favored mild policies, as did another new inspector, a young lawyer from Newburgh named Benjamin Mace. Two other appointees of the incoming Wright administration were conservative in their approach, but the fifth inspector swung the balance against them. This was John Bigelow, who not only worked for humanitarian methods at the men's prison but also became a strong source of assistance to the matron.

[30] Ibid., 69th Session (1846), Vol. IV, No. 139, pp. 113–122.
[31] Ibid., 70th Session (1847), Vol. VIII, No. 255, Part 2, p. 62; DS, 70th Session (1847), Vol. I, No. 5, p. 89.
[32] See New York Tribune, March 18, 1844; April 11, 1844; Feb. 25, 1846; and Jan. 28, 1847.

Bigelow was young, well educated, and idealistic. He had tried his hand at being a lawyer, a writer, and a journalist, and at this stage of his career was dissatisfied with his accomplishments. At first, he appears to have accepted the inspectorship primarily as "an office which without complicating my position in politics establishes me in the confidence and respect of men whose consideration it is desirable to maintain," but he soon became genuinely interested in penal problems. Ambitious, and not afraid to suggest new ideas, he was determined to "make a mark" on the development of penitentiary methods before leaving his post.[33] Throwing his weight on the side of Powers and Mace, he helped to decrease the incidence of flogging until by the end of 1846 the prison went through an entire month in which not a single lash was administered.[34] Punishments, he held, were of two classes: those which "quicken the moral sensibilities," and those which "merely afflict them." The former helped the convict to acquire self-respect, and the latter caused him to lose it. In Bigelow's words, "all punishment which merely insults, depraves."[35]

Bigelow's receptivity to new ideas was exemplified by his reaction to an experiment being conducted at Auburn and at the new ironmaking prison in the Adirondacks, where inmates were being given rations of chewing tobacco. To the young inspector this appeared to be a good means of allowing a "gentle stimulant" to men who were deprived of normal sexual outlets, the companionship of friends, and even the right to speak. In February, 1846, he submitted a report to his fellow board members advocating such a concession, and secured its

[33] Ms. diary of John Bigelow, New York Public Library, entries of April 20 and May 11, 1845; Margaret Clapp, *Forgotten First Citizen: John Bigelow* (Boston: Little, Brown, 1947), pp. 3–39, 41; John Bigelow, *Retrospections of an Active Life* (New York: Baker & Taylor, 1909–1913), Vol. I, pp. 67–68.

[34] See DA, 69th Session (1846), Vol. IV, No. 139, p. 105, and 70th Session (1847), Vol. VI, No. 160, p. 1, Table 3, and p. 5. It should be stressed that the trend was steadily, but not precipitously, downward. The general decline of lashing from 1843 through 1848 is shown by the statistics given in DA, 71st Session (1848), Vol. I, No. 10, p. 17.

[35] Bigelow diary, entry of March 15, 1846.

approval. "It was highly complimented," he confided to his diary, "& it will be the source of great happiness to the poor devils."[36]

Actively sympathizing with the changes Eliza Farnham was putting into effect in the woman's prison, Bigelow was soon able to help the matron in a way highly displeasing to some Sing Sing staff members who favored humane methods but were strongly opposed to what they regarded as radical ideas, especially phrenological ones. Most prominent among these moderates was the prison chaplain, John Luckey. By the middle of 1846, internal bickering at the penitentiary had produced a crisis which foreshadowed the eventual collapse of the reform administration less than two years later.

It is not surprising that Mrs. Farnham and Luckey failed to get along with one another, for the matron's background was not calculated to promote friendship with clergymen. She had been brought up by a stepmother who was a self-professed atheist, and her childhood reading included a number of books by freethinkers. Later, as a student at a Quaker boarding school, she had been unenthusiastic about meetings she had attended, recalling in later years the "musty moralities," "religious saws," and "ancient truisms" which were "alternately aired, in dolorous sing-song tones." After being reunited with other members of her family who had been reared in religiously orthodox surroundings, she had shocked them with her lack of faith.[37] She appears to have become more moderate in her views over the years; as matron, for instance, she had a group of religious singers perform at the prison and wrote approvingly to a friend about the effects produced by such songs as "My Mother's Bible," sung in "half-tremulous tones."[38] On the other hand, she objected to "forcing theology on the prisoners," and opposed the efforts of an assistant who was bent upon converting Catholic convicts to Protestantism.[39] Her espousal of phreno-

[36] DS, 70th Session (1847), Vol. I, No. 5, pp. 10–11, 16–22; Bigelow diary, entries of Feb. 6 and 10, 1846.

[37] Farnham, *Eliza Woodson*, pp. 74, 236–246, 311–314, 349–350; see also the matron's *Life in Prairie Land*, pp. 233–235.

[38] New York *Tribune*, April 22, 1845.

[39] Kirby, *op. cit.*, p. 199.

logical doctrines which seemed at variance with biblical concepts of free will and moral responsibility, as well as her encouragement of novel-reading among the inmates under her
charge, were not popular with the Methodist chaplain and his
wife, Dinah. It is clear from Mrs. Farnham's correspondence
with Bigelow that by December, 1845, if not sooner, she and the
Luckey family were on bad terms.[40]

Bigelow became involved in the Luckey–Farnham dispute by
helping the matron to publish an American edition of some
writings on criminal behavior by Marmaduke B. Sampson, an
English phrenologist. Among other things, he gave her permission to have an artist visit Sing Sing to make outline drawings of convict head-formations for inclusion in the volume.
Much to Luckey's disgust, the chaplain's office was selected to
be the studio for this effort.[41] When the book was finally published under the title *Rationale of Crime*, neither the deterministic outlook of Sampson nor the editorial comments of Mrs.
Farnham could be approved by the Methodist parson. Although
the matron hedged a bit on the problem of moral responsibility,
asserting that "the possession of a faculty in any degree implies
some capacity to use it," she made it clear that she had a rela-
tivistic conception of guilt.[42] Not surprisingly, the work met a
storm of denunciation by such newspapers as Webb's *Courier
and Enquirer* and the New York *Observer*. "They say it destroys
accountability," wrote Bigelow contemptuously. "Let them
slide."[43]

In addition to broadcasting her skepticism about free will,
Mrs. Farnham also encroached upon the prison library, which
had previously been Luckey's preserve. Nobody had defended
the inmate's right to read more vigorously than the chaplain, but
this advocacy did not extend to the novels of Dickens, Combe's
Constitution of Man, and such works as Orson Fowler's
Amativeness: or, Evils and Remedies of Excessive and Perverted

[40] Farnham to Bigelow, Dec. 28, 1845, Bigelow Papers.
[41] Clapp, *op. cit.*, p. 42; Farnham to Bigelow, Aug. 6, 1846, Bigelow
Papers; New York *Sun*, Sept. 23, 1846.
[42] Sampson, *op. cit.*, p. 15 and *passim*.
[43] Bigelow diary, entry of Nov. 17, 1845.

Sexuality. Deeming these books potentially harmful to the minds of the convicts, he tried to prevent them from being kept in the library, against the matron's stalwart opposition.[44] By July, 1846, the situation had become so bad that either Mrs. Farnham or the chaplain had to go. In a showdown before the board of inspectors the position of the former prevailed, and Luckey was relieved of his job.[45]

Neither Luckey nor his supporters accepted this outcome without a fight. The New York *Sun* took up the chaplain's defense, praising him as "a much esteemed Methodist Clergyman" and charging that he "was dismissed from his position simply because he exercised his judgment in excluding immoral and irreligious books from the cells of the prisoners." Mrs. Farnham's phrenological doctrines, it was alleged, were designed to keep the inmates subdued "by gratifying the very tastes which brought them under her charge."[46] Bigelow's support of the matron brought down upon him bitter letters from defenders of Luckey, one of them reminding him that his "constitutional power as Inquisitor" did not extend beyond the limits of Sing Sing.[47] Luckey himself took his case to the public through the press, telling of "innumerable petty annoyances and embarrassments" to which he had been subjected and maintaining the unjustifiability of his dismissal through the "connivance of a majority of the Board of Inspectors."[48] When Matthew Gordon, a young graduate of Union Theological Seminary in New York City, was appointed to take the chaplaincy, it was charged that he disbelieved in the divinity of Christ.[49]

When the New York Prison Association sent an inspection team to Sing Sing later in the year, the whole affair became

[44] See especially New York *Sun*, Sept. 23, 1846.
[45] See Farnham to Bigelow, July 20, 1846, and to Rev. C. H. Halsey, Aug. 1, 1846, Bigelow Papers.
[46] New York *Sun*, Aug. 19 and 22, 1846.
[47] T. W. Niven to Bigelow, Aug. 8, 1846; B. W. Morse to Bigelow, Aug. 10, 1846; and Rev. C. H. Halsey to Bigelow, Aug. 18, 1846, Bigelow Papers.
[48] New York *Sun*, Sept. 23, 1846.
[49] Niven to Bigelow, Aug. 8, 1846, Bigelow Papers.

the subject of a special hearing. Dinah Luckey accused Mrs. Farnham of inculcating "a love for novel reading averse to labor," and asserted that the Scriptures had not been sufficiently emphasized under the matron's regime. She very sternly disapproved of discussions which she had heard among the inmates on the subject of women's clothing fashions. The Luckey group also protested the reading of *Nicholas Nickleby* and *A Christmas Carol* to the convicts, even though defenders of Mrs. Farnham gravely assured the investigators that these stories had been bowdlerized before the prisoners had heard them. It was also charged that the matron had made personal use of state property, that she had unlawfully employed inmates to work for herself and her family, and that she was capricious and unjust in her administration of discipline.[50]

The Prison Association took no action on these complaints. In following this course it incurred the animosity of Luckey's supporters and became identified with the views of the matron and Bigelow. The ex-chaplain made public his loss of confidence in the organization and said that he would hereafter go directly to Albany with his complaints. The N.Y.P.A. was also castigated by Alexander Wells, who was once more happy to censure a Democratic prison administration, even one espousing policies diametrically opposed to those practiced by the regime he had condemned before. The Prison Association, he charged, was but the complaisant tool of Mrs. Farnham and John W. Edmonds.[51] Meanwhile, the matron's edition of Sampson's writings continued to come under public attack despite the pleas of such men as Horace Greeley that it be given a fair hearing. If its doctrines were invalid, the New York *Tribune* urged, they should be rejected "dispassionately and under the influence of reason, not in a tempest of obloquy and passion."[52]

Soon trouble was brewing again at Sing Sing. The new chaplain, Gordon, quickly aligned himself with the Farnham–Bigelow group, and before long he was having differences with

---

[50] DA, 70th Session (1847), Vol. VIII, No. 255, Part 2, pp. 50, 52, 57.
[51] *Ibid.*, pp. 64–65; DS, 70th Session (1847), Vol. I, No. 5, pp. 90–91.
[52] New York *Tribune*, Nov. 11, 1846.

Harman Eldridge, who had replaced Lynds as principal keeper in 1844. Like Luckey, Eldridge was a moderate. Although he had been attacked in the press on one occasion for alleged cruelty, he had been exonerated by Edmonds, and even Mrs. Farnham had called him a man of "humanity and good judgment."[53] His association with the Auburn system, however, stretched back as far as 1826, when Gershom Powers had singled him out as an especially valuable keeper at the Cayuga County institution, and his long habituation to old ways hardly fitted him to sympathize with ideas as advanced as those held by the Farnham group.[54] The precise grounds of his difficulty with Gordon are not clear, but it is possible that he was disgruntled over the firing of Luckey and critical of the new chaplain's youth and inexperience. His position forced him to work closely with whoever occupied the chaplaincy, which had been placed under his general supervision by a law passed several years before.[55]

Whatever the causes, the dispute between the chaplain and the principal keeper was clearly in evidence by early 1847, and Mrs. Farnham was just as clearly embroiled in it. In February, she carried the matter to Bigelow, informing him that a conspiracy was under way between Eldridge and an assistant matron whom Mrs. Farnham described as a "most unscrupulous and . . . accomplished liar."[56] A short period of administrative infighting was followed by the principal keeper's resignation, although there was dissension among the inspectors and a countermove to fire Gordon. Bigelow, of course, threw his weight in favor of the chaplain, who with but nine months'

---

[53] Ibid., May 18 and 28, 1844; Sampson, op. cit., pp. xx–xxi. See also DA, 69th Session (1846), Vol. IV, No. 139, pp. 106–107; 70th Session (1847), Vol. VIII, No. 255, Part 2, pp. 74, 78–79; and New York Tribune, Feb. 21, 1845, characterizing Eldridge as "mild and kind," but "by no means deficient in firmness."

[54] Gershom Powers, A Brief Account of . . . the New-York State Prison at Auburn (Auburn, 1826), p. 76. On the conservatism which tempered Eldridge's views, see especially Edmonds' comments in DS, 69th Session (1846), Vol. IV, No. 120, p. 17.

[55] DA, 65th Session (1842), Vol. IV, No. 65, p. 106.

[56] Farnham to Bigelow, Feb. 20, 1847, Bigelow Papers. Italics are Mrs. Farnham's.

experience was soon elevated to the position Eldridge had vacated.[57]

The triumph of the Farnham–Bigelow group now seemed assured, but such was not the case. The victories over Luckey and Eldridge had been won only at the cost of alienating reformers whose humanitarianism was tempered with a distaste for phrenology and moral relativism. The extent of this alienation was clearly revealed in 1847 when the senate prison committee was authorized to conduct an investigation of the situation at Sing Sing.

This committee, composed of Frederick Backus, Saxton Smith, and Abraham Gridley, was far from subscribing to the views of Elam Lynds and Robert Wiltse. Only a year before, Backus and Gridley had helped to prepare a bill to restrict the amount of corporal punishment that could be administered to a convict. Backus himself wanted the flogging power completely removed.[58] The three men, however, issued a caustic report on the state of affairs at the Hudson Valley prison. The institution, they maintained, was "under a feeble state of discipline," and there was "nothing *masculine* in its composition." The rule of silence was almost completely disregarded when the inmates mingled, and was generally unobserved in the shops. The convicts were saucy and worked only reluctantly; as a result, the value of their labor was diminishing. The time was coming when the contractors might fail to renew their agreements with the prison and legislative appropriations would be required to keep it in operation. Indeed, it was over $29,000 in debt already. The committee believed that a mild philosophy could be implemented without impairing discipline, and cited recent happenings at the Charlestown penitentiary in Massachusetts to substantiate this claim. On the other hand, the senators de-

[57] Bigelow diary, entry of March 7, 1847: DS, 70th Session (1847), Vol. IV, No. 153, p. 4; DA, 71st Session (1848), Vol. I, No. 10, p. 15. The assembly document dates Gordon's accession to the principal keepership as May 14, which may be an error in view of the fact that Eldridge's resignation came in early March. Eldridge remained in penal work, becoming superintendent of the New York Workhouse (see DA, 73rd Session [1850], Vol. VIII, No. 198, pp. 50–53).

[58] DS, 69th Session (1846), Vol. IV, Nos. 120 and 121, *passim.*

clared in sarcastic words obviously aimed at Bigelow and Gordon, such an administration could not be maintained without
"the aid of full grown *men* to superintend its introduction, and
carry it into full operation."

The committee then assailed phrenology and its disciple,
Eliza Farnham. Referring sarcastically to the matron's activities
in examining convict head-formations, the members asserted
"that the State cannot afford to sustain so large an institution
for a course of experiments on so baseless a theory," and called
for a return to common sense and "old fashioned wisdom." The
next object of attack was the New York Prison Association,
which the legislators believed had been a pernicious influence at
Sing Sing. Members of the reform organization, animated by
an undue sympathy for felons, spied upon and annoyed keepers
who were trying to maintain a "mild but healthy discipline,"
and thus made the convicts impudent and hard to control.[59]

The fact that such a document could be written by penological moderates shows clearly the lacerated feelings that had been
produced by the squabbles of the preceding two years. The reform front had been split wide open. This could not help but
encourage conservatives who did not subscribe to the views of
either the moderates or the Farnham–Bigelow group and who
wanted to see a return to severe methods. Late in 1847, Amzi L.
Dean and John Fisher, who as inspectors at Sing Sing had been
outvoted by the Powers–Mace–Bigelow coalition, refused to
sign the annual report of the board and sent the legislature a
minority statement denying that reformation was the chief end
of penal treatment and subjecting Farnham and Gordon to
merciless criticism. In places their declaration was reminiscent
of the harsh philosophy expressed in 1825 by Hopkins, Tibbits,
and Allen when those men attacked the alleged softness of
Thomas Eddy's generation. In the words of Dean and Fisher:

Let prisons cease to be a terror to the depraved, and a warning to
others who may be disposed to wander from the highway where
travels [sic] the good and virtuous—let a phrensied sympathy excite
the passions and swell the bosom of community in soothing the

[59] *Ibid.*, 70th Session (1847), Vol. IV, No. 153, pp 4–6.

imaginary wrongs of criminals, and misguided philanthropy seek to mitigate the ills of mankind in converting our penitentiaries into schools for the instruction alone of its inmates—let the principle that punishment is no part of our prison system, and moral suasion and reformation obtain the ascendancy over the calm judicious observance of an "enlightened policy"—a policy that would be a terror to the depraved and evil doers, and terrify the youthful rogue, and prevent a continual drain upon the treasury for the support of those who [sic] the taxpayers are under no obligation and should not be compelled to support, and then the period will arrive when insurrection, incendiarism, robbery, and all the evils most fatal to society and detrimental to law and order, will reign supreme.[60]

Under severe attack from within the prison and without, the experiments of such leaders as Mrs. Farnham and Bigelow soon came to an end. The reform tempo slowed in November, 1847, when the matron restored the silent rule at the women's prison. Three new inmates had escaped, and she felt it advisable to reaffirm the old regulation. In addition, she reluctantly suspended other personal freedoms and confined the convicts to closed rooms when they were not working. An added retrogression was the discontinuance of the morning lectures which had previously been given to the women, a step necessitated by the consummation of a contract to employ the inmates in button-making.[61]

The heaviest blow of all, however, was undoubtedly Bigelow's failure to secure another term on the board of inspectors. A new state constitution drawn up in 1846 had made such posts elective rather than appointive. Legislation passed in 1847 stipulated that the voters were to choose three men to supervise the entire New York penal system and that the terms of office were to be staggered so that a vacancy would occur each year. When Bigelow tried to secure a Democratic nomination to become a member of the new group, he was defeated, possibly because of his Free-Soil leanings.[62] Already facing serious dis-

---

[60] DS, 71st Session (1848), Vol. I, No. 17, pp. 2–5.

[61] Ibid., Vol. I, No. 10, pp. 74–75, 80–81.

[62] Laws of the State of New-York, Passed at the Seventieth Session of the Legislature . . . 1847 (Albany, 1847), p. 396; Clapp, Forgotten First Citizen, p. 44.

couragements, Mrs. Farnham clearly had little future at Sing Sing with her chief supporter on the way out, and left the penitentiary early in 1848. Soon she was in Boston, helping Samuel Gridley Howe care for such handicapped patients as the celebrated Laura Bridgman at the Perkins Institution and Asylum for the Blind.[63] The great reform period at Sing Sing was coming to an end.

Despite disagreements and setbacks, however, moderates and radicals alike could find grounds for satisfaction in one final achievement capping the humanitarian trend that had been in existence since the scandals of 1839. Late in 1847, at the very end of the reform cycle, the state legislature abolished flogging in the prisons of New York. Although public sentiment had been growing against this form of punishment throughout the decade, its final abandonment came about in large measure because of a highly controversial whipping that occurred at Auburn in January, 1846, followed by the death of the inmate who suffered it, a felon named Charles Plumb.

Plumb had earned his flogging by behaving in an undeniably bad manner. He had emptied his night tub down the stairs of a cellblock, smashed two windows, and littered a workshop with containers of ink, turpentine, paint, oil, and varnish, besides threatening to "split the brains out" of a keeper who attempted to pacify him. After being punished for this conduct, he tore up his Bible, a library book, and his bed clothing. It was not clear that his death shortly thereafter was directly attributable to the lashing he received, and the official cause was stated to be "bilious intermitting fever." Nevertheless, local citizens became deeply aroused because of the incident, and by March the principal keeper, Hiram Rathbun, had been forced out of his job. An attempt by reformers to end flogging once and for all by legislative proscription, however, failed of adoption, much to the gratification of the Auburn inspectors. Corporal punish-

[63] See Eliza Robbins to Samuel Gridley Howe, Feb. 20, 1848, Letters in Blindiana Library, 1848–1849, No. 18, Perkins School for the Blind, Watertown, Mass.; Farnham to Bigelow, June 29, 1848, Bigelow Papers; New York *Tribune*, Dec. 16, 1864; Maud H. Elliott and Florence H. Hall, *Laura Bridgman: Dr. Howe's Famous Pupil and What He Taught Her* (Boston: Little, Brown, 1903), pp. 232–233.

ment, they stubbornly insisted, was necessary if a proper state of discipline was to be maintained.[64]

But the fight against the whip continued. "There is no degradation like the lash," asserted an article in the *Democratic Review*. "We confess that if we believed it to be indispensable, we should be prepared to abandon the whole system. . . . The other improvements in our prison discipline are overshadowed, and sink into comparative insignificance, before this towering atrocity."[65] Two special reports were submitted to the state senate on the matter of corporal punishment, one favoring legal restrictions on flogging and the other advocating outright prohibition.[66] The New York *Tribune*, which had called for the abolition of whipping at the time of the Plumb scandal, reiterated its feelings on this score early in 1847 in the course of an article praising the virtual abandonment of flogging at Sing Sing.[67] Later in the year the assembly committee on prisons rejected the entire theory of deterrence, criticized the use of the lash, and envisioned a time when penitentiaries would become "great MORAL HOSPITALS, where the State, like a good Samaritan, binds up the wounds and heals the maladies which *sin* and *ignorance* have engendered."[68] Meanwhile, dissension among the inspectors at Auburn over the merits of whipping had been revealed when Luman Sherwood, a member of the board, came out against the "cat."[69]

As the 1847 session of the legislature neared its close, the lawmakers responded to such pressures by enacting a lengthy and detailed statute which abolished flogging and formally sanctioned some of the innovations that had been taking place in the state prisons. Thenceforth, blows could be inflicted upon inmates only "in self-defence or to suppress a revolt of insurrec-

[64] DA, 69th Session (1846), Vol. III, No. 83, *passim*, and 75th Session (1852), Vol. I, No. 20, pp. 7, 74; DS, 70th Session (1847), Vol. I, No. 11, pp. 2–3.

[65] Anonymous, "Prison Discipline," *op. cit.*, p. 138.

[66] DS, 69th Session (1846), Vol. IV, Nos. 120 and 121, *passim*.

[67] New York *Tribune*, Feb. 4, 1846, and Feb. 25, 1847.

[68] DA, 75th Session (1847), Vol. VIII, No. 241, *passim*. Italics and capital letters are as given.

[69] DS, 70th Session (1847), Vol. I, No. 12, p. 11.

tion." Unusual punishment, when deemed necessary, should consist of solitary confinement on stinted rations. The act directed Sing Sing, Auburn, and Clinton prisons to erect special cells for such contingencies, and also stipulated that convicts suffering from insanity were to be removed to the state asylum at Utica. Penitentiary administrators were ordered to respect inmate property by taking care to return upon discharge all money and other articles which had been received from a convict at the beginning of his sentence. In addition, the going-away allotment was to be increased by three cents for each mile between the penitentiary and the home or place of conviction of a released offender. In another move the legislators directed the prisons to hire part-time instructors for the education of inmates and authorized annual grants of $100 to each institution for the purchase of library books, maps, and writing supplies.[70]

This act would have been a milestone in the history of correctional policy in New York had it done nothing more than abolish the whip. In addition, it consolidated some of the gains that reformers had made in the prison since the beginning of the decade. On the other hand, its significance should not be overestimated. In the first place, it reflected the recent past more than it foreshadowed the immediate future. Most of the officials who took over the penitentiaries in the remainder of the ante-bellum period were men whose outlook differed materially from that of Seymour, Edmonds, Farnham, and Bigelow, and who could find ways to circumvent the law when it suited their purposes to do so. The act of 1847 was also of limited usefulness as far as rehabilitation was concerned, even though it represented an improvement over the previous situation. The addition of five part-time teachers under its provisions was an inadequate answer to the educational needs of inmates in three (or if the women's penitentiary is counted separately, four) different institutions. The sum of $100 per year allotted to each prison for educational supplies was also manifestly small; in

<hr>

[70] *Laws*, 70th Session (1847), pp. 600-608.

the case of Sing Sing, with approximately one thousand inmates, it amounted to about ten cents per convict.

In short, the statute passed in 1847 was the last noteworthy
accomplishment of a reform era that was about to end. Although short in duration, this period was vital and significant.
For the greater part of a decade, the former emphasis upon
deterrence and repression had given way to faith in the reformability of the offender and concern for his essential dignity as a
human being. In the attempt to bring out the best in prisoners,
resort had been made to kindness rather than to intimidation.
The use of the lash had been curtailed and finally abolished.
The convict's isolation from society had been partially alleviated
by allowing him to read books, to write and receive letters, and
to have occasional visitors from the outside world. An energetic
reform group, the New York Prison Association, had been
founded to spread new ideas, to investigate improper penal conditions, and to assist ex-convicts who needed jobs, lodgings,
clothing, and advice.

Eventually, matters progressed too far and too rapidly to suit
reformers whose humanitarianism was tempered by a fear of
becoming too lenient with offenders and a distaste for moral
relativism. New theories stressing the physical and environmental basis for crime seemed at variance with traditional concepts
of guilt and personal accountability. When such persons as Eliza
Farnham attained positions of leadership, a struggle ensued,
ending in bitterness and recrimination among reformers who
shared a common desire to rehabilitate but who disagreed irrevocably about what this goal meant and how it could best be
achieved. By 1848, this factionalism had produced wounds that
would be slow to heal.

Had the reform movement of the 1840's continued on into
the decades that followed, the Auburn system might have come
to an end in the mid-nineteenth century. As it was, the system
had been modified by 1847, but its essential features remained.
With the exception of the unsuccessful attempt to introduce
communication under Mrs. Farnham at the women's prison,
nothing had been done to alter the rule of silence. The labor

law of 1842 had shaken the industrial program, but the old ideal of the self-sustaining penal system had not yet been discarded. The lockstep, the stripes, the cramped and lonely cells, the monotonous and dehumanizing routine were all present, and remained as part of the ordeal to be faced by the ordinary adult offender while the state progressed in its treatment of misdemeanants, first-term convicts, and juvenile delinquents. The lash was gone, but equally painful instruments of coercion could be, and were, substituted in its place. If a new order was to be achieved, much remained to be accomplished. That this was not to be done in the near future, however, can be observed by taking a brief glance at the penological backwater of the 1850's.*

* This is precisely what Lewis does in the following chapter of his book. —Eds.

REFLECTIONS
ON HANGING

Arthur Koestler

In 1966, the United States, a country long committed to the death penalty, executed but one unfortunate victim; and, in the remaining three years of the decade, there were only two more executions. This is in happy contrast to the 199 prisoners put to death in 1935. The United States is not alone in evincing this trend. England, the home of the "Bloody Code," with more than two hundred crimes punishable by death as late as the first decades of the nineteenth century, declared a five-year moratorium on hanging in 1964. And, in 1969, when the moratorium expired, the ban was made a permanent one. During the first full year of the British experience, there was a decline in the homicide rate, rather than the steep increase prophesied by the police and by some latter-day judicial heirs of Lord Chancellor Jeffreys, who, in 1685, sent over three hundred men and women to the gallows during the mockery of justice known as the Bloody Assizes of Winchester.

In the United States, what arguments have proved sufficiently convincing to cause traditionally punitive legislators to outlaw the death penalty in thirteen states, to cause judges in other jurisdic-

Source: Arthur Koestler, *Reflections on Hanging* (New York: The Macmillan Company, 1957), pp. 137–170. Copyright © 1957 by The Macmillan Company. Reprinted by permission of the publisher.

tions to impose alternative terms of imprisonment, and to cause governors in several states to announce publicly their determination that no judgment of death would be executed during their administrations? And, indeed, what impelled the voters of Oregon to end the death penalty in that state by an overwhelming popular referendum, and what has caused the interviewees of the national opinion polls to switch from retention to abolition of capital punishment in the last decade?

One thing is certain. The energetic, well-organized campaign carried on by the American League to Abolish Capital Punishment and its affiliated state committees, strongly supported by the Quakers and almost every major religious denomination, has had major impact. Augmenting the League's efforts, the almost unanimous abolition consensus among criminologists has insured a continuous flow of graduates from our universities who are strongly opposed to the death penalty. More specifically, however, both bench and bar, legislators and public have responded to the well-documented evidence that in all too many cases justice has miscarried and innocent men have been sentenced to death, having, in some cases, been "hanged in error." Attention, too, has more recently been focused on the discriminatory aspects of capital punishment, with Negroes comprising more than 50 per cent of all victims since 1930. The evidence has been compelling that the indigent, defended by court-appointed counsel, were far more likely to be convicted and executed than the more fortunate defendants who were able to retain private counsel.

The moral arguments, questioning the right of the state to take human life as a punishment for crime, although ably stated by very prominent thinkers, such as Albert Camus, Archbishop Bernard Sheil, Albert Schweitzer, and Martin Buber, did not so much win new adherents as reinforce the thinking of those men already convinced of the immorality of public murder. Far more persuasive to those in decision-making positions have been the repeated demonstrations that the death penalty is no more effective a deterrent than are other more socially acceptable methods of dealing with offenders; that abolition states enjoy on the whole lower homicide rates than death-penalty states (and that the lives of police and prison officers are somewhat safer therein); and that eliminating the death penalty speeds up trials, does away with time-consuming appeals and commutation-pardon hearings, and greatly reduces the costs of criminal justice administration.

Arthur Koestler, one of the great social critics of our time, perhaps best known for his novel and play, *Darkness at Noon*, a penetrating study of the minds of old Bolsheviks who confessed during the Stalinist terror to crimes that they had not committed, has raised an eloquent voice in the long fight to end the anachronism of hanging in England. His *Reflections on Hanging*, two chapters of which are here reproduced, has provided ammunition for abolitionists on both sides of the Atlantic.

The Alternative to Hanging

The Nightmare

Dostoievsky says somewhere that if in the last moment before being executed, a man, however brave, were given the alternative of spending the rest of his days on the top of a bare rock with only enough space to sit on it, he would choose it with relief. There is indeed a Kafkaesque horror attached to an execution, which goes beyond the mere fear of death or pain or indignity. It is connected not with the brutality but with the macabre, cold-blooded politeness of the ceremony, in which the person whose neck is going to be broken is supposed to collaborate in a nice, sensible manner, as if it were a matter of a minor surgical operation. It is symbolized in the ceremonial handshake with the executioner; it is present in the delinquent's knowledge that in the embarrassed stares of the officials he is already mirrored as a dead man with a blue face and ruptured vertebrae; and that what for him is the final, violent termination of life is for them merely an unpleasant duty, followed by a sigh of relief and a plate of bacon and eggs. The Romans deprived their victim of the dignity of death by throwing him to the beasts in the arena with a clown's mask attached to his face; we put a white cap over his head, and if the victim is a woman she is made to put on waterproof underwear on the morning of the execution.[1]

[1] Letter to *The Lancet* by a medical practitioner, Aug. 20, 1955.

Officialdom wishes to make us believe that the operation itself is always quick and expeditious. This is not true. The truth is that some prisoners struggle both in the condemned cell and under the noose, that some have to be carried tied to a chair, others dragged to the trap, limp, bowels open, arms pinioned to the back, like animals; and that still other things happen which should only happen in nightmare dreams. In the Commons debate of 1948, the then Mr. Beverley Baxter mentioned one case which the Home Office did not succeed in hushing up, the case of a sick woman of twenty-eight whose insides fell out before she vanished through the trap. Everybody who took part in that scene suffered some damage to their nervous system. The executioner, Ellis, attempted suicide a few weeks later. The Governor of Holloway, Dr. Morton, was described a few days later by a visiting magistrate: "I think I have never seen a person look so changed in appearance by mental suffering as the Governor appeared to me to be." The prison chaplain, the Rev. Glanville Murray, said of the scene of the execution: "When we were all gathered together there, it seemed utterly impossible to believe what we were there to do. . . . My God, the impulse to rush in and save her by force was almost too strong for me." When it was over, the Deputy Governor of Holloway, Miss Cronin, who was "not at all a sensitive or easily moved person," remarked of the hanged woman: "I think if she had been spared she could have become a very good woman."[2]

These nightmare scenes are not exceptional. When Pierrepoint, the hangman, was asked by the Royal Commission, "You must in so many executions have had things go wrong occasionally?" he had at first lied: "Never." Pressed further whether he had had any "awkward moments," he climbed down and said that he had had one awkward moment "with a foreign spy who had to be carried to the gallows strapped to a chair." Pressed even further, he said he had "probably three more" such cases "like a faint at the last minute or something like that, but it

[2] Statement by Miss Margery Fry to the Royal Commission on Capital Punishment (1949–53). Minutes of evidence, pp. 282, 283. Hereinafter referred to as R.C.M.

has not been anything to speak about."³ It may not be much for Pierrepoint to speak about, but it should be enough for the nation to think about. For if it is proper that these things should be done in its name, then it is proper that it should hear about them.

The horror of the operation remains even if there is no struggle or dementedness in the condemned cell. The preparations on the previous day when executioner and assistant discreetly take the measure and weight of the victim to determine the length of the drop; the dress rehearsal of dropping a stuffed sack of the same weight to make sure that the estimated length of rope will neither strangle the victim too slowly nor tear his head off; the jolly domino game in the condemned cell while the preparations go on and the hour draws nearer; the stratagems to make him sit with his back to the door through which the executioner will enter; the brisk, businesslike opening of that door, the pinioning of the hands behind the back and the walking or dragging him in solemn procession to the execution shed and on to the white chalk mark on the trap; the tying of his legs while two officers stand at his sides on planks thrown across the trap, to hold him up; the fixing of the white cap and the noose with its sliding brass ring—in a few years' time, with God's help, all this will appear as unthinkable as drawing, quartering and pressing to death appear to us today.

The Royal Commissioners were preoccupied with the question how long the penultimate act of the nightmare took, from the entering of the executioner to the drop. Mr. Pierrepoint, always an optimist, answered "the longest time" was twenty to twenty-five seconds. The commissioners, no doubt acquainted with the secret Home Office instructions how to answer suchlike questions, were somewhat skeptical and insisted on witnessing a mock execution. The result apparently confirmed their skepticism:

Q. Did not today's execution take a little longer than usual? —A. That was not really an execution; the atmosphere was not there; and we had no assistant.

³ R.C.M., 8402–10. (The numbers refer to paragraphs, unless preceded by "p." or "pp." referring to pages.)

Q. What do you mean by saying that the atmosphere was not there?—*A.* You gentlemen there made the atmosphere different. We had no assistant executioner for another thing. You have not got the man there to perform on, you have to imagine a bit, and it all upsets your calculations a little bit. That this morning was very slow.

Q. As compared with the real thing?—*A.* Yes.

Q. Do you wear anything special in the way of clothing, like gloves?—*A.* No, just as we are.[4]

Q. . . . So it really means that you go into the cell, you tie up the man's hands, and you tie them up quicker than you did the officer this morning?—*A.* Yes.

Q. But he was much more willing to be tied?—*A.* He was not as willing, believe me.

Q. I should have thought he would have been more willing? —*A.* I should have thought so too, but he was not.

Q. So that took longer than usual, because he was unwilling? —*A.* Yes.[5]

As for the final surgical act itself, the Home Office states that "as now carried out, execution by hanging can be regarded as speedy and certain." The emphasis on "now" refers to the improved technique of a drop of variable length, and of the sliding ring which is supposed to hold the knot of the noose in its place under the left jaw. Before this innovation, the agony of slow suffocation without loss of consciousness could last up to twenty minutes, not to mention various forms of mutilation and lacerations, jaws torn off by hitting the edge of the trap, gashes torn in the neck, heads partly or entirely torn off, and people being hanged twice or even three times in succession. All that, we are told, are matters of the past; the new method is infallible; it causes instantaneous loss of consciousness by "a physical shock of extreme violence."[6] As a result of the improved method, the first, second and third cervical vertebrae are fractured or dislocated; the spinal cord is crushed or lacerated or torn from the brain stem, and if the initial shock is not fatal, the process is completed by strangulation. There is no chance, we are told, "of

4 R.C.M., 8477–80.   5 R.C.M., 8483–86.
6 Royal Commission Report on Capital Punishment (1949–53), 732.
Hereinafter referred to as R.C.R.

a later recovery of consciousness since breathing is no longer possible. The heart may continue to beat up to twenty minutes, but this is a purely automatic function."[7]

Let us hope that this is true, or at least true in the majority of cases; though one is entitled to a certain skepticism regarding the infallibility of the improved method from the medical point of view, particularly where the extremely complex neurological problem of consciousness, and the loss thereof, are concerned. The *Encyclopaedia Britannica*, 1955 edition, which was published after the Royal Commission's investigations, expresses this skepticism in an indirect way:

> *It is said* that the dislocation of the vertebrae causes immediate unconsciousness . . . the heart may continue to beat for up to twenty minutes but this is *thought to be* a purely automatic function.[8] (Italics mine.)

The fact is: we do not know for certain. A violent shock of this type is as a rule, but not always, followed by instantaneous unconsciousness. One classic example to the contrary is the so-called crowbar case, known to all neurologists and surgeons —a laborer whose brain was pierced from crown to jaw by a two-inch crowbar, and who walked, fully conscious, for medical help with the crowbar inside his brain.

A second reason for being skeptical about official assurances regarding the swift and painless character of the operation is that, like any other operation, the efficacy of breaking a neck depends entirely on the skill of the surgeon. On this point we can rely on the firsthand evidence of Pierrepoint. Questioned about the Scottish method of hanging which differs from the English, Pierrepoint said:

> The Scottish [method] is very good, but I think it is very, very old, antediluvian. It is about time it was altered in Scotland.
> Q. What is the difference?—A. The apparatus is very old . . .
> Q. So it is much less exact?—A. It is not perfect. It is all right if you understand the job and you can work these things out, but a stranger can soon make a blunder of it.

[7] R.C.R., 714.
[8] *Encyclopaedia Britannica*, Vol. XI (1955), p. 151.

Q. It is a question of getting new apparatus?—A. They want it badly in Scotland, badly, but their ideas are very good without that. . . .

Pierrepoint was then questioned on the English method:

Q. The knot, as you showed us this morning, must always be under the angle of the left jaw?—A. Yes.

Q. That is very important, is it?—A. Very important.

Q. Why is it very important?—A. If you had the same knot on the right-hand side it comes back behind the neck, and throws the neck forward, which would make a strangulation. If you put it on the left-hand side it finishes up in front and throws the chin back and breaks the spinal cord.

Q. It depends on where he is standing on the trap?—A. No, I do not think so. The knot is the secret of it, really. We have to put it on the left lower jaw and if we have it on that side, when he falls it finishes under the chin and throws the chin back; but if the knot is on the right-hand side, it would finish up behind his neck and throw his neck forward which would be strangulation. He might live on the rope a quarter of an hour then.[9]

In one case, at least, we have direct evidence of a bungled execution, quite recently, after introduction of the improved technique: in case "L 1942" the report of the Coroner on a Pentonville hanging contains the significant words "noose slipped on jaw."[10]

When the operation is over, the victim is buried within the prison walls. Unlike in America, the body is not handed over to the relatives, for a technical reason which sums up the obscene ignominy of the whole thing: in the words of the Royal Commission Report, "hanging . . . leaves the body with the neck elongated."[11]

Whereas in spite of all this evidence British belief in the "humaneness" of hanging remains unshaken, America takes a more realistic view. The Canadian Joint Committee recommended last year the substitution of electrocution for hanging, after the Canadian official executioner had explained in a statement that in "95 per cent to 98 per cent of cases" death was instantaneous,

9 R.C.M., 8412–13, 8417–18, and 8428–31.
10 R.C.M., p. 627.   11 R.C.R., 732.

caused by the breaking of the spinal vertebrae, but in the remaining cases it was caused by strangling. Several American states switched to electrocution or lethal gas precisely because of the haphazardness of hanging. Thus, for instance, the Attorney General of Oregon stated in his written answer to the British Royal Commissioner's questionnaire:

In 1937, lethal gas became the means of executing the death penalty. . . . In the use of the prior method . . . which was hanging, there were mishaps, two of which were horrible.[12]

If hanging is a modern form of the godly butchery, the alternatives of electrocution or the gas chamber are no better, and possibly worse, because of the long and ghastly preliminaries. Regarding electrocution, the following account of the procedure, practiced in the state of Washington, appears in the Royal Commission Report:

The execution takes place at 10 A.M. At midnight on the preceding night the condemned man is taken from the condemned cell block to a cell adjoining the electrocution chamber. About 5.30 A.M. the top of his head and the calf of one leg are shaved to afford direct contact with the electrodes. (The prisoner is usually handcuffed during this operation to prevent him from seizing the razor.) At 7.15 A.M. the death warrant is read to him and about 10 o'clock he is taken to the electrocution chamber. Five witnesses are present (including representatives of the press) and two doctors —the prison medical officer and the city coroner. The witnesses watch the execution through a grille or dark glass and cannot be seen by the prisoner. Three officers strap the condemned man to the chair, tying him around the waist, legs and wrists. A mask is placed over his face and the electrodes are attached to his head and legs. As soon as this operation is completed (about two minutes after he has left the cell) the signal is given and the switch is pulled by the electrician; the current is left on for two minutes, during which there is alternation of two or more different voltages. When it is switched off, the body slumps forward in the chair. The prisoner does not make any sound when the current is turned on, and unconsciousness is apparently instantaneous. He is not, however, pronounced dead for some minutes after the current is dis-

[12] R.C.M., p. 788.

connected. The leg is sometimes slightly burned, but the body is not otherwise marked or mutilated.[13]

The preparations for gassing are even more ghoulish. The following description in the Royal Commission Report of the procedure in North Carolina is typical:

A chamber or room, when the doors are closed, is hermetically sealed to prevent leakage of cyanide gas. This room contains two observation windows. One window is for observation by the required witnesses and the other for officials required to be present at the execution. . . . In this room is a wooden chair with leather straps for strapping the prisoner's arms, legs and across the abdomen to the chair. In the seat of this chair is a trap door electrically controlled which releases the cyanide pellets.

Prior to the execution all equipment is double checked and a pound of sodium cyanide pellets is placed in the trap in the seat of the chair. Twenty minutes before execution three pints of U.S.P. sulphuric acid and six pints of water are carefully mixed in a lead container. The container is covered with a lid of similar material and is placed under the chair in a position to receive the pellets when dropped.

There are two copper pipes adjacent to the chair which lead under the floor outside the physician's stand. At the end of the pipe in the chamber is a rubber hose which is to be connected to the head of a Bowles stethoscope strapped to the prisoner's chest. Attached to the other end of the copper pipes at the physician's stand are the earpieces of a stethoscope for determining the time of the prisoner's death.

The prisoner has been previously prepared in his cell in this manner: clothing removed, with the exception of shorts; the head of a Bowles stethoscope strapped over the apex of the heart with broad strips of adhesive.

After the above preparations the prisoner walks to the execution chamber preceded by the chaplain and followed by the warden or one of his deputies. He is then strapped in the chair under the supervision of the warden or deputy; a leather mask applied to the face; the stethoscope head connected with aforementioned tube; the chaplain's prayers completed and all officials leave the chamber. The last person leaving the chamber quickly removes the cover

[13] R.C.R., 717.

from the acid container. The doors to the chamber and ante-room are quickly closed and the pellets dropped in the acid by the electrically controlled switch. . . .

When this method was first employed, medical opinion was not unanimous about it; there were some who thought that the gas had a suffocating effect which would cause acute distress, if not actual pain, before the prisoner became unconscious. It seems to be now generally agreed that unconsciousness ensues very rapidly.[14]

The report adds: "No sedatives, narcotics or any other drugs are administered to the prisoner before execution."

The alternative to capital punishment is imprisonment "for life." This really means imprisonment for a length of period determined by the demands of public safety and the rehabilitation of the prisoner.

The arguments most often heard against this alternative can be classified as follows: (a) It is *unsafe*. The murderer serving a life sentence is usually let out after a number of years and may commit another murder. (b) To keep a murderer, who cannot be reformed, in prison to the end of his life is *more cruel* than a quick death. (c) Imprisonment is *not cruel enough*; modern prisons pamper the criminal instead of punishing him —plus the subsidiary arguments about the burden to the taxpayer, the strain on prison wardens, the danger of escape.

Murderers as a Class

That it would be *unsafe* to let murderers live is an argument in which many well-meaning people believe, though they loathe the idea of hanging and would rather do away with it. But the public's idea of the murderer is modeled on exceptional and untypical cases (Heath, Haig, Crippen, Christie), which receive the widest publicity and are part of the national folklore. The murderer is either thought of as a homicidal maniac, or a hardened criminal, or a monster planning the "perfect murder." But these popular figures who impress themselves on the public

[14] *Ibid.*, 720 and 722.

imagination are no more typical of murderers as a class than Lawrence of Arabia was of British subalterns as a class.

The figures . . . show that during the fifty years 1900–49 only in one out of twelve cases was the murderer found so dangerous for public safety or his crime so "unpardonable" that he was executed—that means only 8 per cent of the total. In Scotland, the proportion was even lower: 4 per cent. Every analysis of the motive and circumstances under which the crime was committed shows the extreme rarity of the cold-blooded type of murder. Half a century ago, Sir John Macdonell, Master of the Supreme Court, analyzed the criminal statistics from 1886 to 1905 and found the following result: 90 per cent of the murders were committed by men, and nearly two-thirds of their victims were their wives, mistresses or sweethearts. The peak day for murder is Saturday, and the peak hours 8 P.M. to 2 A.M. Approximately 30 per cent of the murders were caused by drink, quarrels and violent rage, another 40 per cent by jealousy, intrigues and sexual motives, and only 10 per cent by financial motives. Sir John Macdonell concludes his survey in the following words (my italics):

I hesitate to draw any conclusions from imperfect data as to matters of great complexity, but I am inclined to think that this crime is *not generally the crime of the so-called criminal classes* but is in most cases rather an *incident in miserable lives in which disputes, quarrels, angry words and blows are common.* The short history of the large number of cases which have been examined might be summed up thus: Domestic quarrels and brawls; much previous ill-treatment; drinking, fighting, blows; a long course of brutality and continued absence of self-restraint. This crime is generally the last of a series of acts of violence.[15]

Half a century later, the Royal Commission examined the statistics of the years 1900–49 and came to the conclusion that they "confirm Sir John Macdonell's statement that murder is not in general a crime of the so-called criminal classes."[16]

[15] Quoted by E. Roy Calvert, *Capital Punishment in the Twentieth Century* (5th ed., London: Putnam, 1936), p. 32.
[16] R.C.R., Appendix 6, p. 4.

The Behavior of Murderers in Prison

Next, let us examine, from the point of view of public safety, the conduct of murderers who have been convicted and reprieved. The people best qualified to decide this question are evidently the prison governors, warders, prison chaplains and Home Office experts. These were heard both by the Select Committee and by the Royal Commission. Their opinions are quoted below; they were unanimous and without dissent. Since this point is of great importance in correcting popular misbeliefs about murderers as a class, I am quoting in full the relevant passages from both reports. First, the Select Committee of 1930:

High tribute was paid to the general conduct in prison, and on release, of reprieved murderers. . . . The testimony of the Home Office witnesses was as follows:
"A very large number of murderers are, in other respects, perfectly decent people, and a very large proportion of them, if they were let out, would be very unlikely to commit any other murder or any other crime. They are really a class by themselves; they are quite different from the ordinary criminal as a rule. . . . It is certainly not common experience that a murderer who has been released after serving part of a life sentence returns to prison . . . as to . . . committing further murders on release, that might be entirely ruled out."

Lord Brentford [Home Secretary, 1924–29] said of the reprieved murderer that he was a man who had committed one crime and, not being of a criminal type or of a criminal mind, he made a very good prisoner. He did not think he had come across a single case of a reprieved murderer committing another murder.

Colonel Hales, Governor of Parkhurst Prison, could not recall one who, from the moment he was discharged, had not made good. The same testimony was given by Revd. William Lewis Cottrell, M.A., Chaplain at Wormwood Scrubs, by Mr. Walter Middleton, Chief Officer of Pentonville Prison, and by Captain Clayton, Governor of Dartmoor.[17]

[17] Report of the Select Committee on Capital Punishment (1929–30), 237–40. Hereinafter referred to as S.C.R.

None of the prison governors or officials dissented from this opinion, although the majority were probably anti-abolitionist. Twenty years later the Royal Commission came to the same conclusion:

There is a popular belief that prisoners serving a life sentence after conviction of murder form a specially troublesome and danger-ous class. That is not so. Most find themselves in prison because they have yielded to temptation under the pressure of a combina-tion of circumstances unlikely to recur. "Taking murderers as a class," said one witness [Major Benke, Governor of Wandsworth Prison and Chairman of the Panel of Prison Governors], "there are a considerable number who are first offenders and who are not peo-ple of criminal tendencies. The murder is in many cases their first offense against the law. Previous to that they were law-abiding citizens and their general tenor of life is still to be law-abid-ing. . . ."[18]

In August, 1952, there was a total of 91 reprieved murderers among the prison population of England and Wales, out of which 82, that is, more than 90 per cent, belonged to the star class.[19] Thus the large majority of reprieved murderers are un-usually well-behaved model prisoners. What happens when they are let loose on society after serving their sentence? Do the re-formed lambs turn into wolves again?

Murderers Turned Loose

The answer is given in the statistics of the Home Office, of Scotland Yard and of the Central After Care Association. Dur-ing the twenty-year period 1928–48, 174 people were sentenced to life, and of these 112 had been released at the end of the period in question.[20] Of these 112, only one was alleged to have com-mitted a second murder: Walter Graham Rowland; and he was . . . one of the most probable victims of mistaken identity.

[18] R.C.R., 617.
[19] R.C.R., 627. The text says that there were seventy-nine prisoners of the star class, but the subsequent figures in the same paragraph seem to indicate that the Commissioners made a mistake in adding up.
[20] R.C.R., 650.

Yet Rowland is, as far as one can gather from existing reports, the only case of a "sane" reprieved murderer being convicted of a second murder in the United Kingdom in the course of the twentieth century. None of the other released "lifers" during the twenty-year period ending in 1948 committed crimes of violence against the person; and only five committed offenses against property. In Scotland, eleven reprieved murderers were released during the same period: only two of these were reconvicted, one for theft and one for "lewd practices."[21]

The evidence before the Royal Commission from the Commonwealth countries and the U.S.A. was as follows:

New South Wales: In general such prisoners after release behave well. Very occasionally . . . the murderer with a previous record of criminality . . . will again come into conflict with the law, but seldom for a serious offense.

Queensland (capital punishment abolished): In the fifty years 1900–50, four released murderers committed subsequent offenses: one attempt to kill, one indecent assault, one infliction of bodily harm, one cattle stealing.

South Australia: No prisoner released after life sentence has been returned for breach of conditions.

Canada: The average of failures is estimated to have fluctuated around 3 per cent.

Ceylon: No accurate information available, but cases where murderers returned to prison are exceptional.

New Zealand: So far as memory goes, no prisoner released after a conviction of murder has broken any of the conditions of his release or committed any offense or been returned to prison.

South Africa: Recommittals of this class of prisoner are extremely rare occurrences.

U.S.A.: Generally speaking, I doubt if there are any facts which would indicate that persons originally convicted and later commuted and released under parole have any higher degree of failure on parole than any other group. There have been a few notorious cases where persons have lapsed into delinquency again, but it is usually a comparatively minor sort of crime as compared to the one which originally got them into trouble. Cases of murder committed by persons pardoned from the death penalty are rare if not almost unknown.[22]

[21] R.C.R., 650. R.C.R., Appendix 15, pp. 486–87.
[22] R.C.R., Appendix 15, pp. 487–88.

It may be objected that this unanimous body of evidence refers only to the more harmless type of murderers who were reprieved precisely because they were considered harmless. But the experience of countries which have abolished capital punishment and where, therefore, every murderer is automatically reprieved, whether considered "harmless" or not, is exactly the same as in countries where murderers are still being executed.

Regarding the Dominions, . . . in Queensland and New Zealand, both abolitionist during the period in question, only one case is known of a reprieved man attempting murder in the last fifty years. In Europe, the Royal Commission's inquiry embraced six countries: Belgium, Denmark, the Netherlands, Norway, Sweden and Switzerland. *In these six countries altogether six convicted murderers have committed crimes of violence after their release in the course of the last thirty years.* The Royal Commission concludes:

> Even in countries which have abolished capital punishment the protection of society is rarely thought to require that murderers who are mentally normal should be detained in prison for the remainder of their life or even for very long periods. . . . The evidence that we ourselves received in these countries was also to the effect that released murderers who commit further crimes of violence are rare, and those who become useful citizens are common.[23]

These facts are so amazing and contrary to public belief that they call for some explanation. It is partly contained in the statements of the prison governors and Home Office experts which I have quoted: namely, that with rare exceptions, murder is not a crime of the criminal classes, and that the average murderer is *not* an "enemy of society" in the broad sense. This general statement was borne out by the statistics on the motives and circumstances of murder. It was confirmed by the experience of abolitionist countries which show that released murderers are less apt to relapse into crime than other offenders. Broadly speaking, it boils down to this: that the vast majority of murderers are either "crazy" in the elastic, nonlegal sense of

[23] R.C.R., 651.

the word, or momentarily "crazed" ("mad" in American par-
lance); because a normal person in a normal state of mind just
doesn't commit murder. Hence murderers are, by and large,
either mentally abnormal, or acting under abnormal circumstances. The former belong not to prison but to an institution;
the latter are easier to reform than any other type of criminal.

There remain the rare exceptions—the Christies and Haigs—
who, in all likelihood, cannot be reformed and would have to be
kept safely locked away to the end of their natural lives. But
these "monsters," who so much agitate public imagination,
form such a small percentage as to be almost negligible as a
social problem. Moreover, they do not affect the question we are
discussing—life imprisonment as an alternative to the death
penalty—because they do not belong to prison but to an institution. The Royal Commission says about them: "We agree
with the Home Office that any convicted murderers whom it
would be unsafe ever to release are likely to be in the category
of the mentally abnormal."[24] They belong to a category apart,
since the protection of society against them becomes the responsibility not of the legal but of the medical profession.

The practical consequences of abolition would in fact hardly
be felt or noticed by the country. The cessation of the death
penalty would simply mean that on an average thirteen persons
per year would be added to the British prison population. Even
the Home Office, traditionally opposed to abolition, agrees that
these people "would not be likely to give any exceptional trouble to prison officers."[25] And furthermore, that those who could
not be safely released in due time would form a very small proportion of the whole, and would be found in the category of
the mentally abnormal and in that category alone.[26]

For the thirteen men and women who are annually hanged
with the nation's tacit consent are by no means "monsters" and
"irretrievables." We saw how the rigidity of the law and the
anachronism of the M'Naghten Rules transform justice into an
unholy roulette game. Mrs. Ellis, Mrs. Thompson, the boy
Bentley, all of whom were hanged, were no more "irretrievable"

[24] R.C.R., 652.   [25] S.C.R., 246.   [26] R.C.R., 658.

than mace-bearer Martin, who was spared. The late Sir Alexander Paterson, Director of Convict Prisons, had this to say about the thirteen whom we annually hang: "If the estimate of [the condemned person's] character, formed by those who have to look after him for several weeks while awaiting sentence, could be taken into account by those who have to advise the Secretary of State, a considerable number might be respited."[27] And the Chaplain at Wormwood Scrubs Prison, the Rev. W. L. Cottrell, summed up his experience as follows:

Of the fifteen men whom I have seen executed I have felt very much indeed that a proportion of those men, perhaps half of them or even more, might really have been allowed to live, and had they been allowed to live I have felt that they would really turn into decent honest citizens. That is not emotional sentiment that has carried me away, but it is the real hard facts of the men whom I have known, because a chaplain gets very intimate with these men before they die, and I have felt that many of them, like so many reprieved murderers have done of whom I know today, would really have been quite decent honest citizens and could have taken their place in the world and in society.[28]

The precautions taken by the Home Office, before a man sentenced to life is released, will be discussed later. But the evidence of the extreme rarity of the cases where a murderer found fit for release committed a second crime is in itself sufficient to show that the risk run by the community, through the substitution of life for death sentences, is almost entirely an imaginary one. It is certainly smaller than the joint risk of executing innocent people and of letting guilty people off because the jury is not certain enough to hang the man, but would send him to prison in the knowledge that the case can be reopened. We have seen that these are the inevitable consequences of an outdated law, and the chances are that there are more murderers at large for this reason in England than in countries where capital punishment was abolished.

[27] S.C.R., 244.
[28] Minutes of the Select Committee on Capital Punishment (1929–30), 844.

The Length of a Life Sentence

We now come to the argument that a quick death is less cruel than a long prison sentence. It comes from two categories of people: those who rationalize their sadistic tendencies by a pious "break his neck for his own good," and from genuine humanitarians who, ignorant of conditions in modern prisons, base their apprehensions on vague notions of jail life in Dickensian days.

The person best qualified to judge whether prison is preferable to execution is evidently the prisoner himself. Sir Basil Thomson, an outstanding authority, wrote that "no Governor has ever yet met a condemned prisoner who would refuse a reprieve or who did not ardently long for one." Calvert quotes another ex-prison official as stating "that of the thirty reprieved murderers whom, in the course of his duties, he had come to know intimately, there was not one but had testified, after years of imprisonment, to his thankfulness for the respite."[29] Yet at that time prison routine was much grimmer and more depressing than nowadays.

The actual length of a "life" sentence is determined by the Home Office. It is not decided in advance, but according to the reports received on the prisoner's character and conduct. Each case is reviewed at least every four years. In exceptional cases the reprieved prisoner may be released almost instantaneously. Home Office statistics[30] show that during the decade 1940–49, 93 people were released from serving commuted life sentences. Of these, six had served less than a year—among them a woman who had gassed her son, a hopeless imbecile of thirty who had to be nursed like a baby; and a Jewish refugee woman from Nazi Germany who, together with her mother, tried to poison herself during the war for fear of a German invasion. The mother died, the daughter survived and was convicted of murder as a survivor of a suicide pact.

Of the others, on an average five persons were released each year between their second and sixth year in prison. This makes

[29] Calvert, *op. cit.*, p. 194.
[30] R.C.R., Appendix 3, Table XII.

a total of 32 persons out of 93, released after serving less than
seven years. All of these were obviously pathetic cases, who
could not be of the remotest danger to society. The peak years
of release were between the seventh and eighth years after conviction—36 cases, amounting to 40 per cent of the total. Of the
remainder, ten persons were made to serve nine years; eight persons, ten years; two, eleven years; three, twelve years; one, thirteen years; and one, fourteen years. Nobody was released who
had served more than fourteen years. The table does not say
how many prisoners there were who had served more than fourteen years and were *not* released; but the Home Office states
that "only most exceptionally would anybody serve more than
fifteen years under the present practice; the normal is much less
than that."[31] From this we must conclude that most of the
"over-fifteen-years," i.e., the irretrievables, are in Broadmoor.
Yet, as we saw, there was only one case in England, Wales or
Scotland, during the last fifty years, of a released "lifer" committing an act of violence—and that was the enigmatic case of
Rowland.

How a Life Sentence Is Spent

So much for the length of time spent in prison by reprieved
murderers before they are considered to have expiated their
crime, and safe to be released. How is that time spent?

Long-term prisoners in England are divided into two classes:
"star" and "ordinary." The star class comprises all first offenders
unless they are considered a bad influence, but also prisoners
with previous convictions if they are supposed to become a good
influence; there is no rigid rule.

In August, 1952, the prison population included, as previously
mentioned, 91 reprieved murderers, 82 of whom were in the star
class. The men of the star class were serving their term partly at
Wakefield, partly at the new "open prison" at Leyhill; the
women, either at Aylesbury or at the "open prison" at Askham

[31] R.C.R., 646.

Grange. Others were undergoing hospital treatment, or waiting for their transfer from local prisons.[32]

The "open prisons" are a recent experiment, dating back to 1946. There are no walls around the prison, no bars on the windows, no locks on the doors, and no guards are posted. Leyhill houses on the average 250 to 300 prisoners, of whom, in 1952, 20 were reprieved murderers. Escape is, of course, child's play —but it is not in the interests of the type of prisoner sent to an "open prison." In 1947, the first year after the experiment was started, fourteen escaped; in 1948, eight; in 1949, five; in 1950, one; in 1951, one; in 1952, nil.[33]

Yet the great majority of reprieved murderers serve part of their sentences—often a large part—in "open prisons."

The major part of the day—seven to eight hours—is spent by the prison population much in the same manner as by the ordinary free population: on work. "Work" for the prisoner under the old regime meant "the treadmill, the shot drill and the crank, of which the deliberate intention was to be irksome, fatiguing and—because totally unproductive—degrading."[34] Today "work" means nearly anything in the prisoner's own trade or a trade learned in prison: from farming and market gardening to printing and bookbinding. At Wakefield, prisoners are engaged in weaving, tailoring, precision engineering, bricklaying, foundry work, painting and decorating. At Leyhill, in carpentry, shoemaking, printing and binding. Some Leyhill prisoners work on local farms, or at road-mending, or as bricklayers and builders. They bicycle to their places of employment without any escort, and work without prison supervision. Other prisons send out parties of up to twenty prisoners with a single officer accompanying them, to do agricultural or forestry work. In women's prisons, the main trades are needlework, dressmaking, knitting, cleaning, painting, gardening and laundering. Some prisoners manufacture fishermen's nets, others footballs, others gloves and pullovers. The customers of their produce are the prison administration itself, other government departments, public and local bodies and, to a small extent, private firms.

[32] R.C.R., 627.   [33] R.C.R., 626.   [34] R.C.R., 624.

All prisons in which long sentences are served have vocational courses for those prisoners who had no skill or trade, or who wish to acquire a new one. They take the form of a six-month's course of both practical and theoretical instruction based on a Ministry of Labor syllabus. They include, for men, precision engineering, carpentry, fitting, bricklaying, painting and decorating, foundry work, weaving, printing, bookbinding. For women, there are courses in cookery and general housewifery, tailoring, and so forth.

The pay is very small. It normally does not exceed four shillings a week. The idea behind this seems to be that the surplus value of the prisoner's work should pay for his upkeep. On the continent the rates of pay are generally much higher: in Belgium, prisoners earn up to thirty shillings, in Denmark up to two pounds a week, half of which can be spent in prison, the other half kept until release. However that may be, the system answers the old idiotic argument that abolition of the death penalty would increase the taxpayer's burden. The average of thirteen broken necks per annum costs the taxpayer ten pounds per neck to Mr. Pierrepoint, plus the fee to his assistant, to which have to be added traveling expenses for both; not to mention the outlay for warders going sick after each operation; maintenance of the apparatus, wear and tear of the rope, and so forth. The reprieved convict, on the other hand, earns his keep, plus a surplus for the prison administration. The costly prisoners are those who serve short sentences in local prisons, such as vagabonds and petty thieves. From the anxious taxpayer's point of view, it would be more logical to hang these.

Outside working hours there is a large and growing program for various activities in both the field of education and entertainment. There are lectures, theatre performances, film shows and concerts. In some prisons the prisoners have their own orchestras and dramatic societies. All have libraries, but prisoners may also receive books and periodicals from outside and subscribe to correspondence courses for any trade or hobby. Games are played at weekends, and physical training is given to younger prisoners. At Wakefield there are five courts; at Leyhill, the cricket and football teams play against the local clubs; the inmates can have their own gardens, competing in the annual flower show; they have a putting course, a deck-tennis court, a swimming pool, ping-pong, billiards and a wireless room.

It can hardly be said that detention under these conditions is "a doom far worse than death," as the Lord Chancellor of the day, Lord Jowitt, and the previous Lord Chancellor, Viscount Simon, said in the House of Lords debate in 1948. These worthies, whom I had occasion to quote before, were referring to some long bygone horrors of the Belgian and Italian prison systems as the only conceivable alternative to hanging. It is worth a digression to listen to the Lord Chancellor:

> In Belgium the position is that a murderer who is sentenced nominally to imprisonment for life is usually allowed out after some twenty-five years, but he serves the first ten of the twenty-five in solitary confinement. . . . Speaking for myself, I do not for a moment doubt that these are fates worse than death, and I am quite certain that nobody in this House or in another place would for one moment tolerate the conception of any such penalty as that.[35]

The facts are that even in Belgium, which has a harsher prison regime than any other European country, solitary confinement "has been gradually abandoned since 1920. . . . It must be emphatically stated that solitary confinement in Belgium . . . no longer exists."[36]

But even if the Lord Chancellor's information had been correct, and not outdated by twenty years, why on earth would England have to imitate just that one example? Lord Jowitt had thought of this objection, and had the following answer to it:

> Logically, one is perfectly entitled to say, "Look at what has happened in Belgium." One can say, "Well, you see, the abolition of the death penalty had no ill effects; there are no more murderers." On the other hand, if one says that, then, logically [sic], one must be prepared to say, "I will accept the Belgian remedy." Yet none of us would accept that. Therefore, I come to the conclusion that, logically, it is fallacious to rely on the experience of foreign countries, unless one is to accept the remedy which they propound.[37]

[35] Hansard (Minutes of Parliament), Apr. 27, 1948, col. 397.
[36] R.C.R., Appendix 14, p. 4.
[37] Hansard, Apr. 27, 1948, cols. 397–98.

I have said before that the strongest case for the abolition of the death penalty is to be found in the arguments of its upholders.

Pampering the Murderer

The majority in the House of Lords which in 1948 defeated abolition for a trial period was based on a holy alliance between those who proclaimed with the Lord Chancellor that a life sentence was a cruelty "worse than death," and those who thought with Lord Sandhurst that it was not cruel enough.

Unless we look out (that noble Lord warned the House), prison will become a home away from home, and the next thing will be that they will be giving the beggars weekend leave. . . . We have to remember that quite a large proportion of the criminal population come from, and are the result of, bad housing and bad homes. The effect would be to make prison more comfortable than home, and even now such people know that when they go to prison—and the magistrates' courts produce evidence of this—at least they will be warm throughout the winter. . . . The general view of the police is dead against this suggestion [suspension of the death penalty]. I think it was well summed up by the Commissioner when he said that it is safer to commit murder than to cross the road. At the present moment, that is perfectly true. If you commit murder, you know that you will be out of danger of everything except of a natural death for the next ten or fifteen years. Not one of us in this House can say that. So long as we are free to roam about the streets freely, as some people do, we are liable to come to a sudden and abrupt end at any moment.[38]

Which proves that Hansard can be funnier than P. G. Wodehouse. For if there are people in this nation living under such wretched conditions that even prison is preferable to them, then decency demands that housing conditions should be improved and not that prison conditions should be made more wretched. Fortunately, people attracted to prison on these grounds exist mainly in the noble Lord's imagination, and among picturesque characters in Dickens's and Joyce Cary's novels.

[38] *Ibid.*, cols. 454–55.

But this kind of nonsense apart, it may still be thought that the swimming pool and dramatic society of Leyhill mean going too far toward coddling the criminal. The answer is that conditions even in the most modern prison seem more idyllic when one reads about them than if one has to live in them. A quarter-century ago, before the great prison reform got under way, Sir Alexander Paterson told the Select Committee:

Whatever means of education, stimulation and recreation may be employed, however you may seek to ring the changes on handicrafts and literature, skittles or chess or ping-pong, despite the invaluable labors of most devoted voluntary workers, it requires a superman to survive twenty years of imprisonment with character and soul intact.[39]

Since this was said, prison conditions have been radically changed, and terms of detention shortened. Yet even so, detention for six, eight or ten years is a very dreadful thing. It is a modern purgatory with welfare services, skittles and ping-pong, yet a purgatory nevertheless which those who never lay in jail cannot really visualize even if endowed with sympathy and imagination. In its matter-of-fact language, the Royal Commission says that:

The deterrent effect of imprisonment on the individual offender lies primarily in the shame of being sent to prison and the fact of being in prison, with all that that fact in itself implies—complete loss of personal liberty; separation from home, family and friends; subjection to disciplinary control and forced labor; and deprivation of most of the ordinary amenities and intercourse of everyday life. An offender is sent to prison *as* a punishment and not *for* punishment.[40]

However terrible the act that landed him in limbo was: the cracking of a human skull or the stopping of a human breath, the delinquent is chewing the cud of his deed and vomiting it out and swallowing it again at least once a day, multiplied by 365, multiplied by 5, 6, 7, 8, 9, 10, repeating to him or herself

[39] R.C.R., 653.   [40] R.C.R., 622.

"if only at that moment I hadn't. . . ." Atonement consists in the knowledge, or the illusion, that one could have acted otherwise than one did; purgatory is the internal combustion of the missed chance. It is not a continuous process. It may stop after a while, or diminish and then start again in a furious crescendo: "if only . . . then I wouldn't be here." Until gradually, with ups and downs, periods of depression and periods of excitement, which are all in a day's, week's, year's work, gradually the past is burned out and the future becomes real again; and the "I wouldn't be here" is replaced by "when I get out." At its worst, prison is limbo; at its best, it is a forced residence for adult, full-blooded and mostly temperamental people in a kind of boarding-school-cum-Y.M.C.A.-cum-Salvation-Army-doss-house, mitigated by lectures, skittles and games on Sunday.

The worst of it is not the absence of sex, or drink, or even of the family. The first two lose their sting after a while, and at times surprisingly quickly; and the intense friendships and tensions of a convict community substitute for the third. The worst is the loss of one's adult manhood or womanhood—in the non-sexual, purely human sense. A prisoner feels as if he were castrated—not because he can't sleep with women, but because he has been deprived of the dignity of his manhood and reduced to a schoolboy or ward, to an infantile and helpless state, no longer the master of his destiny but its victim, deprived of responsibility, under constant observation: a marionette in a fair and enlightened puppet-player's hands, yet still a marionette. Even when working without supervision or playing soccer, convict team against village team, he feels that he is not quite human—a man not exactly despised, yet not exactly trusted, crippled in his rights, diminished in his self-esteem—a star prisoner, treated with benevolence, in a word a creature *almost* human.

Whatever reforms are introduced, even if the bars vanish and the prison is an open one, this basic defect cannot be remedied because it is the essence of the prisoner's condition, the irreducible core of his punishment. That is why that very wise White Paper says: "An offender is sent to prison *as* a punishment and not *for* punishment."

That is also the reason why "lifers" are so reasonable and well behaved, and give less trouble than the small fry. The primary motive is not the hope for privileges and remissions—though, of course, the earning of privilege and remission is for the prisoner the equivalent of the freeman's pursuit of career and material gains. The true reason is that the only way open to the prisoner to save the remainder of his human dignity, and to avoid further humiliation, is to be a model prisoner. That means not only outwardly obeying the rules, but inwardly accepting them as a condition of existence; or, which amounts to the same thing, to treat the rules as if they were nonexistent by conforming to them, thus avoiding that they be enforced. Moreover, well-behavedness among long-termers is not regarded as "sissy," nor is unruliness and showing off regarded with approval, for it makes life more difficult for everybody, and because every disciplinary action makes a prison more grim and prisonlike. On the other hand, correct and disciplined behavior will, apart from its practical benefits, gradually earn the prisoner the respect of the warders. This, in turn, will raise his self-respect and diminish the span between the almost-human and the human condition —which he will only re-attain when he is set free.

To quote the saying about the repentant sinner who causes more rejoicing, and so forth, would be sentimental and out of place. But it is no exaggeration to say of a man who has been condemned to die and has worked himself through purgatory and finally regained his freedom, that he has earned every moment of it at a much higher price than ordinary mortals, born under kinder stars.

The Return to Freedom

When the prisoner has served his six, or eight, or twelve years, according to the case, he is not simply turned loose with a "go and sin no more." Steps for his reintegration into society start in fact as soon as he arrives in prison. At that stage he is interviewed by a representative of the Central After Care Association (a voluntary body under a Council appointed by the Home Secretary), who discusses his future plans with him and henceforth visits him regularly to help and advise. His progress is reviewed periodically by the Governor, medical officer and prison chaplain. Where the need arises, the cooperation of the local authorities and of the Ministry of Education or Labor is obtained. As the end of his term of imprisonment approaches, he may be granted permission to go home on leave for periods of five days, not earlier than four months and not later than two months before the date of discharge. The object of this innovation (which dates from 1951 and follows the practice of other countries) is "to contribute to the restoration of the prisoner's self-confidence by placing trust in him under conditions of complete freedom, and to give the prisoner an opportunity before his final release from prison to make contact with prospective employers, to deal with domestic problems and to renew his home ties, in order to facilitate as far as possible his absorption into society."[41]

According to the Central After Care Association's report to the Royal Commission, during the fifteen years 1934–48, the number of male prisoners convicted of murder and discharged after serving their sentence, in England and Wales, was 129. Out of these, 112 "settled down immediately." The corresponding number of females was 27, out of which 19 settled down "immediately", and four "fairly well."[42] Some prisoners are released on a license which binds them to report any changes of address to the After Care Association, and to comply with certain other conditions, but they are the exception, not the rule. The general tendency is that once an ex-murderer is considered worthy and safe to be released, he should be allowed to resume a normal life without ties and reminders of the past.

It is reassuring to note that the police who, as a body, are the stoutest supporters of the death penalty, are most cooperative in helping a man who has escaped that fate to find his feet again. The directors of the Central After Care Association were unanimous in testifying that they have found the police in all cases most helpful, and that sometimes they go out of their way to be so. The same paradox applies to the Home Office, which stubbornly defends capital punishment and yet engages in bold, humane experiments, like "open prisons" to ease the life of those who have been spared.

[41] R.C.R., 643.   [42] R.C.R., Appendix 15 (i).

The Answer to Straffen and Christie

A special problem is the category of murderers who are mentally abnormal, but not technically insane. As we saw before, the Home Office and the Royal Commission agree that in this class "and in it alone, are likely to be found any prisoners whom it would be unsafe ever to release."[43]

But the Christies and Straffens are not the only type who belong to this borderline category. "These prisoners do not form a homogeneous group. Some are suffering from minor forms of mental disease or mental defect, from neurosis or some kind of epileptic condition; others are psychopaths. It is this latter group with whom we are particularly concerned, since . . . there is no recognized and accepted method of treatment that can be applied to psychopaths, and many doctors believe that no treatment is effective. In the first group there are types of disorder which may respond to psychiatric treatment; of those in the second some improve as they grow older, but some never improve and are always a danger. They constitute a more solidly intractable problem than the first group, and are a persistently disturbing element in prison society."[44]

The only possible solution for this group is confinement in a special institution, halfway between ordinary prison and mental hospital, where they are treated and kept during an indeterminate period—which in some cases means to the end of their lives. A special institution of this kind is now in the process of being created in this country. On the Continent, there are several of them—the best known at Herstedvester, in Denmark. Sex offenders form the largest group; in Denmark and Holland they may be castrated on their own wish, and as a rule this leads to the extinction of the criminal impulse. But otherwise the chances of cure and release for sex offenders and psychopaths are small; whereas in other categories they are better. At the worst, a part of the mentally sick must be regarded as the drones of society, as we regard their brothers and sisters in misery, the certified insane. The distinction between the two is a matter of

[43] R.C.R., 658.   [44] R.C.R., 659.

technical definitions, and since we regard it as a barbarity to kill
the insane, it is equally barbarous to kill those whose sickness
our courts deny on the strength of a diagnostical rule, established by lawyers in 1843.

The matter is simple enough. But not so to the Ellenborough-
Goddard axis. . . . Let us return, for the last time, to the Lords'
debate in 1948, when Lord Goddard had, among other things
already quoted, this to say on the subject:

If the criminal law of this country is to be respected, it must be in
accordance with public opinion, and public opinion must support
it. . . . In my humble opinion, I believe that there are many, many
cases where the murderer should be destroyed. . . . Let me give your
Lordships two instances to justify my view that some of these bestial
murderers should be destroyed. Last November, I tried a case at
Bristol. The prisoner, thank God, was not a British subject. He was
a Pole, but he had been here for quite a long time. On his own confession, having finished his supper, during which he had only a
moderate quantity to drink, he said that he had an overwhelming
desire for sexual intercourse. He went out and, finding no young
girl near his camp, went to a village alehouse on the outskirts of the
village, kept by an old woman of seventy-six. He entered that
woman's house at dead of night, he went into her room, he raped
her, he committed another nameless offense on that poor creature's
body, and he killed her. At the end of last sittings, another case
came before me in the Court of Criminal Appeal. I regret to say
that this time the prisoner was a British subject. In a mining village
in South Wales, a young man about twenty-two years of age who
had had a little to drink—not much, for no one suggested he was
drunk—while pushing his way down an alley knocked against an
old woman who reproached him—reviled him, if you like, for I
expect she used strong language at him. He struck at her so that she
fell on the sidewalk and fractured her skull. Then he kicked her to
death and raped her as she was dying on the pavement. . . .[45]

It is somewhat odd that both cases which the Lord Chief
Justice selected to regale their Lordships with were sexual murders commited on old women. It would be even odder if he
did not realize that a lad of twenty-two who raped an old

---

[45] Hansard, Apr. 28, 1948, cols. 492–93.

woman *on the pavement* and kicked her to death, and the other man who raped a woman of seventy-six and committed "another nameless offense" on her, were both pathological, mentally sick cases. He did not deny that they were insane; he merely concluded that some cases were so awful that the prisoner should be destroyed. And he made his meaning unmistakably clear in his evidence before the Royal Commission when he stated that though he knew that Ley was insane, he "thought it very proper that he should have hanged."[46]

Both the law of the land and the law of humanity take the opposite view: that disease of body or mind is not a reason to destroy a man. The Royal Commission went out of its way to reject the philosophy of the highest judge of the country:

We make one fundamental assumption, which we should hardly have thought it necessary to state explicitly if it had not lately been questioned in some quarters. It has for centuries been recognized that, if a person was, at the time of his unlawful act, mentally so disordered that it would be unreasonable to impute guilt to him, he ought not to be held liable to conviction and punishment under the criminal law. Views have changed and opinions have differed . . . but that principle has been accepted without question. Recently, however, the suggestion has sometimes been made that the insane murderer should be punished equally with the sane, or that, although he ought not to be executed as a punishment, he should be painlessly exterminated as a measure of social hygiene. . . . Such doctrines have been preached and practiced in National-Socialist Germany, but they are repugnant to the moral traditions of Western civilization and we are confident that they would be unhesitatingly rejected by the great majority of the population of this country.[47]

THE MONTHLY SACRIFICE

In 1938, a Gallup poll on the question whether the death penalty should be maintained or not, showed 50 per cent "ayes" in favor of hanging, and 50 per cent "nays" and "don't knows." Nine years later, in a similar poll, the "ayes" in favor of hanging had increased to 68 per cent. Another eight years later, in

[46] R.C.M., 3251.　　　[47] R.C.R., 278.

July, 1955, the *Daily Mirror* arranged a new poll which revealed a complete reversal of public opinion: 65 per cent voted against the death penalty—about the same proportion which previously had voted for it.

Such wild fluctuations of public opinion are unusual in a country where the floating vote amounts only to a small fraction of the total, and general elections are decided by narrow margins. There is, no doubt, a steady, gradual increase in the number of people who favor a more humane administration of the law; but this slowly mounting tide does not account for the violent gales which blow now in one direction, now in the other. When the vision of the gibbet appears on the nation's horizon, opinion swings and twists like the body suspended from it; eyes bulge and reason is strangled. If the last victim happens to arouse pity—a feeble-minded boy for instance, unhinged by the movies, or a mother of two children, half-crazed by gin and jealousy—up go the "nays" of mercy like a flight of doves; if he is a cool customer like Christie, up go the "ayes" like a swarm of vultures. Let us agree that this is not a dignified or desirable state of affairs.

The manner in which governments and politicians handle the problem of the death penalty is no more dignified, though less excusable. Public opinion swings, moved by passion and pity, but Home Secretaries, as we saw, obey a peculiar swing-rule of their own. In recent Parliamentary debates, Home Secretary, Major Lloyd George, who, in 1948, had voted for the abolition of hanging, defended it on the familiar grounds: its unique value as a deterrent, the difficulty of finding a satisfactory alternative punishment and, lastly, that public opinion is opposed to abolition. All this is as old as Methuselah and no more need be said on the first two points; but the third, alas, cannot be dismissed. It is true, of course, that governments only use public opinion as a shield when it is convenient to them. When public opinion demanded that Bentley be reprieved, the Government disregarded it. On a previous similar occasion, the then Home Secretary, Lord Brentford, explained that "no Secretary of State worthy of his name could permit himself to be influenced in a matter of that kind by public clamor." Mob mercy, he continued, was as bad as mob execution. There was no difference between a lynching mob and a mob trying "to usurp the office of the Minister" by petitioning for a Royal reprieve.[48] Thus the argument proved to be beautifully reversible: Heads I win, tails you swing.

An example of this double-think was given by the Home Secretary in a recent debate. A few minutes after he had refused to consider abolition because the public was in favor of hanging, he was asked the following question:

Mr. Price (Lab. Westhoughton): Does he realize that British public opinion was shocked and scandalized by the gross commercialism of certain showmen in Blackpool who put on exhibition an effigy of Ruth Ellis, one day after she was hanged at Holloway Gaol?

Major Lloyd George: . . . It would hardly be practicable or indeed desirable if every departure from public opinion . . . in this country was made the subject of legislation.[49]

Thus hanging cannot be stopped, because we must listen to public opinion; and the desecration of a dead woman cannot be stopped because we must not listen to public opinion.

Nevertheless, public opinion is still the strongest passive support of the hang-hards. The main reasons for this are ignorance, traditional prejudice and repressed cruelty.

The public's ignorance of the facts and arguments of the issue is of course artificially fostered by official spokesmen and other oracles. The bogies conjured up by Ellenborough have not lost their effect even after a century and a half. The public is made to believe that only the hangman can protect them against "the hardened robber"; that it is quite impossible for an innocent to be hanged; that no mentally sick person is hanged; that all the burglars of the realm are impatiently waiting for Abolition D-Day to arm themselves with guns, and that the day of the hanging judges is past. They are also being given the impression that hanging is a normal thing outside England in the contemporary world, that only some small freak nations, like Switzer-

[48] Quoted from Charles Duff, *A New Handbook on Hanging* (London: A. Melrose, 1954), p. 56.
[49] Quoted from Manchester *Guardian*, July 22, 1955.

land or Norway, have engaged in freak experiments of penal reform, that all murderers are Haigh-type monsters, that sex maniacs must either be hanged or turned loose, that thirteen reprieves per year would cost the taxpayer millions and that the dislocation of the cerebral vertebrae and rupture of the jugular vein is a humane and instantaneous procedure which is always carried out swiftly and without a hitch.

The effect of this official smokescreen is that the stark reality of the gallows is hidden in the background, and, at the same time, the public is led to believe that the whole subject is a highly controversial one in which the arguments of both sides are evenly balanced and can only be judged by experts. Once the smokescreen is dispelled, people will realize that hanging is simply a stupid and cruel relic of the past, much more stupid and cruel than they ever imagined. About half a dozen books were written in the last few years crammed with facts in favor of the abolition of hanging. Why has nobody written a book in defense of it? I believe the reason is, as I have tried to show, that the strongest case against capital punishment is to be found in the arguments of its defenders. I challenge them to produce quotations from abolitionists as silly or ignorant or dishonest as the collection of pro-hanging quotations in this book.

Ignorance can be cured, but not callousness. Those who feel strongly that this nation should continue to break people's necks or strangle them to glory, display a curious mixture of insensitivity and sentimental traditionalism which makes them impervious to reasoned argument. They believe that legal murder prevents illegal murder, as the Persians believed that whipping the sea will calm the storm. They will say that England cannot do without hanging, and when you point to the example of other countries which get along perfectly without it, they will say that foreigners are different. They will say that English justice makes hanging by legal error impossible, and when you quote names of people who were hanged in error, they will answer that you cannot expect any system to be perfect. They will say that hanging is the most humane method of execution, and if you quote cases of a man having to be carried to the drop "strapped sitting in a chair" or women dragged to it in a free-for-all fight, they will answer that mentioning such matters is in bad taste. As a former Home Secretary said: "The less said at the inquest, the better; it is preferable to draw a veil over these cases."[50] What matters is that the victim is dead, not the manner in which he was made to die, and the nation is busy washing their hands.

Those who are determined that this barbarity should continue are to be found in all classes and professions, from retired colonels to bus drivers; the boundary is not defined by income or education. George Bernard Shaw wrote that the treatment of the "human vermin in the Commonwealth," including idiots and morons, ought to be "kill, kill, kill, kill, kill them." His arguments were essentially the same as the charwoman's "What I always say is let 'em swing; that's what I always says"; which again are essentially the same as certain speeches I have quoted from the House of Lords. The division is not between rich and poor, highbrow and lowbrow, Christians and atheists: it is between those who have charity and those who have not. The Bishops who in 1810 voted death for a five-shilling theft had no more charity than the atheist Shaw.

In this age of mass production, charity has come to mean dropping sixpence into a box and having a paper-flower pinned on one's lapel. But originally it had a different and revolutionary meaning: "Though I speak with the tongues of men and of angels, and have not charity, I am become as sounding brass, or a tinkling cymbal. And though . . . I have all faith, so that I could remove mountains, and have not charity, I am nothing. And though I bestow all my goods to feed the poor, and have not charity, it profiteth me nothing." Charity in this ancient meaning of the word is about the most difficult virtue to acquire: much more difficult than equity, mere kindness, or even self-sacrifice. For true charity presupposes a rare combination of gifts: humility-plus-imagination. Humility without imagination makes the pious bore; imagination without humility makes the brilliant cynic. But where the two appear together, they are an

[50] Statement by Sir William Joynson-Hicks in the House of Commons, June 23, 1927. Quoted from *The Case Against Capital Punishment* (London: The Howard League, 1953), sheet 17.

active healing force for the ailments of man and the wounds of society—and a burden on him who is blessed and cursed by possessing it. For his motto must then be. *homo sum: humani nihil a me alienum puto*—I am human and nothing human is alien to me. And one must be very humble indeed, and very imaginative indeed, to accept this; for it means that neither Hitler nor Christie, neither young Bentley nor old Mr. Pierrepoint, can be excluded from the demands of charity—since what we dislike in them is merely an extreme development of some of the less palatable aspects of ourselves, of some human quality in which we all share. The test of one's humanity is whether one is able to accept this fact—not as lip service, but with the shuddering recognition of a kinship: here but for the grace of God, drop I.

This guilty recognition of an inner kinship may, however, be repressed from consciousness and turn with a vengeance into the opposite of charity. When Ruth Ellis had shot her lover in a frenzy of jealousy and resentment, women were in general less inclined to demand a reprieve than men. Many of them, involved in similarly unhappy circumstances, may have felt some unconscious envy at the thought that if they were denying themselves the luxury of murdering a faithless lover or husband, then those who indulge in it ought to pay the price. Their apparent moral indignation was a mixture of envy and vindictiveness. Sexually frustrated women will persecute their luckier sisters under the same cloak of moral righteousness.

There also exists a kind of pseudo-charity, expressed in sayings like "you ask for sympathy for the murderer, but what about the poor victim?" The answer is that we sympathize with the victim but we do not wish to add a second crime to the first. We sympathize with the victim's family, but do not wish to cause additional suffering to the murderer's family. We did not abolish drawing and quartering for lack of sympathy with the victim, but because cruelty is incompatible with the notion of charity.

There is a spoonful of sadism at the bottom of every human heart. Nearly a century ago, Charles Dickens wrote that "around capital punishment there lingers a fascination, urging weak and

bad people toward it and imparting an interest to details connected with it, and with malefactors awaiting it or suffering it,
which even good and well-disposed people cannot withstand."
His contemporary, John Bright, knew that "capital punishment,
whilst pretending to support reverence for human life, does in
fact, tend to destroy it." And even earlier, Samuel Romilly said
that cruel punishments have an inevitable tendency to produce
cruelty in people. The image of the gallows appeals to their
latent sadism as pornography appeals to their latent sexual
appetites.

There is a famous saying by a press tycoon that what the
newspaper reading public wants is blood, sex (he used a more
anatomical expression) and the national flag. It was the *Daily
Mail* version of Freud's discovery that the sexual instinct and
the instinct of aggression are, beside tribal loyalty, the most
powerful biological drives. Civilization obliges us to keep the
little Stone Age man inside us under strict control; but while
the sexual appetites find a reasonable amount of authorized or
tolerated outlets, aggression has almost none. Competitive
sports are supposed to provide such an outlet, but it does not
amount to much: cricket and soccer do not allow scratching,
biting and strangling. So, on peaceful Sunday mornings, before
setting out for Church, we avidly gulp down the *Dirt in the
World*. True to Northcliffe and Freud, the largest space in the
popular press is given to divorce and murder cases, catering to
the two basic instincts. Some fifty million readers of the popular
press express their unctious disgust about this state of affairs, yet
they lap up the contents of the slop-basin to the last drop, for
homo sum and such is human nature.

The point is not to deny the existence of the fur-clad little
man in us, but to accept him as part of the human condition,
and to keep him under control. Newspaper editors who have to
earn money for the proprietors cannot be expected to stop
making the most of hanging, so long as hanging exists. In
countries from which the death penalty has vanished, this dirty
sensationalism has vanished too, and murder trials do not get
more publicity in the press than cases of burglary or fraud now
get in this country. For the fascination of the murder trial, and

its appeal to unconscious cruelty, lies in the fact that a man is fighting for his life like a gladiator in the arena, and in the thrilling uncertainty whether the outcome will be thumbs up or thumbs down. One only wonders why the bookmakers and tote do not come in.

A short time ago, there was a national outcry against horror comics, particularly from the judges who defend the real horror of hanging. Yet a horror comic is always less exciting, because it deals with fictitious events, than the matter-of-fact statement that a real person, whose photographs we have seen, whose words we have read, has been officially strangled. The drawings of monsters and mad sextons enamoured of drowned blondes are less pernicious, because of their science-fiction remoteness, than the studiedly sober report about the traces of brandy found in the executed woman's stomach. Moral deterrent, public example, reverence for human life—what bloody hypocrisy! So long as there are bull fights there will be *aficionados*, and so long as there are gladiators there will be a circus audience. There is a poisoned spray coming from the Old Bailey which corrupts and depraves; it can only be stopped by abolishing its cause, the death penalty itself. Two centuries ago, visitors to this country were puzzled to find the road to London dotted with grizzly gibbets. They are still puzzled by the same contradiction between the Englishman's belief in the necessity of hanging and his proverbial virtues of tolerance to man, kindness to animals, fussing over plants and birds. They fail to understand the power of tradition, his reluctance to abandon any of his cherished prejudices. Tradition has a hypnotic effect which commands blind belief, an instinctive recoil from any new departure as a "dangerous experiment," and unwillingness to listen to reasoned argument. This is why the principal defenders of hanging have always been the most tradition-bound bodies of the nation: the House of Lords, the Bishops' bench, the upper ranks of the gowned and wigged profession. Yet in spite of their power and influence over the public mind, chunk after chunk of sacred tradition has been wrenched from their hands: the pillory and the ducking chair, the stake and the gibbet, the cat-o'-nine-tails;

and within the next few years the strangling cord will be wrested from them too.

For despite the inertia of man's imagination and its resistance to reason and fact, public opinion is at long last beginning to realize that it does not need the hangman's protection; that the deliberate taking of life by the state is unjustifiable on religious or philosophic or scientific grounds; that hanging by mistake will go on as long as capital punishment will go on, because the risk is inherent in its nature; that the vast majority of murderers are either mentally sick and belong to the mental sick ward, or victims of circumstance, who can be reclaimed for human society; and that the substitution of the life sentence for the death penalty exposes the peaceful citizen to no greater risk than that of being killed by lightning in a bus queue, and considerably less than the risk of being a passive accomplice in the execution of an innocent or a mentally deranged person, which the citizens of this country run on the average thirteen times a year.

It is not only a question of the thirteen individual lives which we offer annually as a sacrifice to the stupid moloch of prejudice. The gallows is not only a machine of death, but a symbol. It is the symbol of terror, cruelty and irreverence for life; the common denominator of primitive savagery, medieval fanaticism and modern totalitarianism. It stands for everything that mankind must reject, if mankind is to survive its present crisis.